AF560760

PATRIOTISM, PARTITION AND THE PERSECUTED

PATRIOTISM, PARTITION AND THE PERSECUTED

Social Biography of Victims of Partition

DEBAL K. SINGHAROY

MANOHAR
2023

First published 2023

ISBN 978-93-91928-78-0

Published by
Ajay Jain *for*
Manohar Publishers & Distributors
4753/23 Ansari Road, Daryaganj
New Delhi 110002

Typeset by
Ravi Shanker
Delhi 110095

Printed at
Replika Press Pvt. Ltd.

Dedicated to

FAKIR AND JAMAL

the victims of partition

Contents

Acknowledgements

The idea to write this book emerged from my long drawn non-academic interactions with a section of people, who were the victims of communalism and the Partition of the country in 1947. Their feelings of victimhood, sufferings, nostalgia about the left behind motherland that has remained on the other side of the border, moved me to get engaged with this topic.

I started working on this book with a lot of hesitation as it involved consulting and collecting vast array of information, documents, literatures and other related materials, on the one hand, and putting them in a social science's perspective, on the other. Though I am a sociologist and not a historian, I became cautious that I should not venture into history. Even though I would be writing a social biography, using some historical materials and historical literatures, I had to be careful about treading into a space that was not very familiar with. However, I received enormous help, cooperation and encouragement from several corners. Many helped and encouraged me even unknowingly simply by showing interest to know more about the narratives in this book. I am extremely thankful to all of them.

This book has come out of my prolonged and sustained interaction with Fakir and his family, who were uprooted from their own country due to the Partition of India in 1947. The interaction was a difficult task as most of the narratives were full of emotional expressions related to separation, humiliation, violent attacks, and also friendly cooperation. Many letters, documents, personal diaries were consulted while going into the depth of this social biography. I am extremely thankful to Fakir's family for sharing these documents, incidents and stories and for kindly agreeing to allow me to write their story.

I am extremely grateful to Professor Ellie Chambers and Professor Andy Northedge, both Emeritus Professors at UKOU Milton Keynes, United Kingdom, for encouraging me to write this book. I am especially thankful to Professor T.K. Oommen (Professor Emeritus), Maitrayee Chaudhari, Professor of Sociology, JNU, New Delhi, Professor Tulsi Patel, Professor Abhijit Dasgupta, both Professors of Sociology (retd.), Delhi University, for their encouragement and to my former departmental colleagues, Professor Nita Mathur, Professor Rabindra Kumar, Professor B. Kiranmayi, Professor Archana Singh and Dr R. Vashum for their support and encouragement.

I am also thankful to Nehru Memorial Museum & Library, New Delhi, for providing me the Affiliated Fellowship in 2021. I took the opportunity to finalise the manuscript during my stay there.

I am thankful to Mr Ramesh Jain and Mr Ajay Jain of Manohar Publishers & Distributors, New Delhi for publishing this book and the editorial team members, Mr Sanjay Kala and Mr Subin Sabu for their valuable suggestions.

Finally I must thank my wife Prava, daughter Purbali, my son-in-law Deepam Vashisht, and my son Anirudha for their constant encouragement and inspiration. I am also thankful to Rajesh Sharma, Joginder Kumar, and Sonia for typing the manuscript and correcting errors without any complaint.

New Delhi DEBAL K. SINGHAROY
December 2022

Introduction

Seventy-five years ago, in 1947, India was partitioned on the religious line. This Partition immediately created two sovereign nation states – the secular Republic of India and the Islamic Republic of Pakistan with its two constituents, the East and West Pakistan. With a significant turn of history, this Partition further paved the way for the creation of People's Republic of Bangladesh out of East Pakistan, within the twenty-five years of creation of the Islamic Republic of Pakistan. Notwithstanding such political developments, Partition has remained a reality for over half-a-billion people living on both sides of the borders of these three sovereign nations. This has remained as a living testimony of communal divide and hatred for these nations and the people who have historically lived together, but have experienced indescribable trauma of partition related communal victimhood both during and after the Partition. The collective memory of the victims of Partition is often crowded with the vivid image of forced migration, communal violence, mob rampage, looting, abduction, rape and murder that they encountered as religious minority across the border. The religious majorities were not untouched by such trauma either. This Partition has remained rooted in the ontology of the people and the society, in their collective memory of painful separation from their *'janmabhumi'* (the motherland/birth place), family, friends, neighbourhood, and acquaintances alongside a longing for reunion with old friends, relatives, left behind motherland and sweet-old memories. Partition continues to hurt and hunt people of this subcontinent till now as the experiences of sufferings and horrific memories of Partition are transmitted from one generation of victims to the succeeding generation. As Batliwala (1998) writes, '... Partition was not, even in my family, a closed chapter of history—

that it's simple, brutal political geography infused and divided us still. The divisions were there in everyday life...' (Batliwala 1998: 1-2).

Partition followed the unprecedented trail of violence, that was unleashed with the resurge of communalism, a dark force that swayed the most parts of the society across the border. Many got carried away with the upsurge of this brute and ugly force creating a sense of horror in collective memory. However, standing against the tide of this dark force many also created pleasant collective memories by upholding at time and places the human spirit of peaceful living together with age old friends and neighbours of other faith, giving these vulnerable the much required protection, safety and help even risking their own lives in those crisis, uncertain and tense torn moments of Partition. They have silently gone against the overall flow of communal hatred and violence to repose intercommunity trust, cooperation and support in the moments of such brutal crisis those operated overtly across the space. These have created diverse memories of Partition for many. As underlined by Ishtiyaq Ahmed (2011), many people were reluctantly compelled to unleash violence against 'others'. Simultaneously, there are also incidences of one community saving the life and property of other community (Ahmed 2011: 7). These have also remained part of collective memory, but are seldom documented or documented very scantly.

In Indian subcontinent, a good body of literature is produced on the processes, reasons and outcome of Partition, for instance J.B. Kripalani (1976), A.I. Singh (1987), A.K. Neogoy (1987), B. Parekh (1989), I. Ahmed (1996), U. Butalia (1998), G. Pandey (2001), S. Mahajan (2000), A.G. Noorani (2000), K.A. Khalique (2002), S. Settar and I.B. Gupta (2002), A.I. Singh, P. Moon, G.D. Khosla, and M. Hasan (2004), B. Chakrabarty (2004), W. Gould (2005), M. Godbole (2006), J. Chatterji (2007), K. Roy (2011), I. Ahmed (2011), J. Basu and A. Roland (2011), G. Pandey (2012), B. Chakrabarty (2012), S. Bandyopadhyay (2014), S. Sarkar (2014), A. Jalal (2014), D. Sengupta (2016) , B. White-Spunner (2018), R. Ali, T.K. Saint, and D. Sengupta (2017), A. Malhotra (2018), J. Chaterjee (2019), A. Ahmed (2020), B. Bhaswati (2021), M. Bhatia (2021) are some of the numerous contributions made on India's independence struggle and Partition of the country.

Why and how did the Partition happened?, Who are responsible for the Partition?, What was the role of communal politics in the Partition? These are some of the major questions sincerely addressed in many of these works. Intense narratives are produced on the Partition of India focusing on the divide and rule policy of the British, communal mobilisation of the All India Muslim League, and the Hindu Mahasabha, rigidity of the Congress party and its failure to uphold the unity of the country. Based on rich archival data, historians have argued that the Partition of India was one of the four Partitions by the imperial British; the other being the Ireland, Mandatory Palestine, and the Cyprus, and that Partition of India and the creation of a sovereign Pakistan 'signaled the triumph of Muslim Communalism or Pakistani Nationalism and a failure for the Congress and its ideal of "secular Indian Unity"'. Many Indian historians have blamed the divisive policies of the British, and British have blamed Nehru's ideological rigidity for alienating Muslim League in 1937, and 1946 (Singh 2006: 5). It is also argued by the nationalist historians that Muslim League's act of communalization of politics since 1930 with British encouragement, the victory of the Congress in 1936-37 election and the subsequent formation of Indian National Congress Government in most of the provinces, the dependence of the British on the Muslim League for cooperation during the World War II in the wake of non-cooperation by the Congress resulted into the Partition of the country. However, the revisionist school, specially emerging from Pakistani academia argued that 'the right wing among the Congress and the Hindu communal forces pushed the Muslim league to a corner and Muslim league and Jinnah used the demand for Pakistan as a bargaining counter point with the Congress' (Roy 2012: XVI, Jalal 2014).

Scholars such as Chakrabarty, (2004) has emphasized on the Hindu and Muslim identity construction as the cause for the Partition of the country. It is argued that members of both communities were united as separate entities during the campaign for Partition. 'What brought them together was perhaps a well-nurtured feeling of hatred and intolerance for those outside the communal boundaries' through the processes of fission and fusion of their identity. The articulation of distinctive Hindu and Muslim identity and identity consciousness contributed to the shaping up of powerful campaign for separate Muslim state into British Indian provinces (Chakrabarty 2004: 27).

On the contrary, Pakistani historians like Ayesha Jalal has blamed the resurgence of Hindu communalism for the Partition of India. Jalal points out that Jinnah's claim of Indian Muslims as a nation was founded on the internationalists discourse on territorial nationalism and doctrine of self-determination, and that 'Jinnah's recourse to Islam was a product of political necessity – need to win support of the community having no prior history of organizing on a single platform'. To Jalal, recourse to Islam made sense to a politician and a party ... Both the politician and the party needed to steal the populist march on the rivals. It was his manipulation not of religion, but of politics that enabled Jinnah to steer the course of the League (Jalal 2014: 29).

Against the popular perception that the religious and cultural diversities have been the fertile grounds for the germination of communal differences in India, it argued that religious traditions and cultures associated with religion themselves have never been responsible for communal conflict in India. 'But the ways those traditions are processed, represented, and propagated by Congress nationalists (and then the way those syntheses were interpreted by non-Congress person) were often communally divisive' (Gould 2005: 274). It is underlined that the connection of Congress leaders with Hindu Mahasabha and Arya Samaj at different levels, use of Hindu idioms during the Civil Disobedience and thereafter, adoption of *Vande Mataram* song, tricolor national flag, Gandhi's *Harijan* fast in response to communal backlashes helped reconfigure communitarian identity in the name of religion. 'In a struggle to represent itself as a national institution, Congress as a movement became an open house for whole range of political actors and ideologies. The Congress mobilization through religious festivals and expressions opened field to political operators with more communal agendas, and reinforced the League's acquisition that Congress power represented the Hindu Raj (ibid: 265-6).

To Joya Chatterjee (1996), the difference between the Hindu Mahasabha and Congress was 'withered away during the 40s, and in Bengal, Hindus evolved a parallel separatism of their own, even though the Partition is generally belief to have been consequence of the separatist policies of Muslim minorities'. Chatterjee argues that the Hindu Mahasabha and the Congress worked closely together in the cause of Partition and the Bengal Provincial unit of Congress unquestionably took the lead in orchestrating the campaign successfully for the division of the province on communal lines (Chatterjee 1996: 22).

Sucheta Mahajan (2000) has effectively focused her blame on the British and the Muslim League for the partition of the country. Mahajan documents that after the 1945-6 election, when the Congress won in most of the Provinces and in the Central Assemblies, the British could have accepted the claim of Congress to be the main representative of the Indian opinion. But the very success of the 'divide and rule policy of the British that propping up the Muslim league to combat the Congress contributed to their final failure to leave behind the united India'. To Mahajan (2000), Jinnah was still useful to the British as a counter force against the Congress. British was unsure of united India's role in the future Commonwealth and wanted to keep Pakistan an alley. 'The Partition decision to be seen both as the first act of the drama of Commonwealth diplomacy and the closing scene of divide and rule.... It was part of Britain's future in India as well as her past. The acceptance of Partition was thus only the final act of a process of step-by-step concession to the Muslim League's intransigent championing for a sovereign Muslim state' (Mahajan 2000: 386-9).

Though the political dimension of the Partition is well documented, what has remained underreported or has acquired lesser status is, as called by Uruashi Butalia (1998), 'the human dimensions of the Partition'. The impacts of Partition on the common man especially on the questions focusing on 'how families were divided, how friendships endured across borders, how people coped with the trauma, how they rebuilt their lives, what resources, both physical and mental, they drew upon, how their experience of dislocation and trauma shaped their lives', have got very limited in the conventional history (Butalia 1998: 4-7).

In recent years, however, there have been growing attempts by an important section of the scholars to investigate into the plights of the common man who became the victims of the Partition and also simultaneously experienced 'the loss and sharing, friendship and enmity, grief and joy, with a painful regret and nostalgia for loss of home, country and friends, and the determination to create them afresh (Ibid. 1998: 4). Efforts have also been to emphasise on the hitherto 'unimportant fragmentary episodes' in order to provide narratives of the common man and their struggle as marginal group and the refugees to rebuilt their lives alongside the great political turmoil . Hence, going away from the classical narrative on how and why India was divided, these scholars are concerned with the consequences of Partition especially how the refugees re-ordered their lives after 1947. These scholars have given emphasis on empathy with the common mass 'to reconstruct the varied experiences of Partition, meaning they ascribe to it with the aid of folklores, oral interviews, fictions, poems, short stories, and other writings. It highlights the trauma of Partition of the innocent common masses who experienced threat, separation, and attempt to life, refugeehood and persecution due to Partition in 1947' (Roy 2012: xvii).

Going away from the conventional archival documents, and based on the oral history collected through interviews, Uruashi Butalia (1998) provides a first-hand and vivid account of the victims of Partition of India in 1947, including the members of her own family who have experienced the horror of partition. These are as much the personal narratives of the victims of partition as much revealing of the other side of the history. Butalia has passionately shown the innate urge of these victims to secure the protection and dignity of the family members in the wake of the outbreak of communal atrocities that followed the Partition. She has also sensitively documented the 'silent stories of rebuilding the family after the Partition'. Importantly, gender question has remained a focus of her narratives. Regarding her approach to this study she writes 'I have come to this work through a political—and personal—engagement with history, contemporary communalism, and a deep and abiding belief in feminism' (Butalia 1998: 9).

For Gyanendra Pandey (2001), though experiences of violence, dislocations and the collective memories surrounding these are important components of the history of the masses, the historiography of the ruling class seldom address such serious moments of dislocation in the history. Though memories of common people are important source to reconstruct history, these very often than not get side lined or ignored. Following Pierre Nora (1996), he argues that 'there has been decisive shift in the writing of history from historical to psychological, from social to individual, from concrete to message to subjective interpretation.... Memory has become the discourse that replaces history as another communicator' (Pandey 2001: 17). Turning to the Partition of India, he points out that there is a need to 'recover the history of Partition not of large and historical processes alone ... but also history of struggle of people fighting to cope survive and to rebuild a new history as a history of everyday....While individuals and families recreate themselves in change situation and conditions, they are unable to forget memories of violence quite easily (ibid: 17-21).

Ahmed (2011), focusing on the Partition and its aftermath, elucidates the victimhood of common man through their first-hand account. He narrates how many Hindus, Muslims and Sikhs got engaged in arson and killing of and violence against 'others' and were reluctantly compelled to unleash violence against 'others'. He also documents the incidences of one community people saving the life and property of other community and the good and bad memories of Partition those are making people to undertake post-Partition visits to left behind land and to avoid such visit based on old bad memories (Ahmed 2011).

Literature, poetry, drama, memoirs have also widely contributed to construct the realities of sufferings of Partition on the people. D. Sengupta (2016) founded on selected Bengali novels, has analyzed the traumas of Partition as encountered by people being the member of particular caste group, gender and class and critiqued the hegemonic tendency of the nation state. She has developed candid narratives of formation of Hindu-Muslim identity, the Kolkata and Noakhali riots, post-Partition displacement, issues of settlement of Bengali refugees, post-Partition life of the commoners and such related concerns. In another similar work, Ali, Saint and Sengupta, (2017) based on Urdu, Punjabi, Hindi and Bengali essays, poetries, dramas, short fictional stories and memoirs from India, Pakistan and Bangladesh, have brought out new insights into the realities of Partition and its afterlife. These writings forcefully narrate the feelings of nostalgia, emotion, separation and urge for reunion of the displaced people across the border.

In social sciences, memory has always remained an important component of data collected for social analysis. Many of the case studies and life histories are developed founded on memories, and integrating those memories with other varieties of empirical data. In recent decades, memory has got a pace of prominence in developing narratives surrounding life stories of the victim of Partition as a welcome come addition to write and rewrite social histories. When the archival data is inadequate or absent to present the depth of pains, plight, pleasures, sufferings and celebrations of the common man, memory and oral history come in big way to reflect on their history from below. By establishing connection between events and the people memories construct identity with a shared past. It is possible that individual memories may differ as individuals are differently located as historical actors. However, a large part of shared memories of broad historical upheavals of Indian subcontinents have remained associated with the identity of the marginal people e.g. refugees, migrants, natives, and insider and outsider.

It is acknowledged that the study of memory has always remained problematic because of its subjective and multi-faceted orientations. Memories are founded on events or series of interrelated events, and those are also witnessed and experienced in real time by different people who are subject to their own subjective biases. Here, Batliwala points out that the way people choose to remember an event are not self-evident givens. They rather are interpretations, 'as remembered or recorded by one individual or another' (Batliwala 1998: 8). Notwithstanding the issue of subjectivity and interpretations, memories on Partition have remained to be social facts for the millions people who have experienced the trauma of Partition. The state and the historians and the social scientists often give their own facts and interpretations. Many of those are contradicting and conflicting in factual and interpretative terms. However, while dealing with the memories social scientist have the option to counter balance it with related oral histories founded on memory. These altogether can provide a new perspective on construction of social history founded on memory.

The present study is founded on both individual and social memories those are shaped out of the broad process of communalisation of politics, Partition of the country, condition of staying back of a Hindu family as a religious minority in East Pakistan, their experiences of getting heart touching cooperation and support from Muslim neighbours and friends to thwart repeated communal attacks in difficult situations, coercive episodes of migration from East Pakistan and Bangladesh to India, shocks and plights of uncertainties and refugeehood, and processes of naturalizing within the liberal plural socio-cultural fabrics therein. It has illustrated the intertwining of the local (family, neighbourhood, village(s)) dynamics of patriotism, communalism and nationalism with the wider (regional and national) social and political processes through a social biography. This social biography presents the trajectories of lives of members of a Hindu family who have undergone the experiences of articulation of the ideologies of communalism and ethno-nationalism, threats of communal violence and support of patriotic Muslims in time of brutal communal attacks on them, their shifting status of nativity, acquiring the status of Hindu minority, their migration to India as refugee with part family, their isolation, pains of family separation and joy of reunion, their hope and despair in everyday existence in the pre and post-Partition of Indian subcontinent. It has presented this social biography by applying the technique of life history founded on memory and lived in experiences those have taken shape in the historical contexts surrounding Partition of India.

In the Indian subcontinent, the historical interrelationships between the ideologies concerning patriotism, nationalism, ethnocentrism, communalism, and the event of Partition in 1947 remain deeply rooted politically. These relationships have got reconstructed and reoriented over the centuries and have brought forth far-reaching social, cultural and economic ramifications to people living on both sides of the borders of this divided subcontinent for several generations. Many have been persecuted through these processes by either becoming refugees or staying back as religious minorities, and losing their homeland, livelihood, and security, in return, by encountering everyday threats of murder, riots, rape, and the cultural, humanitarian and emotional crises following the Partition of the country in 1947. These, in many ways, have remained embedded within their experiences as collective memories of victimhood of communalism and the Partition of the country, despite being committed to the patriotic and nationalistic ideals in their aspirations.

Most important, the colossal sense of victimhood by the vast section of people is linked to the evolving politicality of constructing ideologies, such as patriotism, ethnocentrism, nationalism and communalism and their evolving courses across the globe. Patriotism, as an ideology, has always stood for an all-encompassing and unconditional love for the motherland and its people, and has inherently remained grounded in an inclusive and apolitical commitment for the collective being in the formation of society and the country. However, with the expansion of modernity, followed by the industrialization, colonization, de-colonization, political transitions and other situational exigencies of the societies, the country has experienced a phenomenal transition.

In the historical trajectory of such transition of the country and the modern-state formation, some components of patriotism have altered their course by taking forms comprising ethnocentrism, nationalism and communalism. Despite its shift from its course in some of its elements, patriotism, for many, is still continuing as an expression of love for the country and fellow citizens irrespective of religion, sect, ethnic, linguistic, regional and such other biases, in its orientation and expression.

Though nationalism, as such, is founded upon emotional and political constructions, it has emerged to be a unifying factor in its nature; moral and ideal epitome for selfless sacrifice in its essence. Similarly, it has also taken various forms across the globe in the form of cultural, political, secular, civic, communal, and constitutional nationalisms. While, nationalism was a liberating force against the colonial and other non-sovereignal forces, it has also become an instrument for a section of political forces to mobilize and unite people and to achieve sectarian and communal political goals. Nationalism, by taking a communal and exclusivist form, has contributed in production of unprecedented communal hatred accompanying with threat, isolation and intolerance resulting in the division of communities and partition of the countries in the name of ethnicity and religion. It has transformed the social and natural differences into politically and culturally defined nomenclatures, comprising of 'we' and 'them' and the 'common friends' and 'enemies' with respect to classification of communities. Thus, it has forced relegation of millions of people to be religious and linguistic minorities in their own motherland across the border and to bear the brunt of communal backlash based on cultural and economic spheres and, thereafter, the forced migration to the unknown and uncertain destinations as 'refugees'.

With the upsurge and consolidation of communal forces and communal nationalism India attained Independence in 1947 through the Partition of the country. However, the 1947 Partition of India and the mass exodus across the borders were not a one-time phenomenon, nor was it ever conclusive. Despite the horrific experiences, many affected families were undecided and preferred to stay back as a religious/ethnic minority with the hopes of normalization and reversal of situations, following their historical and a lifelong emotional attachment to their motherland and their native habitation. Also, their closeness to their neighbours and friends, and fears of loss of livelihood are other such factors for staying back. Following their staying back, accompanied the victimhood experiences, insecurities, regular menaces, ignominy and persecution on an everyday basis in their struggle for survival; many also experienced abundant love, deep emotional support, assurances and security at the individual level from their good old childhood and family friends-cum-neighbours hailing from various religious groups. Many also risked their own lives to provide safety and security to these religious minorities who stayed back as a matter of attachment to the motherland. For these insecure religious minorities, these supports and protections were the sole lifelines in the unfolding 'new land' consisting of 'many enemies' and 'few friends'.

Over the years, new generations born in the religious minority families also experienced the heightening communal threats and tensions on the one hand, and friendly cooperation and support from their friendly neighbours on the other hand. Inter-community cooperation also emerged as living examples of coexistence of the religious minority and majority sections in the newly created countries, based on their inheritance of common pasts comprising cultural and ethnic pluralistic values. However, in the wake of widespread political and communal tensions taking shape at the wider level of the society, the individual and inter-community support and securities were appearing to be too fragile to overshadow the realities of communal apprehensions and perils for the religious minorities living in theocratic states. As a result, many of them became compelled to migrate to the opposite side of the border initially with half of the family members, and thereafter, with the entire kinsfolk severing all sorts of societal ties. After migrating to the new land, many lived as survivors who were persecuted and uprooted; remained stigmatized by the society as refugees or half-refugees, accompanied by their haunting old memories, and departed with pains of detachment-cum-unfulfilled desires of reunion with their abandoned motherland.

This book, in the context of consolidation of the ideology of nationalism, covers the arousal of ethnocentrism, communalism and exclusivist nationalisms emerging from the late nineteenth century up to the attainment of Independence of India, followed by the Partition of India in 1947, supplemented with large-scale exodus across the borders of the newly created sovereign states—India and Pakistan. It narrates the experiences of persecution of a Hindu minority family hailing from East Pakistan, their part-family migration and refugee status in India, and their struggle for survival and integration with the large pluralistic Indian identity.

Based on the biography of this particular Hindu religious minority family from East Pakistan, it specifically narrates the circumstances of their staying back as a member of the religious minority community; along with their experiences of everyday victimhood and menaces on the one hand, and the cooperation and protection from their Muslim friends and neighbours during the times of crisis on the other, which created a new meanings with respect to inter-community trust and conflicts. It elucidates the episodes of serial attacks and humiliations on the family members, followed with the forced and sudden migration of part of the family members to India as refugees and their augmentative sufferings, struggles and encounters with several political forces on both sides of the border as half families.

The book also depicts against the backdrop of the famous 1971 Bangladesh war of independence, and thereafter, the resurgence of religious fundamentalism, the brutal killing of the Muslim friends associated with the Hindu family there and the final exodus of their remaining family members to India. It chronicles the feeling of pain with regard to estrangement from their motherland, and the desire to unite with the left-behind motherland and a faint hope of reunion to stay on the other side of the border. Finally, this book illustrates how these successive generations became the victims of the Partition for upholding the spirit of inter-community trust.

The book is presented in six chapters concerning: (a) the issues of patriotism, ethnocentrism, communalism and nationalism; (b) the emergence of nationalism, the resurgence of exclusivist communal nationalism and the historical processes concerning the Partition of the country in 1947; and (c) the victimhood and persecution experienced by the people because of Partition in 1947 and their unending suffering, thereafter. Chapter one entitled, 'Patriotism, Ethnocentrism, Communalism and Nationalism: Changing Courses and Emerging Discourses' unfolds the essential components, progression and interrelationship between the ideologies concerning patriotism, ethnocentrism, communalism and nationalism.

The second chapter titled, 'Communalism, Politics and the Partition of India in 1947: Belying the Patriotic Tradition', elucidates how the resurgence of communalism and the communal politics submerged the plural ethos of the country leading to its Partition in 1947.

The following three chapters, i.e. 'Partition and Persecution: Fakir and his Family as Minority in East Pakistan', 'Laltu's Journey to India with Half Family: Struggles against Persecution on Other Side of the Borders', and 'Reunion of Half Families and Legacies of Laltu in India' present a case of a stayed back Hindu minority family in East Pakistan which was forced to migrate to India as refugee after eighteen years of Partition. It showcases through the biographic sketch of a person who was born and brought up in eastern part of Bengal of undivided India, his experiences of the intra-community friendship, succeeded by gradual alienness, tribulations, the forced migration to India and the episodes of further post-resettlement struggles.

India had experienced the processes of consolidation of the forces of nationalism on the one hand and communalism and ethnocentrism on the other during the anti-colonial struggle. However, nationalism has changed its course with the manifestations of communalism and ethnocentrism making India experience the proliferation of multiple nationalities, propagation of two nation theory and ultimately the division of the country. The division of the country showed the victory of the exclusivist communal nationalism forcing a vast section of people of newly designated religious minority for mass exodus across the border with unprecedented human tragedy. The realities of patriotism got subdued for many in the wake of forceful manifestation of communalism and exclusivist nationalism. Many patriots got collectively identified as religious minority and aliens in their own land where they were born and lived for generation, while the other became majority through the new political discourse and the Partition of the country. While a vast section of religious minorities migrated to the other side of the border to look for security and a new life, a section stayed back notwithstanding all threats and insecurities because of their traditional attachment to motherland or perhaps they had no option to go elsewhere. Many of them who stayed back, besides encountering regular humiliation, threat, and insecurities for generations, also received unconditional love, support, help and security from the patriotic people of other communities. Though the spirit of patriotism and love for the motherland were eclipsed by the overflow of communalism, these were not erased from the mind of people for ever as they have the eternal urge to remain rooted to their own land, people, culture and habitat. Thus, despite getting uprooted, tortured, humiliated, and socially, economically, politically and emotionally persecuted through the politics of Partition of the country, many upheld the intercommunity cooperation and friendship and retained the strong desire to get united with the left behind motherland even during the last days of their lives on the other side of the border. These never sung common men have encountered the lived history of communal politics of India by upholding the spirit of patriotism by making several sacrifices as common Hindus and Muslims.

This social biography is presented through the life history of Fakir and his family, who lived as a religious minority after the division of the country in 1947 till 1974 in the Bheramara Thana of Kushtia district (erstwhile Nadia) district of East Pakistan, now in current Bangladesh by collecting information following the techniques of in-depth interviews, unstructured open ended discussions with Fakir and his family members, consultation of their personal letters, telegrams, diaries and notebooks, property documents etc. The interviews and discussions and their own narratives were very lengthy and were full of emotional expressions. I am a part of Fakir's family and have been a witness of many of their sufferings, pains and pleasures as an insider. I am aware that my attachment with this family has influenced me in many ways in writing this book. Fakir was a poetic person and was fond of instantly composing small couplets to express his emotion. Those have inspired me to compose poetries to express the feelings of the respondents and their association with old memories, those are parts of their lives and their social history. Except for Fakir, all other names are not revealed in this book due to professional reasons of the respondents and their requests for anonymity. One of the reasons for such anonymity, as one member of Fakir's family said 'I want to forget the past, as those memories gives us pain, and bring feeling of horror in our existence. I only wish those parts of history and life are not repeated in our lives again…'

I am not a historian. My attempt, however, has not been to reconstruct history in the conventional sense of the term. In many ways it may be considered as idealized, a personal and one-sided narrative. But it is not a faceless fiction, but a social biography. By putting this local social biography in a wider context this book has only tried show how the communalism induced Partition of the country has pushed common men to their victimhood as religious minority to encounter communal violence and everyday threat to life, how they faced tortures, how the Muslim friends and neighbours protected them in the crucial situation by even risking their own lives, how were they forced to migrate to India as refugee and marginalized; how the family get separated and reunited after years of sufferings and isolation, what efforts they made to create the space for their safely, security, and to rebuilt their future, how they got socialized and naturalized in liberal and plural fabrics of India, what are the legacies left behind by the elderly generation of victims, how are those practiced by the succeeding generation of victims, and what challenges they encounter in becoming inclusive in society. Thematically, it locates this social biography in the contexts of nurturing of inherent patriotism of Indian society, articulation of ethnocentrism and communalism thereon, changing facets of nationalism and the historicity of the Partition of India in 1947 and its consequences on the common man.

The identities of patriotism, ethnocentrism, communalism, exclusivist, communalism and civic nationalism are overlapping and their boundaries are often fuzzy as these frequently shuttle between cultural essentialism and situational/political constructionalism. In a situation of politically induced urgency when some sections of people by using the identity of exclusivist communal nationalism construct social binary to isolate the religious minorities, attack them brutally, threat life, property and their dignity and force them to leave the country, notwithstanding the communal tension, some people came out openly by upholding the eternal spirit of the identity of patriotism to protect the vulnerable minorities, giving them the much required assurance of their safety, security and belonging even risking their own lives. These create both for the protector and protected victims an enduring lived-in-experience and memory of assurance for dignity, belongingness, inclusion, love and fellow feeling. These acts and experiences are subjective and emotional and reflective of inherent collective conscience founded on patriotism. Many compatriots and especially the victims of communalism induced partition cherished those memories despite having unfair past, try to replicate those experiences of support and cooperation even paying costs for it. They indeed discover celebration of life in the process of paying those costs. In that sense their lives have not gone a waste. They have left behind a legacy of inter-community mutual trust, deep sense of accommodation and empathy to emulate by the next generation.

CHAPTER 1

Patriotism, Ethnocentrism, Communalism and Nationalism
Changing Courses and Emerging Discourses

Motherland and Patriotism

Men and women are born in a family. They also simultaneously get linked to and associated with various local and major social groups like kin, clan, neighbourhood, ethnicity, religion, motherland, the country, state, market and so forth. An individual's association with each of these groups develops a distinctive sense of identity, interests and expectations, and thereby, attracts a specific attention, commitment, love and loyalty. Among all these, one's relationship with one's motherland or place of nativity (*janmabhumi*) is distinctively different from others. Such association is grounded on the ideals of patriotism. It is a multi-faceted manifestation of a deep-seeded feeling of moral and emotional attachment, uncompromising love and loyalties for the sake of dignity and integrity towards the motherland. This patriotic feeling is simultaneously embedded in the strong sense of admiration for boundless resources and accumulation of pride for its cultural heritage and historical legacies, inherent glory and fathomless beauty of their motherland. Since ages, it has bestowed numerous people a sense of distinctive identity, a perspective, a doctrine, an ideology or a way of life, that connects them with their land, water and air, environs, its people and food habits, culture, art, music, folklores, norms, values, stories and moorings with everyday sense of sharing and reciprocity. It sustains and permeates among them, through its presence a sense of longing; providing a lived-in feeling of rootedness, completeness, encompassing bondage of 'we-ness' and 'own-ness' collectivity with a larger identity of their motherland. Also, it creates a sense of melancholy and nostalgia in its absence.

Patriotism is not only a poetic imagination and description, or a military conqueror's zeal, but also an existential and spiritual attachment to their land, nature, people, history and culture of motherland by the commonfolk. It is grounded on their ontology and an inherent spirit of accommodation, fellowship and commitment for all the people living in the motherland (or fellow compatriots) egalitarianism, absence of hostility to others, inclusivity of identity, and apoliticality of social concerns.The emotions and concerns are as much psychological as is it in literal sense. With respect to the subjective articulation, the geographic boundary of motherland is often natural; and covers all irrespective of their religion, colour, language, caste, class, occupation and creed, and sharing the same topography. Though, one's mother tongue is the prime principle of rootedness to the motherland, other tongue/dialects are also nurtured in this natural habitat showing mutual respect for each other.

Throughout the Indian vernacular lexicography, the term 'motherland' is widely mentioned as *desh, desham, nadu, bhumi*, and the inhabitants are termed as the *deshbasi, deshermanus, bhumiputra*, etc., irrespective of one's religion, language, caste, class, occupation and political orientations. From the Indian perspective, the concept of *desh, desham, nadu, bhumi*, in its essence, is an accommodation of natural inhabitants speaking multiple dialects, practicing diverse customs, norms, faith and belief systems in a geographical area, unconcerned with the political underpinning of the state and society. Social heterogeneities seldom acquire the shape of political divisions, as these diversities are often inter-linked through a common thread of cultural, historical ethos, heritage and practices.

Ethnocentrism

In a multicultural society, the terms *desh, desham, nadu, bhumi*, etc. may not be restricted to a particular linguistic, cultural, religious, and ethnic group. There may be articulation of feelings of cultural neglect, collective insecurity, social marginalization, economic exploitation, and the threat of domination among some ethnic groups over other groups. Again, there may be an arousal of aspiration to preserve cultural distinctiveness, economic and political autonomy, without the interference of other group(s) in their affairs in an identified territory. These factors may lead to the development of ethnocentrism among some ethnic groups with the belief that they are distinctively different and superior to others, or they are excluded, threatened and dominated by other ethnic communities. There may be assertions of ethnic identity(ies) by few ethnic groups highlighting the distinctiveness of their inherited common religious, historical, linguistic, territorial, racial, cultural origins. Claims of these common origins may also provide the basis for the creation of a sense of separatism thereby creating a separate identity within a community.

It is widely realized that ethnic distinctiveness not only exists, it is also constructed. Ethnicity is founded on multiple grounds and collective principles of common origins through religion, language, history, colour, culture, region of the people and so forth. It also involves intersectionality of similar mindsets of people intertwining at each other's principles of common origins for their existence and construction of new identities or meanings. Since the members of ethnic groups often find more than one principles, but on the occasions of collective assertion, they make a choice. While in one situation, such choices may be conditioned by subjective value of an individual's association with one specific ethnic principle, but in another situation it may be steered by rational calculation of interests with another ethnic principle. Putting together, this creates 'ethnicity' as a matter of heart in one place and mind in another (Barks 1996, cf. Jenkins 2007: 1478). Ethnocentrism in one situation may be formed on the basis of cultural principle for seeking cultural exclusivity and in another situation, on a political principle aspiring for political autonomy, and benefitting economic interests to a group from the state machinery, on the other. Thus, ethnocentrism may acquire political connotation over a period of time, and may articulate demand for separate nationality causing the development of ethno nationalism and formation of ethno-statehood.

Therefore, ethnocentrism as an ideology acquires distinctiveness from patriotism in its expression in the forms containing exclusivity of identity, initiation of boundary for specific group within the larger communities. It articulates subjective feeling of admiration and well-being, accommodative spirit and compassion and egalitarianism for own identified group. However it constructs sense of hierarchy and segregation for outcasts, becomes expression of politicality around social concerns, and develops hostility to others giving rise to association with the specific territory and developing aspirations for nationalism and nation-state formation. It is often underlined that, when a particular ethnic group identifies itself with a territory and adopts the same as their homeland by transforming their 'outness' into 'ins' and acquires legitimate moral claims over an area, it transforms into a nation. And, when a nation secures its political jurisdiction in their homeland, it becomes a state. Thus, the formation of nation based ethnic claims comes forth before the formation of such state (Oommen 1997: 36).

Communalism

Communalism has developed its roots in ethnocentrism. It shows exclusive fondness, loyalty and commitment to one's own ethnic community, gradually, developing a deep sense of segregation, antagonism and intolerance against the other communities. Communalism begins with the belief, that people can be organised and clubbed together for the economic, political and social purposes around their religious identities (Chandra 1993: 148). Besides religion, the communal lines are used based on racial and linguistic identities to organise people. Communalism is, thus, community specific within a larger society, while the basis of this community may be religion, language and race. In the process of its progression, communalism has propagated the belief that the cultural identities and the political and economic interests of one's group are distinctively different from those of the other religious groups. And, that particular group have been conditioned to be isolated, neglected, victimised, marginalized by other groups in the process of their cohabitation in a larger society, that they are under constant threat of further victimization in the society; that they need to carve out a political space for their existence and progress in the society. As highlighted by Castells, it may take the form of 'exclusion of the excluded, by the excluded' (Castells 1997: 7). Thus, communalism becomes an ideology of looking at the society and the politics; and communalists are keen to spread communal belief system and violence as a means to spread their respective ideology. Consequently, communal violence is the end result of the spread of communal ideology (Chandra 1993: 151).

Communalism in an essence is an organizing tool for recognizing collectively, with exclusive love for own community and exclusion of the other community, accompanied with distrust, hatred for other, and thereby, developing binaries. It implies threat or victimhood from others as tools for the propagation of its ideologies, lay emphasis on glorious historical or/and religious past to strengthen its societal base, and thereupon, recasting into a form of political ideology to capture power, influences the course of formation of nationalism in a country.

However, the universal forms and apolitical values of love and commitment of patriotism have a very limited scope of expression in ethnocentrism and communalism, as these are confined by the consolidation of communities within the communities with political aspirations. There are overlapping trajectories of ethnocentrism and communalism in terms of their expression and collective assertion, and both have their lasting impact on the expression of nationalism. In the South Asian context, with reference to India, in particular, the dominant basis of communalism has historically been the religious identities since the middle of nineteenth century and has enormously influenced the process of shaping up the spirit of Indian nationalism.

Communalism has two facets as highlighted by Chandra (1993)—the liberal and the fascist. The liberal communalists accept the views that both Hindus and the Muslims have divergent economic, political, social and cultural interests, which must be reconciled and adjusted through pressure and negotiations. These communities have shared political, social and cultural interests, which have made them part of a common nation, and that they must be united to achieve these interests, for political independence, economic development and alleviation of poverty. On the contrary, the fascist communalists, argue that the interests of Hindus and Muslims are not only divergent, but antagonistic and irreconcilable, and for which they argued for a two-nation theory and formation of a separate state in which the religious minorities would lead a subordinate, subservient, and experience a level of second-class existence (ibid.: 149). In the multi-ethnic society, such communalism may take a distinct form of nationalism like that of communal or separatist nationalism and keep on mobilising people for its long-term sustenance on the society. However in the political trajectory, it may achieve different destinations. In the South Asian context as highlighted by Ahmed, it may fail to mobilise substantial support from among the group on whose behalf it is staked, or it can wither away under the impact of overall socio-economic change, or be accommodated within the same autonomy formula, or assume threatening proportions in the form of secessionist bids. The important thing to note is that states almost invariably resist breakaway attempts.... The group tension and conflict in modern multi-ethnic societies underline political separatism (Ahmed 1996: 1). At this point, let us have a clarity on the concept and dynamics of nationalism.

Nationalism

In the developmental trajectory of the society and the state, with the expansion of colonization, westernization and modernization, patriotism has encountered social, economic and political forces. Since the ambiguous boundaries of land and lives of the people get politically influenced, many noble principles of patriotism started getting restrained within the principles of ethnocentrism and communalism and, thereafter, nationalism. Nationalism, hence, produces an overarching collective political identity by overlapping many of the pre-existing ethnic-cum-community identities. However, by its operational principles, it may not function in an autonomous manner with other identities that have pre-existed in the society. It carries forward many collective identities having a complementary relationship at some points of time, may develop contradictions, with many other identities in the due process. Over the centuries, many components of patriotism, ethnocentrism and communalism were also captured within the onward march in the modernization process of nationalism. Most social groups, which are either looking forward to preserve their autonomy and aspiring independence from aggression of other forces, construct or apply nationalism as an organizing, mobilizing and motivating force of connecting people to espouse their particular cause. Most importantly, while patriotism contains no historical veracity, the ethnocentrism, communalism and nationalism expanded with certain stages of historical development of the society.

Nationalism elucidates itself as an ideology through construction of a collective identity and a set of imageries; and upholding the ideology, identity and symbols creates a deep sense of pride and desire, even at the cost of death or to kill for its protection and preservation. It makes people raise themselves as a collectivized entity above their individual concerns and subsume their existence within the all-encompassing ideology, identity and symbols of nationalism. In many ways, nationalisms and nation states in the contemporary world have emerged to be realities for articulating unity and differences among humankind despite of diverse operational principles and discursive perspectives.

Though nationalism as an ideology has emerged to be a universal phenomenon, it has taken assorted forms and crossed eclectic trajectories. Every nationalism is founded on particular historicity and have some inherent contractions in it. Here, Pandey (2001) underlined that nationalism has been the product of distinctive histories and it has been as profound 'as its leading class or classes; visionaries as well as practical men and women aspiring to rule or to unify people, mobilize resources and transform economic and social political conditions in a new progressive spirit and like every other major development in history it has been sought through its own contradictory impulses'. Pandey further asserts that 'given the contradictory claims and achievement and the necessarily contradictory quality of its conditions of existence, we can scarcely accept at face value of the self-representation of a particular nationalism of nationalist ideologies (Pandey 2001: 18-19). It is now acknowledged that, over the centuries, nationalism has revealed its diverse shades and there have been diverse perspectives in comprehending it.

Perspectives on Nationalism

The concept and ideology of nationalism has remained one of the most powerful forces in the contemporary world, in spite of acquiring host of complexities attached to it. It has been ambiguous in its orientation and direction to be unitary, cooperative, integrative, inclusive, sympathetic, moral, spiritual, sacrificing force and so forth on the one hand, and divisive, disintegrative, exclusivist, detestation, intolerant, and egocentric on the other. Perspectives on nationalism have been diverse across the globe based on the spatial, historical and varieties of other considerations. The Western English scholar J.S. Mill has invoked the elements of sympathy and cooperation among people to encapsulate the ideals of nation. Mill considers nation as 'a portion of mankind, who are united among themselves through common sympathies to cooperate with each other more willingly than with other people, and cherish the desire to be under the same government by themselves' (Mill 1861/1958 ed.: 16). For Ernest Renan (1882), the ideal of nation is also linked to the formation of a principle and a conscience of high order as he defines nation as a soul and a spiritual principle. It is a great solidarity constituted by the feeling of sacrifices made and those that one is still disposed to make. This is founded on the moral conscience and spiritual principles, are not simply constructed mechanically (Renan 1882/1992). However, a nation can't be formed without some essential features and aspirations in common. E.H. Carr (1939) defines a nation as confined by certain common characteristics, particularly languages, developing a certain degree of common feeling, will and closeness among its members and an idea of a collective government etc., and clearly distinguishes one nation with other national and non-national groups (Carr 1939: 7).

It is widely asserted that people get linked to a larger community through their association with the entities of nation and nationalism. This relationship is depicted as much through their actions and is much more than its imagination. Through nationalism, many derive the legitimacy of one's thoughts and actions and their ontological connotations. This implies that the ideal of nationalism is an emotional and romanticised imagination. For Anderson (1983), a nation is 'an imagined political community and imagined as both are inherently limited and sovereign. It is an imagined entity because the members of even the smallest nation will never know most of their fellow beings. Yet, in the minds of each life lies, the image of their communion. It is imagined as a limited identity because even the largest nation has limits too, and boundaries ahead, other nations. No nation imagines itself coterminous with humankind. Ultimately, it is this fraternity that makes it possible, over past two centuries, for so many millions of people, not so much to kill, but willing to die for such limited imagining' (Anderson 1983: 57).

Nationalism, in its modern sense, though originated in the Western world in the seventeenth century, has also reached other parts of the globe subsequently. While such a movement has been observed by a section of Western intelligentsia as an imposition of a high Western culture on the rest of the world leading to the emergence of concepts such as nation-state and liberation movements, its also been seen by many Eastern scholars as abominable in the world. Gellner (1983) considers the process of achieving the ideal of nationalism as a general imposition of a high culture on a particular society, where low culture once prevailed. It has also been seen as the establishment of an incognito impersonal society, with a manually substitutable atomized individual, held together, above all, by a shared culture of this kind, in lieu of a previous complex structure comprising local groups sustained by folk cultures, which are replicated regionally and distinctively by the micro-groups themselves (Gellner 1983: 57). Significantly, in Gellner's formulation, the nation-state and nationalism are congruent in nature. However, Eric Hobsbawm (1990) considers these formations to take place in context with social and historical sequences. Here too, the western bias is reflecting extensively. Hobsbawm further elaborates that, across the world, nationalism is constructed essentially from above, and 'national consciousness' is developed varyingly among various social groups and regions in a country. In its initial phase, it was purely cultural, literary and allegorical in nature, without any particular political implications. Over the years, the participation and political campaigning by leaders and radicals, the 'idea of nationalism' emerged into a literal shape. Simultaneously, nationalism acquired mass support from the middle-class sections, factory/industry workers, and peasants by organizing movements, leading to the formation of nation-state system. As a matter of course, nationalism comes much before the creation of nation state. On the contrary, Hobsbawm (1990) was very critical on the issue of establishment of nationalism in the Third World countries. He argues that in the Third World countries, the idea of nationalism does not take shape even after the formation of nation states (Hobsbawm 1990: 121-2).

Dark and Diverse Shades within Nationalism

Though nationalism expanded as a liberating force, it has also brought forth several dark sides of human being with its progression. It is accompanied with social divisions, separatism and hatred towards fellow human being in the name of nationalism. Rabindranath Tagore (1950) was disturbed by the increasing rifts in the world and the growing lust for various vested economic and political interests for the sake of nationalism. For Tagore,

> A nation, in the sense of the political and economic union of a people, is organized for a mechanical purpose. It is an end in itself. It is for self-preservation. It is merely the other side of power, not of human ideals.... The Nation, with all its paraphernalia of power and prosperity, its flags and pious hymns, its blasphemous prayers in the churches, and the literary mock thunders of its patriotic bragging, cannot hide the fact that the Nation is the greatest evil for the Nation... (Tagore 1950: 5-18).

He further elaborates that

> Men, the fairest creations of God, came out of the National manufactory in huge numbers as war-making and money-making puppets; ludicrously vain of their pitiful perfection of mechanism .... It is the aspect of a whole people as an organized power. Nationalism is a great menace (ibid.: 26, 66).

Tagore was highly apprehensive about the tyrannical powers and encaging liberties by the shallow motive games in the name of nationalism.

Over the years, nationalism has taken a diverse course, both in terms of content, and its operations. There are distinctions between the progressives and traditionalists, benign and malign, Western and Eastern, civic and cultural, liberal and conservative forms of nationalism (Spencer and Wollman 1998: 255-7). Over the centuries, nationalism has emerged to be a paradoxical force of love and hatred. However, the democratic world had always tried to condition it through institutionalization of various democratic elements and structures. Though, the general emphasis has been on the creation of a civic character of nationalism in the democratic world, i.e. the creation of civic citizenship and common civic culture, legal and political communities, equality, fraternity and justice for all members, major forms of nationalisms are found to be double-sided. It moves both in forward and backward directions, healthy and morbid, progression and regression from the starting point (Nairn 1977: 347-8, Ignatieff, cf. Smith 1995: 99).

With this notion, nationalism creates a sense of classification, i.e. 'we' and 'others'. Initially, the 'others' are designated to be the alien rulers, invaders and their administrative stratagems. The notion of 'others', gradually develops ethnic, linguistic, religious and regional dynamics. Nationalism thus, by creating and recreating the conditions for 'we' and the 'other', in turn is leading the 'good' forms of nationalism into a 'bad' nationalism (Spencer and Wollman 1998: 256). The classification of emotions of 'we' and 'others' have also taken the form of binaries. In the contemporary world, these binaries have appeared to be real at many instances; and there is an emerging tendency of facilitating the ethno-cultural and exclusivist forms of communal nationalism in the form of political ideology over civic form of nationalism. It invents layers of 'others' by designating the others as 'anti-national' and outsiders as the 'enemies of the nation'.

Nationalism has also changed its course with expansion of industrial revolution, capitalism and colonialism. With the emergence of Industrial Revolution in the Western world, the imperial powers competitively started colonizing the non-industrialized world for the expansion of new markets and trade networks using ethnocentric policies and imperialism as tool for legitimacy. Following the expansion of imperialist powers in the non-western nations, the sovereignty of the latter began to be encroached upon, and they were politically, economically and culturally colonized. However, in the successive years, multi-faceted patriotic spirit took the form of nationalism in most parts of the world as an ideology of resistance against the colonizers. Eventually, nationalism as a distinctive phenomenon, has taken different shapes over the centuries and gradually, it became part of the modernization project in fostering a parallel relationship with the rise of modern nations across the globe (Adria 2010: 7).

Nationalism in the Indian Subcontinent

In the Indian subcontinent, nationalism, though, has evolved within the framework of modernization, and has gained its ground due to its fiercely anti-imperialist stance (Aikant 2006: 170). Nationalism has not been seen as an example of exclusivity, but as a universal struggle of humanity for a larger cause. For Mahatma Gandhi, nationalism was part of a universal struggle and a sacrifice of humanity for justice and equality. He was against the armed nationalism and prejudices against humankind in the name of nationalism. Gandhi, in his words describes that, 'My love for the nationalism or my idea of nationalism is that my country may become free, that if need be the whole of the country may die, so that the human race may live. There is no room for race hatred there. Let that be our nationalism' (Gandhi 1947: 171) .

Throughout India, there had been strong claims, especially by the right-wing political thinkers, to redefine the background of Indian nationalism in terms of inherited common cultural features. V.D. Savarkar (1923) locates the roots of Indian nationalism on the claim of inherited common race, land, history, language, and culture. Savarkar elaborates that 'Hindustan is founded on "one nation" and "one race"—from a common fatherland, and therefore, of common blood'. To him, the Hindus are one because they own a common Hindu civilization (*sanskriti*) and culture and the Sanskrit language has been the chosen means of expression and preservation of that culture and the history of this race. Similarly, he elucidates that the development of Western science, technology, industry and knowledge systems in India are to be used for achieving material prosperity, and for making bombs, weapons, in order to 'militarize Hindudom', and there is a need to 'Hinduize all politics' and 'militarize Hinduism' (Savarkar 1964: 46, Keer 1966: 142, cf. Raju 1993: 1936-7).

It has been widely pointed out, however, by a section of the scholars, that India is built on pluralistic cultural, religious and linguistic foundations; and the cause of Indian nationalism has always stood for a pluralistic cultural framework for inter-connectedness amongst people as nationalized subject, and ensuring justice, fraternity, and equality for each other.

> Nation is understood in India in terms of civilizational unity, belief and cultural heritage of the people that is grown out of the freedom of acceptance and rejection. Thus, even within the ritualistic and religious orthodoxies, the heterodox systems have coexisted in India. It is a mistaken belief that unity of a nation is incumbent upon homogeneity (Aikant 2006: 175).

Verily, there have been uneasy tensions between the cultural nationalism and the Nehruvian vision of secular nationalism. The essence of nationalism has successively changed in the Indian subcontinent since last one-and-a-half centuries. Many highlighted that in 'the 1950s and 1960s, nationalism was a feature of anti-colonial struggles in the Third World. From the 1970s, it had become a matter of ethnic politics of killing each other, thereby making 'nationalism as a dark, elemental, unpredictable force of primordial nature, threatening the orderly claims of civilized life (Chatterjee 1994: 3).

Chatterjee (1994) views that, while contesting the colonial power, nationalism was essentially a cultural 'normalization' project based on universalist justificatory resources, without making any sort of distinctions of language, religion, caste, or class as a matter of difference. It was in the urgency to drive away the huge menacing colonial forces from the Indian soil that the internal differences were de-privileged. But, the post-colonial modern liberal-democratic state has also showed indifferences to these concrete differences for acquiring its legitimacy to rule. This, in turn, produced numerous instances of fragmented resistances amongst the subaltern groups to project the 'limit of the universality of the modern regime of power' (ibid.: 4-13).

After examining the growth path of Indian nationalism within the broad historical context of attainment of Independence and the communal divides, Pandey (2012) argues that the new secular nationalism of India felt the need 'to forge a different kind of (secular) historical tradition for Indian citizen – a past with a lighter burden on community consciousness and greater emphasis on tolerance, integration and on loyalty that tied the individual less to parochial grouping (caste, community village and so on), and more to larger whole (India , Indian state or the Indian spirit)' to contribute simultaneously to counter the construction of India in dogmatically community (especially, religious community etc.) terms. To him, the contradiction between 'these alternative views of nationalism were not settled between 1920's and 1940's, and it has not been conclusively settled to this day (Pandey 2012: 80-1).

Significantly, India has been experiencing uneasy tensions between the civil and cultural nationalisms since the days of anti-colonial struggle. At times, they are so entangled that it is impossible to neatly demarcate each in a tradition-ridden multi-ethnic oriented country. The process of formation of Indian national identity encounters the forces of westernization, colonization, secularization, on the one hand, and the pre-existing religious and cultural practices of various societies, on the other. Indian nationalism, as Pandey underlines 'stood above (or outside) the different religious community and took as its unit the individual Indian citizen and was rigorously conceptualized in opposition to this notion of communalism. Since communalism had come to be seen by 1920s as the politics of the religious community, one might argue the opposite, that nationalism was nothing, but communalism driven into secular channels and not sufficiently driven'. To him, communalism and nationalism arose together and are part of the same discourse (Pandey 2012: 61). To Mahajan (2000), however, communalism and nationalism which are historically opposed and any tendency to equate communalism to nationalism causes causalities to the ideological difference between secular nationalism and communalism, and this effort legitimizes communalism and misrepresents nationalism and its powerful secular credentials (Mahajan 2000: 23). The ideal of a unified national identity born out of multi-religious and cultural diversities demanded a clarified relationship between the religion and nation-states. However, the fundamental question is, whether or not there would be demarcations between the state and religion and whether the Indian nationalism will be founded on a majoritarian Hindu state or religious pluralism. Gandhi, wrote in 1947:

> Free India will be no Hindu *Raj,* it will be Indian *Raj* based not on the majority of any religious sect or community, but on the representatives of the whole people without distinction of religion. They would be elected for their record of service and merits. Religion is a personal matter, which should have no place in politics (Gandhi 1947: 277-8).

He further writes,

> I do not expect India of my dreams to develop one religion that is to be wholly Hindu, or wholly Christian or wholly *mussalman*, but I want it to be wholly tolerant, with its religions working side-by-side with one another (257).... The state has nothing to do with it (religion). The state should look after the secular welfare, but not your or my religion. That is every body's personal affair (ibid.: 278).

Gandhi has advocated not for religious identities and practices, but for co-existence of multi-religious and cultural entities for independent India. His major emphasis was for an India that would be free from divisions between the masses and classes.

Jawaharlal Nehru wrote in 1946:

> In a country like India, which has many faiths and religions, no real nationalism can be built, except on the basis of secularity...We have not only to live up to the ideals proclaimed in our Constitution, but make them a part of our thinking and living and thus build up a really integrated nation. That does not mean absence of religion, but putting religion on a different plane from that of normal political and social life. Any other approach in India would mean the breaking up of India (Nehru 1946: 330-1).

Nehru has strongly emphasized on the 'spiritual and moral legacy of the saints'. To him, the 'Indian sages have always provided a moral foundation and certain moral concepts, which hold together the ideals and our life in general' (ibid.: 530-6). Nehru's idea of a secular state 'does not obviously mean a state where religion is discouraged. It means freedom of religion and conscience, including freedom for those who have no religion, and subject only to their not interfering with each other or with the basic conceptions of our state.... The word, secular, however, conveys something much more to me, although that might not be its dictionary meaning. It conveys the idea of the social and political equality' (ibid.: 327). His emphasis, in all possibility, lies with the inculcation and assertion of citizenship rights. The Constitution of India has underlined the principles of equality, fraternity, justice, secularism, and socialism to be cornerstone of its nationalism. Similarly, it has prescribed equality for all its citizens irrespective of their caste, creed, race, religion, sex and class; and equal treatment to all religious groups to practice their faith. Nationalism is still evolving in India and it is swinging between the poles of civic, secular, cultural, political, constitutional and primordial expressions and aspirations. It has acquired many dynamics and has traveled in many directions and has incurred many costs.

Nationalism has proved to be a double-edged sword in the Indian subcontinent. While at one point, it was a uniting force against the colonial forces during the independence struggle, it has also divided people in the name of religion, language, region, caste and ethnicity. It has become a political tool of unity and divisiveness that has defined the 'we' and 'others' both from within and the outside mostly in the primordial terms. Despite limitations and an inherent duality in its character, nationalism has retained its significance as a dominant political force in the Indian subcontinent. Within the all-encompassing surge, the noble components of patriotism, those comprising the subjective feeling of admiration and well-being for the motherland, inherent spirit of accommodation and fellow feeling and commitment for all; egalitarianism, apoliticality of social concerns and the absence of hostility to others, inclusivity of identity and so forth, get co-opted with the political, cultural and mobilizing undercurrents of nationalism. Such co-option has been very often done through the creation of an atmosphere of national exigencies in defining the 'other' and submerging all other issues and identities within the project of hyper-nationalism. As a normal practice and expectations, patriotism has been put in place along with civic nationalism, but at times a new normal is created to subsume patriotism and nationalism to the service of the state and hyper-nationalism. By redefining new alliances and foes, the role and status of major social institutions introducing culture, religion and ethnicity as a major sources of identification of political collectivity, it tries to replace many of the pre-existing narratives and sustaining new normalities to suffice their political agenda. The country, the society and the people have always paid high cost for such reconstruction of social and political normalcies.

India has borne a witness; not only to the formation of nationalism through its anti-colonial struggle, but also the changing courses of nationalism all throughout its struggle. With the resurgence of communalism and ethnocentric attitudes, India experienced the proliferation of multiple nationalities as a political reality, together with propaganda of a two nation theory based on the religious line, thereby paving the way for separation. In 1947, India achieved its Independence, but paid a heavy price for the resurgence of communalism and exclusivist forms of communal nationalisms and the subsequent Partition of the nation. Several questions emerge within the debates of nationalism and nation-formations that the author questions. What were the contexts and processes of construction of communalism, exclusivist nationalism in India? How the resurgence of communalism and exclusivist nationalism had reconstructed the ideal of a unified country?

A historical account of such contexts, processes, intersection of common man's experience with these processes, their agonies, memories and sufferings are provided in the successive chapters of this book.

CHAPTER 2

Communalism, Politics and the Partition of India in 1947
Belying the Patriotic Tradition

Historically, as a country diverse in its religious, linguistic, culture, ethnic and pluralist identities, India always witnessed the intertwining of intra-community relationships. These relationships have coexisted for centuries with implicit and explicit cultural ethos of unity in diversity, along with the reciprocity and accommodation, inter-dependence and trust at the grassroots of their everyday existence. As an inevitable aspect of this plural coexistence, communities have encountered problems concerning cultural differences and disagreements. But at the same time, it has also produced strong sense of mutual respect for each others' beliefs and practices and toleration of syncretic cultures. Together, these developments gave a new direction to Indian composite social lives and enriched the plural mosaic of Indian society.

The Arrival of Communal Interests and Politics

Notwithstanding the availability and sustenance of such ideal pluralistic ethos, various disagreements and differences have emerged at times of socio-political disputes and conflicts. On numerous instances, external political interventions, new patterns of political and economic interest articulations, arousal of political aspirations and social construction of communal binaries by the community leaders have provided a communal turn and twist for such differences and disagreements. Though, the articulation of communal aspirations, interests and binaries were considered to be momentary and short-lived within the broader framework of the Indian social narratives, various unabated and belligerent political aspirations and misinterpretations of cultural differences since the early twentieth century has changed the political trajectory of Indian history by making it a victim of communal divisions.

The emergence of Hindu-Muslim communal tensions had acquired deep-rooted political connotations during the British rule in Indian subcontinent. Various political characters namely, the British administration, Muslim League, Congress party and other political parties, including the right-wing religious organizations and social reformist organizations have responded to the resurgence of communalism in their own characteristic ways. With the manifestation of communalism and communal nationalism, India witnessed a large-scale articulation of communal politics and interests, collective mobilizations, violence and counter-communal mobilizations in many parts of the country. These brought forth unprecedented damage to the centuries-old tradition of inter-religious coexistence, acculturation and integration in the Indian society.

Since the early part of twentieth century, colonial India had witnessed a series of communal events, along with the introduction of various new colonial rules, regulations and administrative measures. Various political parties sponsored collective factionalism and counter-mobilizations, together with articulation of religious, cultural and secular interests and identities across the space. Many of the vested interests and identities directly or indirectly encouraged the colonial design of 'divide and rule' negating the traditional Indian values of social accommodation and inter-faith coexistences. Hence, the foundational spirit of patriotism gradually started getting replaced with ethnocentrism, communalism and exclusivist nationalism. This chapter aims to bring forth the contexts and the process of emergence of communal politics in India leading to the division of the country in 1947.

I

India: A Confluence of Humanity

Indian traditions have remained associated to the practice of animism and universalism. In addition to Hinduism, India has been the birth place of Jainism, Buddhism, Sikhism and numerous indigenous religions like. Over the centuries, India has also encountered the influence of exogenous religious forces with the arrival of non-Indian faiths like Judaism, Christianity, Zoroastrianism, Islam and Bahaism in the subcontinent. Besides accommodation, India has also experienced the phenomenon of religious conversions of huge chunks of Hindu population to Islam and Christianity under various Islamic and western colonial powers and missionaries respectively. Notwithstanding such religious conversion, Hinduism has not only survived in India, but has also accommodated all other religions in this land by adopting the Upanishadic philosophy of *vasudhaiva kutumbakam*, i.e. 'the world is one family'. Hinduism has emerged to be a land of pilgrims for all rare, religion and culture, and the adherents of Hinduism consider it as a 'way of life'.

Rabindranath Tagore, in his famous poetry *Bharat-Tirtha* writes:

He mor chitta punya tirthe jagore dhire
Ei bharater mahamanaber sagar tire.

My heart, awake in this holy land of India; it is a place of pilgrimage for nations to mingle in a confluence of humanity.

Kehonahi jane kara obhanẹ kato manusher dhara
Durbar srote eloko thahote samudre holo hara
Hethay arya hetha anarya hethay dravir chin
Shak hun dal pathan mogal ek dehe holo lin

Nobody knows who urged them; yet they came from different lands and merged in a single body – the Aryans, the non-Aryans, the Dravidians, the Chinese, the Scythians, the Huns, the Pathans and the Mughals – all of them like so many separate streams flowing irresistibly to lose at the end of their journeys their individual identities in one vast sea.

Paschim aji khuliachhe dwar
Setha hote sabe ane upahar
Dibe ar nibe milabe milibe jabe na phire
Ei bharater mahamanaber sagartire.

Now the West has opened up its gates, all are collecting its prized gifts and the same irreversible process of mutual exchange and assimilation is taking place once again in that holy confluence of humanity.[1]

Shifting Political Regimes and Privilege for Religious Groups

These confluences, however, were not untouched by the political mechanisms of the rulers, and the communal underpinnings. Each ruling group has introduced its own sets of rules to govern the country showing special inclination to its own cultural, linguistic, administrative legacies and religious orientations. Significantly, a particular ruling group has always tried to replace the other, and in the process, one privilege group deprived the privileges of others. Many of these aforesaid actions on the basis of their religious orientations have been a political act, and this has been effectively used to create communal divide, especially by the British Raj.

Many historians have pointed out that the pre-colonial rule in India was characterized by a fair degree of peaceful coexistence among the Hindus and Muslims. Diverse beliefs, faith and customs seldom came in developing harmonious relationship among the religious communities, since religious tolerance was the dominant feature in the earlier times among the members of communities (Chakravartty 1987: 11). Sunderland similarly pointed out that, despite several conflicts between the Hindu and the Muslim feudatories, these were simply inspired from the political conflicts, but not religious conflicts (Sunderland 1928: 1). In the medieval and early modern India, the Muslim rulers had introduced Islamic criminal laws, revenue systems, and introduced Persian language as the court language, thereby making Islam a dominant political force. On the arrival of the British East India Company, they introduced several changes in the political and social arenas. They replaced the existing land tenure system with the Permanent Settlement in 1793; Persian was replaced by English as the official language, they changed Islamic criminal law with the Indian Penal code, and substituted the vernacular education with

[1] *Source*: https://www.boloji.com/blog/477/rabindranath-the-linguist. Accessed on February 2020.

English education to suffice their colonial needs. Since many Hindus quickly mastered the English language and acclimatized with the British systems, they were preferred by the colonial rulers in occupying the major official positions. Eventually, many Hindus became *zamindars* where the former assured revenue collections for the British, thereby upholding the pillars of the British regime (Khalique 2002: 115). The British, however, were antagonistic towards Indian languages, cultures, communities, and Indian civilization itself. As reflected in Macaulay's *Minute on Education*, dated 2 February 1835:

> I have never found one among them who could deny that a single shelf of a good European library was worth the whole native literature of India and Arabia. The intrinsic superiority of the Western literature is indeed fully admitted and I certainly never met with any orientalist who ventured to maintain that the Arabic and Sanskrit poetry could be compared to that of the great European nations. ... It is, I believe, no exaggeration to say that all the historical information which has been collected from all the books written in the Sanskrit language is less valuable than what may be found in the most paltry abridgments used at preparatory schools in England. In every branch of physical or moral philosophy, the relative position of the two nations is nearly the same....[2]

Similarly, many colonial historians have described Indian civilization with negative connotations. For instance, English historian James Mill compared the Hindus with the 'savages of America'; the Indian architectural and sculptural creations were termed as 'barbaric arts'; and India, a 'half-civilized nation'.

The intrusion of western culture brought forth a threat to the indigenous culture. Besides exploiting the local economic resources, the British also imposed several oppressive measures for the Indian masses. A general discontent against the arrogance of British against the local people, and their exploitation was brewing in the society. However, these were not consolidated as political protest against the British immediately. Since the early nineteenth-century India had already witnessed Hindu and the Muslim revivalist movements like Arya Samaj, who preached the Hindus to go back to the Vedas, and by the Wahhabis who advised the Muslims to strictly follow the

[2] *Source:* http://home.iitk.ac.in/~hcverma/Article/Macaulay-Minutes.pdf. Accessed on January 2020.

Quran and the Sunnat. Alongside, the wider fabric of the society also started witnessing a new turn with the arrival of printing press, modern education and modern means of communication and emergence of modernization. The 1857 Rebellion, which is designated by many as the first war of independence, brought a sense of consolidation to the nationalistic forces in Indian subcontinent. From the later decades of the nineteenth century, a thin layer of English educated people from all communities gradually appeared on the scene and colonial India started experiencing an amount of consolidation of the ideals of nationalism, especially among the literati elites (Khalique 2002: 115-16).

The British, in response to the events, adopted the strategy of divide and rule in India. Lord Elphinstone, the Governor of Bombay in Minute, dated 14 May 1860 wrote, '*Divide et imperia* was the old Roman motto, and it should be ours' (Sunderland 1928, cf. Chakravarty 1987: 16). The British depicted India as a divided country, in terms of racial, linguistic, and religious divisions and often underlined the lack of commonalities in the Indian society that was much warranted as the basis for the idea of nationalism in India. The British government, established on the basis of 1881 Census, officially underlined differences among the Indian people, in terms of physiognomic, racial, regional, caste, religious attributes and so forth. Based on the Census report, they identified the Indian communities as the enumerated community of majority and minority communities (Kaviraj 1995: 143) Efforts though were made by the educated elites and the social reform leaders to consolidate the nationalistic feelings amongst the masses irrespective of their diverse backgrounds. The British, however, effectively began using the religious divide to thwart the emergence of Indian nationalism. Along the line of the British's divisive tactics, many communal forces began to erupt in Indian subcontinent.

Organizational Formation for Nationalism and Communal Divides

On 28 December 1885, Congress party was formed for the development of close relations between the workers, dissolution of all races, creeds and provincial prejudices, and for consolidation of national unity. Though Congress was largely broader in its representational values, a section of the Muslim leaders pointed out that the Muslims were not adequately represented. On 28 December 1887, Sir Syed Ahmed Khan opined that Hindus and Muslims are altogether two different nations. Opposed to the Congress, he along with Raja Shiv Prasad Singh of Benares set up the United Indian Patriotic Association in August 1888. Both, the Central Mohammedan Association and Mohammedan Literary Society supported Khan's views. While a section of the Muslim leaders started subscribing to Khan's view, another section of the Muslim politicians joined the Congress. It is noteworthy that there were also contradictions among the members within the Congress party. While Surendra Nath Banerjee stressed on emphasizing the secular approach of the party, the Hindu revivalists like Bal Gangadhar Tilak and others did give a Hindu colour to Congress. Some Congress leaders were also involved in the Cow-Protection Movement and used Congress platform for the Goraksha Sabha meetings. These altogether, started contributing to the alienation of large-scale Muslim representation from the Congress (Chakravartty 1987: 18).

The British engaged with these apparent disagreements among a section of Muslim and the Congress in order to keep the Indians divided. They tactfully applied the perceived communal divides for their administrative convenience, and gave it a concrete shape with the Partition of Bengal province on 16 October 1905. The Muslim dominated area of Bengal and Assam was designated East Bengal, and the Hindu dominated area as West Bengal. Similarly, Lord Curzon crafted the proposal to give the Muslims of East Bengal a higher representation in the government. Through this Partition, the British proposed to 'invest the Mohammedans in East Bengal' as Curzon told on 18 February 1904, to woo Muslims with a unity, which they have not enjoyed since the days of viceroys and the kings (*Muslim Chronicle*, 11 November 1905, cf. Khalique 2002: 120).

Contrary to the British expectations, neither the Hindus nor all sections of the Muslims were in favour of Bengal's Partition. Bengal observed a 'day of mourning' on 16 October 1905 itself. Rabindranath Tagore celebrated the *Rakhi Utsav* ceremony to symbolize unity between the Bengali Hindus and Muslims. Thousands of emotionally charged people of both the communities came to the streets of Calcutta, Dhaka and Sylhet; and tied the *rakhi* on each other's hand as a mark of their traditional unity and symbol of resistance against Partition. The *rakhi* became the symbol of Hindu-Muslim unity and harmony. With this act, Swadeshi movement received a momentum with the participation of workers, peasants and the commonfolk in boycotting British goods. Against this, the Bengal Partition, in many ways, provided an impetus to the communal divisions in the society. Within a few months, India foresaw the birth of All India Muslim League and the Hindu Mahasabha (ibid.: 121).

On 31 December 1906, the All India Muslim League was formed in Dhaka to promote feelings of loyalty towards British government amongst the Indian Muslims; to protect and advance the rights and political concerns of the Indian Muslims, and to foster relations between Muslims and other communities of India (Aggarwal 2014: 2). The first communal party was founded keeping its membership confined to Muslim only, and it imparted a degree of solidarity amongst Muslim communities, which was earlier unknown. All Indian Muslim League after its formation resolved that the partition of Bengal 'is sure to prove beneficial to the Mussalmans community which constitute the vast majority of that province and that all such methods of agitation as boycotting should be strongly condemned and discouraged' (All Indian Muslim League Resolution no. IV 1906, op. cit., A.N. Zaidi vol. I: 393). In 1907, the Arya Pratinidhi Sabha was established to reconvert the Muslims and Christians into the fold of Hinduism. In 1907, the United Bengal Hindu Movement was formed, and later the Punjab Hindu Sabha took initiatives in forming the Akhil Bharat Hindu Mahasabha (Chakravartty 1987: 20).

While the Bengal Partition started gaining momentum, the Muslim League started looking for the opportunity to get representation with the colonial administration. In March 1908, at the Aligarh session of the Muslim League, the party demanded adequate representations and weightages for Muslims in all councils with separate electorates proposing a 50 per cent representation in the Viceroy's Executive Council. In 1909, Morley-Minto Reforms Act, also known as the Indian Council Act of 1909, was passed to introduce separate electorates as a part of these reforms, giving a further impetus to the communalist forces. While the Congress vehemently opposed, the Muslim League welcomed this Act (Khalique 2002: 120). The Morley-Minto Reforms Act of 1909 along with separate electorate for the Muslims in many ways concretized the manifestation of British's divide and rule policy in India (Chakravartty 1987: 19). In fact, by making provision of separate electorates for the Muslims in this Act the seed of separate Pakistan was sown by the British (Ahmed 2020).

Against the backdrop of Bengal's Partition, Aurobindo Ghosh and his compatriots in Bengal, Savarkar in Bombay State (modern day Maharashtra) became very active in their respective regions in igniting the revolutionary-cum-anti-British mass movement. In 1909, Aurobindo Ghosh and others pleaded for Indian nationalism based on the Hindu orientation. In 1909, Punjab Hindu Sabha was formed under the leadership of Arya Samaj leaders like Lala Lajpat Rai and others to safeguard the interest of the Hindus. Subsequently, provincial Hindu Sabhas were founded in other provinces like United Province, Bihar, Bengal, Central Province and the Bombay State. The adherents to Hindu Mahasabha started working to develop a pan-Hindu consciousness. Savarkar asserted for the arousal of the pan-Hindu consciousness throughout the country rising above the caste, sects and creed under the Mahasabha (Prakash 1966: 10, op. cit., Chakravartty 1987: 21).

On 12 December 1911, the Partition plan of Bengal was withdrawn in view of the strong public resistance and the revolutionary zealousness against the British, together with the spread of Swadeshi movement in other parts of the country. On 8 December 1913, the Punjab Hindu Sabha passed a resolution to redevelop into All India Hindu Sabha. Significantly in 1913, the Muslim League invited the Congress leaders to address its session in Lucknow, where the Congress leaders made efforts for rapprochement with the League leaders. However, nothing was achieved significantly out of this meeting (Khalique 2002: 120-3).

Arrival of Gandhi Amidst Communal Conflicts and Consolidation of National Movement

In July 1914, Gandhi returned to India from South Africa under the situation of strained Hindu-Muslim relationship and the increasing plights of the peasant, factory workers and the common folk. He undertook several initiatives to integrate the forces altogether to boost India's independence struggle at the ground level.

A large section of Indian Muslims paid their allegiance to the Sultan of Turkey, who was also the Caliph. In 1914, Turkey declared Britain its enemy. Following this, a section of Indian Muslim supported the Caliph and started mobilizing the Muslim population. This became the greatest turning point in the establishment of Khilafat movement in India. After the withdrawal of the Bengal Partition plan and Britain's changing attitude towards Turkey, the overall communal situation slightly improved, even though the process of consolidation of communal forces continued (Chakravartty 1987: 24). Apart from this, the Muslim League session in Bombay and the Congress' annual session in Bombay in 1915 both coincided together.

In April 1915, Sarvadeshak Hindu Sabha was formed as an umbrella organization of all provincial Hindu Sabhas, which coincided with the Kumbha Mela of Haridwar. Gandhi was also present in the conference. In the separate sessions of both Congress and Muslim League at Lucknow, the Lucknow Pact was formed in December 1916, in which the Congress conceded for the demand of separate electorates and reservation of seats for the minorities in the provincial legislatures, where Muslim populations were a minority. Many observed the Lucknow Pact as the turning point for the Muslims in reversing their aloofness from the Congress. A section of Muslim leaders though were against the move. Gandhi's emergence as a nationalist leader was marked by the emergence of the Hindu-Muslim fraternization. Gandhi's objective was, as he once wrote, to bring about the unison between the Hindus and Muslims that nobody can break. In solidarity with the Khilafat movement, he also asked for the release of Ali Brothers (ibid.: 24-5).

In 1917, the independence movement of India saw a new turn

with the initiation of Champaran Satyagraha concerning rights of the indigo cultivators by Gandhi. In March 1918, he took up the issue of textile mill workers of Ahmadabad and in the same year, he launched Satyagraha for the peasants of Kheda district of Gujarat. With all these major events, India started witnessing the organized discontent against the British government. The British also became politically alarmed with these peasant movements.

In March 1919, the British government introduced the Rowlatt Act with the provision to decide the imprisonment of suspects in political cases without trial. This inhuman Act was strongly opposed by many nationalist leaders. Against the Rowlatt Act, the Congress observed 6 April 1919 as 'a day of national humiliation' throughout the country. Gandhi organized several protest movements where people came out on the streets against this Act. The British government resorted to several brutal measures to put down these agitations. One vivid example of this was the infamous Jallianwala Bagh massacre on 13 April 1919 at Amritsar. Rabindranath Tagore returned his Knighthood as a protest against this massacre. With all these catastrophic events, the nation woke up against the British government.

In 1920, Gandhi supported the Khilafat Movement showing a concern for Muslim causes. He appealed to everybody, including the Hindus, to support the Khilafat Movement. Against the backdrop of the Khilafat movement on June 1920 without waiting for the decision of the Congress, Gandhi launched Non-Cooperation Movement against the British to redress the wrongs related to Khilafat agitation and the Jallianwala massacre and it became a mass movement under the aegis of Gandhi's leadership (Chakravartty 1987: 69-70). However, Gandhi's support to the Khalifat Movement was not welcomed by the Hindu nationalists in India. The situation further deteriorated, when the Khilafat meetings in the Malabar region also took the shape of communalism where the movement turned against the Hindu landlords. Notwithstanding the communal upsurge, Gandhi started taking up the issues of the peasants and the workers and launched mass mobilization against the British government. In 1922, he launched the Civil Disobedience movement against the British. However, he suspended this movement due to outbreak of violence at Chauri Chaura. While the Congress leaders, under the leadership of Gandhi were engaged to espouse the cause of the peasants and workers, the Muslim League simultaneously continued to see the problems in the Indian society through the lenses of Hindu-Muslim divisions (Chakravartty 1987: 71).

India's Independence movement saw several turning points in the early 1920s with the peasant and workers entering in the organized and large-scale collective mobilizations, Congress leaders and workers entering into the village – never before, the demand of underprivileged stated getting raised, massive agitations among the Muslims especially on the Muslim political issues on the fate of Khilafat, the Non-Cooperation Movement, the Hindu and Muslim communitarian mobilization in northern Indian to reclaim victims and protect, and the Hindu Muslim riots from 1923 onwards showing the heightening danger arising from community-based mobilization (Pandey 2012: 59-60).

From the early 1920's, India started to witness widespread communal violence. The Muslim community leaders organized Tablighi Jamaat and Tanzim movements to mobilize the ordinary Muslims, and the Hindu leaders too organized the Shuddhi and Sangathan Movements for the Hindu populations, following which, communal riots took place in many parts of the country (Khalique 2002: 127). In November 1921, Britain and Afghanistan signed the Friendship Treaty, which gave a further major setback to the Khilafat Movement. The Movement was further weakened with the abolition of the Ottoman Caliphate under the Treaty of Lausanne in 1923. Against the backdrop of horrifying Hindu-Muslim communal riots; in September 1924, Gandhi went on a twenty-one days hunger strike. Although, many Hindu and Muslim leaders suspended their grassroot mobilization programme based on religious orientation following Gandhi's hunger strike, the communal politics kept on spewing in many parts of the Indian subcontinent (ibid.: 128).

Besides, there were several Hindu nationalists who disapproved the linking of the Khilafat movement with the independence movement. Keshav Baliram Hedgewar, the founder of Rashtriya Swayamsewak Sangh (RSS), considered that the 'decision to associate the Khilafat cause with the non-cooperation struggle serves only to weaken the cause of the latter; and the Indian Muslims were more concerned with the fate of Turkish Caliph than the Indian Independence'(Curran 1951: 10, op. cit., Chakravartty 1987: 74). Though Gandhi emerged to be popular among the Muslims, Mohammad Ali Jinnah had little confidence and respect for him. At the Muslim League Session in Calcutta on 7 September 1920, he said, 'I would still ask the government not to drive the people of India to desperation, or else there are no other course left open to the people, except to inaugurate the policy of non-cooperation, though not necessarily the programme of Mr Gandhi' (*IAR* 1921, pt. 3: 221, op. cit., Chakravartty 1987: 77).

In the Belgaum session held in December 1924, the Hindu Mahasabha decided to establish wider political role for the Mahasabha and appointed a committee under the chairmanship of Lala Lajpat Rai to ascertain and formulate Hindu opinion on the subject of Hindu-Muslim problem in their relation to the question of further constitutional reforms (Pandey 2012: 76).

In 1925, Hedgewar formed the RSS to bring back the lost glories of the Hindus to ensure the protection of the Hindu *Dharma*. On the other hand, A.K. Fazlul Haq, the leader of Krishak Praja Party of Bengal, who had a significant Muslim following apprehending the rise of Hindu forces, raised the cry of 'Islam in Danger' in 1925. Furthermore, in December 1925, Muslim League intensified its polemical attacks on Indian nationalism and its leaders and insisted on the concept of two separate nations for the Hindus and Muslims. In 1926, leaders like Lajpat Rai, Madan Mohan Malviya, split from the Congress Swaraj Party and established an Independent Congress Party to contest triennial election to the central and provincial legislature against those nationalist who in their opinion paid insufficient attention to the Hindu interest (Pandey 2012: 77).

Notwithstanding Gandhi's sincere efforts, India saw the gradual communal re-orientation of a major section of the Muslim leaders, the growth of Hindu and Muslim communal movements, the reorganization of the Hindu Mahasabha and the inability of the Congress to stop the growth of communal organizations. The increasing number of Hindu-Muslim riots led to the further deterioration of the Hindu-Muslim relations. According to government official reports there were as many as 112 serious communal riots in the country from 1923 to 1928 (ibid.: 138). Due to this, India started experiencing the regular staging of meetings by the Hindu and Muslim radical organizations and the proliferation of provocative publications from both the communities.

In the course of his presidential address at the special Khalifat Conference in Delhi on 29 April 1926, Maulana Sulaiman Nadwi said openly, 'Every Muslim should be exhorted to bear in mind that he has no respect or compassion for a *kafir* (infidel), and even to extend the hand of friendship towards Hindus....They should organize 10,000 volunteers in Delhi ... to safeguard the Muslim interests against the repetition of Calcutta riots.' A month before the Calcutta riots, in the ninth session of All India Hindu Mahasabha held at Delhi on 13 March 1926, Bhai Parmanand moved the following resolution,

> In order to defend the rights and interests of the Hindu community and to further the growth and development of the Hindu Unity...the establishment of an order of Hindu *sewak* is necessary, who would develop whole of their time and energy to the service of the Hindu Nation (*IQR* 1926, vol. 410-12, op. cit., Chakravartty 1987: 154-5).

In March 1927, Jinnah agreed to the institution of the joint electorate under certain conditions and the Congress party too approved Jinnah's proposal after a discussion. While the dominating tendency was in favour of communal unity, the members of Mahasabha and Muslim League took a diametrically opposite turn. At the tenth session of the All India Hindu Mahasabha, B.S. Moonje, a prominent leader of the Mahasabha said, that 'the system of joint electorates generally accepted to be contributive to the growth of nationalism and dissipation of communalism, it was regarded by the Muslim leaders as something bad. However, they were ready to accept, if, sufficient price was paid by the Hindus; and that the Hindus, who were more eager for *swaraj*, must pay the price demanded' (*The Musalman*, 23 March 1927: 8, op. cit., Chakravartty 1987: 166-7). Meanwhile, the issues of religious conversion, cow slaughter, and music before the mosque became more publicized as political issues by both communities. The Hindu Mahasabha passed its resolution in the Madras session on 29 December 1927, urging the Muslim community to ban cow slaughter.

Furthermore, the British got an opportunity to intensify their divide and rule policy. In 1927, the Simon Commission was formed to draft and formalize a constitution for India without any Indian representatives. In 1928 and 1929, while the Simon Commission reached India, it met with vehement opposition from the Congress party and a faction of Muslim League leaders, led by Jinnah. However, the motives for protests were different for the Congress and the Muslim League. The British government appeared to be quite confident of dissuading Hindu Mahasabha from the anti-Simon Commission protest. Lord Irwin, the Governor-General and the Viceroy of India wrote, 'the Hindu Mahasabha, watching the Muslim approach to the (Simon) Commission, has no heart to boycott, and it would not take much to push them off' (cf. 'Irwin to Readings', dated March 1928, Halifax collection, MSS/EUR/F118(107) IOL, op. cit., ibid.: 172).

Most importantly, the question of reservation of seats again became a contentious issue from the early 1928. The Muslim League was in favour of reservation for Muslims, but both Hindu Mahasabha and the Akali leaders were strongly against it. The All Parties Conference appointed Motilal Nehru to draft a report. The Motilal Nehru Committee recommended a joint electorate and proposed non-reservation of seats for the House of Representatives, except for Muslims in the provinces where they were a minority, and for the non-Muslims in North-Western Frontier Provinces; and non-reservation of seats for any community in Punjab and Bengal. The recommendations put forward by the committee further accentuated the communal problems rather than minimizing it. The Muslim League showed reservation to it, while the Hindu Mahasabha endorsed it (ibid.: 177).

Consolidation of Demand for Full Independence and Furthering of Communal Divide

In December 1927, Jawaharlal Nehru, in the Congress's Madras session presented the resolution for a *poorna swaraj*, or complete freedom. It was the first resolution of the Congress to demand complete independence of India. This resolution was dissolved, but this session declared its goals of securing the demands of emancipations of Indians from the British Raj. Annie Besant, the founder of Indian Home Rule movement recognized it as a dignified move and a clear statement of India's goal (Ramu 1995: 25). On 26 January 1929, the Lahore session, under the presidentship of Jawaharlal Nehru, the Congress resolved for asserting complete independence for India; and an Action Plan Committee was worked out under the leadership of Motilal Nehru. The Congress party recommended for a Dominion status for India (e.g. the British Dominions of Canada, New Zealand, and Australia, etc.), and acceptance of constitutional governance as formulated in the Nehru Report.

However, the Muslim League kept on insisting for an executive responsible government as their demand from the British, rather than a complete independence as their collective goal. On 9 March 1929, the Muslim League adopted a Fourteen Point Plan, which was an alternative to the Motilal Nehru Action Plan, and demanded that all legislatures and other elected bodies to be constituted on the definite principle of adequate and effective representation of minorities, especially in the Central Legislative, and the Muslim representation should not be less than one-third.

JINNAH'S FOURTEEN POINTS – 1929

1. Federal System:

   The form of the future constitution should be federal with the residuary powers rested in the provinces.

2. Provincial Autonomy:

   A uniform measure of autonomy shall be granted to all provinces.

3. Representation of Minorities:

   All legislatures in the country and other elected bodies shall be constituted on the definite principles of adequate and effective representation of minorities in every province without reducing the majority in any province to a minority or even equality.

4. Number of Muslim Representatives:

In the central legislature, Muslim representatives shall not be less than one-third.

5. Separate Electorates:

   Representation of communal groups shall continue to be means of separate electorates as at present provided, it shall be open to any community, at any time to abandon its separate electorate in favour of joint electorate.

6. Muslim Majority Provinces:

   Any territorial redistribution that might at any time be necessary shall not in any way, effect the Muslim majority in Punjab, Bengal and NWFP.

7. Religious Liberty:

   Full religious Liberty, liberty of belief, worship and observance, association and education shall be guaranted to all the communities.

8. Three-Fourth Representation:

   No bill or resolution shall be passed in any legislature or any other elected body if three-fourths of the members of any community in that particular body opposes such a bill.

9. Separation of Sindh:

   Sindh should be separated from Bombay Presidency.

10. Introduction of Reforms in the NWFP and Baluchistan:

    Reforms should be introduced in the NWFP and Baluchistan on the same footing as in other provinces.

11. Government Services:

    Muslims should be given adequate share along with other Indians in the services of State.

12. Protection of Muslim's culture and language:

    The constitution should embody adequate safeguard for the protection of Muslim culture, language, religion and civilization.

13. One-Third Muslim Ministers:

    No cabinet, either central or provincial be formed, without being a proportion of at least one-third Muslim ministers.

14. Constitution:

    No change shall be made in the constitution of state except with the concurrence.

(Mujahid 1981: 20-1)

Meanwhile, the members of the Congress Working Committee, at the meeting held on 14 to 16 February 1930, decided to initiate the Civil Disobedience movement at the Sabarmati Ashram. Various constructive programmes and mass awareness campaigns were organized. On 12 March 1930, Gandhi began his Dandi March with his seventy-nine *padacharees*. While on the march, Gandhi declared that he would keep away from the Ashram until *swaraj* was achieved. The march continued for twenty-four days and reached Dandi on the 5 April 1930. Gandhi and his companions proceeded to break the Salt Law by picking up salt heaps lying on the sea shore. Gandhi also decided to raid the salt factories of Dharsana and Chharsada. The British Government arrested Gandhi on 5 May 1930, which created nationwide uproars. Following the Salt March, the Congress Working Committee further escalated the Civil Disobedience movement across the country (Ramu 1995: 28). The Congress occupied the centre stage of political arena, wherein the vast section of Indian population got involved with the Civil Disobedience Movement in some way or the other. However, the Muslim League and the Hindu Mahasabha remained firm in promoting their own objectives of influencing their respective domains.

On 25 January 1930, the leaders of Muslim League urged Muslims not to participate in the Independence Day celebration organized by the Congress, since the Congress leaders have not made any efforts to settle the Hindu-Muslim conflicts. Meanwhile, the British government announced the Round Table Conference with Indian leaders to discuss the future Constitution of India. The Hindu Mahasabha Working Committee passed a resolution on 18 January 1930, stating that, 'the Mahasabha welcomes the announcement of the intention of the British government to hold the Round Table Conference with the representatives of British India and the Indian state, to discuss the future Constitution of India'. The Sabha is of the opinion that, 'the country will not be satisfied with anything less than immediate grant of a Dominion Status'. The Sabha hopes to be able to offer its co-petition to the government to settle the principle of a Constitutional Dominion government which suits to the needs of Indian population at the proposed conference (ibid.: 35, 47). The First Round Table Conference took place on 12 November 1930, between the British government and the Indian political representatives without the representation of Congress leaders, where both Jinnah and Bhim Rao Ambedkar raised their Fourteen Points and the separate electorate for the backward classes respectively.

On 21 January 1931, the Congress Working Committee passed the resolution that it was not prepared to give any recognition to the proceedings of the so-called Round Table Conference and appealed to the masses to carry out programmes to boost the fight for freedom. After the Round Table Conference, the Viceroy initiated a reconciliatory approach and on 25 January 1931, Gandhi and all other members of the Congress Working Committee were released from jail unconditionally. Subsequently, the Gandhi-Irwin Pact was signed on 5 March 1931, and the Civil Disobedience Movement was withdrawn; and the Congress agreed to participate in the future Round Table Conferences. In the Second Round Table Conference, on 1 December 1931, Gandhi participated, but it failed to meet the demands of the Congress. Therefore, the Congress decided to continue with the Civil Disobedience movement.

On 16 August 1932, the British Prime Minister Ramsay McDonald announced the Communal Award that recognized the overwhelming significance of religions, cultural, and caste groups in Indian society in order to prove his point that India was not a nation as a whole. This award, besides providing separate electorates for the religious minorities and giving the Muslim reservation a weightage, also announced separate electorates for the 'depressed classes' and untouchables, and other ethnic and religious minorities like Sikhs, Indian Christians, Anglo-Indians, Europeans and Marathas. Congress opposed this award and spread mass mobilizations across the country against this award by the British Prime Minister and Gandhi and other prominent Congress leaders were arrested. In opposition to the Communal Award, Gandhi, on 20 September 1932, sat on the fast unto death in the Yerwada Jail (Khalique 2002: 135).

Finally, a negotiation was held between depressed class leaders, along with Ambedkar. Poona Pact was signed between Mahatma Gandhi and Ambedkar on 24 September 1932, which ensured the continuance of joint electorate system, and ensured more seats to the depressed classes. This pact sent a strong message to the British government against their attempt to institutionalize the communal divisions; and to the Muslim League's acceptance of separate electorates for the Muslims. Significantly, the Muslim leaders also abandoned the communal attitude for a short duration and engaged them with the larger questions that was affecting India (Khalique 2002: 137, Singh 1987: 2-3). Over the succeeding years, the Civil Disobedience Movement became weaker and the Congressmen became gloomy about the prospects of Congress' primary objectives. Many Congress leaders associated themselves with the removal of untouchability and other social problems of the country. Gandhi began his unlimited fast for emancipation to the untouchables, or Harijans. As his health deteriorated, he was released from the jail unconditionally (Ramu 1995: 45).

Institutionalization of Communal Divides

The British introduced the Government of India Act 1935 in order to represent the elected Indian representatives and the introduction of direct elections too. While Congress and the Muslim League participated in the 1937 provincial elections within the framework of manifesto laid down by the recent Government of India Act 1935, communal divisions took a new political and institutionalized turn in India and communalism impeded all aspects of this initiative ranging from the election campaigns, nomination of candidates, election conduct, structuring and functioning of government system. Conflicts between the Congress and the Muslim League, especially the sharp differences between Nehru and Jinnah became part of the mainstream politics. While the Congress reiterated its struggle to overthrow the colonial power, the Muslim League remained silent on the issue of de-colonization. Both Nehru and the Congress were against the spread of communalism and campaigned for the true representation of Indian people; but for Jinnah, the Muslim League was the sole representative of the Muslims, and communal interest was, therefore, a reality. Though Nehru was critical of the communal characteristics of the Muslim League and its rootless representation among the masses, he welcomed their cooperation for the anti-imperial struggle and general welfare of all the people of the country. Jinnah, however, had a little faith on the secular identity of the Indian nationalist movement. Similarly, he also questioned the Congress's credentials to speak on behalf of entire India (Singh 1987: 1).

In 1937, general elections were held in the eleven provinces on the basis of communal representations and the reservation of seats. Communal aspirations became widespread in the 1937 election campaigns. Congress party swept the polls in most of the provinces and emerged to be the largest single party in the North- Western Frontier Province and formed their government in seven out of the eleven provinces. Later, the Congress formed its coalition government in other two provinces. Bengal and Punjab were the only two provinces, which had non-Congress representations (coalitions headed by Krishak Praja Party and Punjab Unionist Party respectively). The Muslim League contested the elections to various legislative bodies, but achieved moderate success. Out of the 485 of its reserved Muslim seats, the League won only 110 seats. Even in the Muslim-majority provinces of the Punjab, the North-West Frontier Province, Bengal and Sindh, the League was challenged by the rival parties. The Congress contested for 58 of the reserved seats and won only 26 seats.[3]

Post-1937 election results, Muslim League failed in forging a pan-Muslim unity. Following this, Jinnah adopted a reconciliatory approach towards the Congress and offered to cooperate with Congress leaders in the provinces. However, despite attempts by several Muslim leaders to cooperate and merge with Congress, Jinnah, on 30 June 1937, appealed to all the Muslims to 'unite among themselves as they have been ordered to do so by the God and his Prophet' (*Bombay Chronicle*, 2 July 1937, cf. Singh 1989: 13). Other Muslim

[3] *Source:* http://www.shareyouressays.com/essays/provincial-elections-of-1937-and-the-congress-ministries/89872. Accessed on January 2020.

League leaders like Shaukat Ali started pushing the slogan that 'Islam is in danger' and appealing Muslim voters to elect Muslim candidates in the name of Islam. In 1937, a Muslim League candidate got elected from the Bundelkhand region, and this gave Muslim League an extra boost for the issue of Muslim unity in India. In late 1937, Jinnah started making direct attacks on the Congress with the allegations that the Congress was working for a 'Hindu Raj', and 'working for majority community' and appealed for a mass contact programme to thwart the challenges posed by Congress in front of the League. Meanwhile, Fazlul Haq, who took the help of Hindu nationalist, Europeans and the Depressed Caste groups to form a government, joined the Muslim League. He also joined the claim that the Muslim League was the sole representative of Muslims. But the Congress Working Committee rejected the claims that the Muslim League was the 'sole representative of Muslims in India'. Jinnah further sharpened its attack against the Congress and appointed committees to look into the issue of harassment and atrocities against the Muslims in the Congress ruled states. In December 1938, the Congress Working Committee formally declared Muslim League and Hindu Mahasabha as communal parties (Singh 1987: 23).

In the middle of 1937 and 1939, Muslim League published several reports and pamphlets like the *Pirpur Report*, *Shareef Report*, etc. Fazlul Haq's pamphlet titled, *Muslim Sufferings Under Congress Rule* highlighted the plights of Muslims in several parts of the country, and atmosphere that was preventing them to enjoy their cultural and religious rights. The Muslims were compelled to sing *Vande Mataram*, imposing Hindi instead of Urdu, and imposing a ban on cow slaughter, etc. The Report apprehended that 'under the Congress-led Hindu *Raj*, Muslim will always remain weak, powerless and oppressed'.

In the Annual Session of All India Muslim League on Dec. 26, 1938 in Patna in sharp attack to Congress, Jinnah again questioned the Congress's ability to represent the whole of India. He said that the Congress did not represent the Muslim, Christian, Scheduled Caste and the non-Brahmin. He underlined 'I said the Congress does not even the represent all the Hindus....What about the Hindu Mahasabha... The High Command of the Congress is absolutely determined to crash all the communities and culture in this country to establish Hindu Raj. . . . With all the pretension of nationalism it straightway started with the *Vande Mataram*. …it is sung as such and thrust upon others'. Turing the Gandhi, he said 'Gandhi is the man responsible for turning the Congress into an instrument for the revival of Hinduism. His idea is to revive Hindu religion and establish a Hindu Raj in this country' (Yusufi 1996: 908-10).

In September 1939, British India entered into the Second World War and sought cooperation of all the political parties of the Provincial Legislatures. The Muslim League resolved to offer its support to British with a condition that 'the Viceroy takes its leaders into confidence and accept the League as the only organization that can speak on behalf of Muslim India'. The Congress Working Committee resolved to ask for a clarification on the Second World War's aims and the future of democracy and imperialism in India post the War. As the Viceroy declined to specify the war aim, and expressed his willingness to consult the Princely States, Muslim leaders about the constitutional reforms in India post-War, political ambitions of Jinnah got a major public boost. In an arranged discussion between Nehru and Jinnah on 18 October 1939, Jinnah insisted that the Congress give up its anti-imperialist policy. As the Viceroy gave the assurance that full weightage would be given to the views and interests of the minority representatives, the Muslim League's Working Committee supported Jinnah as the President of the League to assure British of Muslim support and cooperation during the War (*National Herald*, 23 October 1939, Singh 1989: 33-4).

The British persistently showed reluctance to make its war aim explicit to Indian public. In November 1939, all the elected Congress party leaders, who ruled in the 8 out of 11 provinces of India, resigned from Provincial Councils. Jinnah found this moment a matter for celebration. On 22 December 1939, he called on the Muslim League to observe the 'Day of Deliverance' and 'Thanksgiving' to celebrate the resignation of the Congress leaders and demanded a Royal Commission inquiry on the 'Muslim sufferings' to keep pressure alive on British and the Congress. The Hindu Mahasabha too supported the Muslim League and other parties to form its provincial governments in provinces like Sindh, North-West Frontier Province and Bengal (ibid.: 54).

Demand for a Separate Nation of Pakistan

The British started effectively using the League and Congress differences to their political advantage; and showed little interest to withdraw their governance after the Second World War. Neither Jinnah was interested in settling with Congress, nor the British government in favour of any discussion with the Congress. In the 27th Session of the All India Muslim league on 22 March 1940, Jinnah in his Presidential address made sharp attack on the Congress with a deep plan in his mind. He said,

> After the World War was declared the Viceroy naturally wanted help from the Muslim League. It was only then that he realize that Muslim League was a power ... when I got this invitation from the Viceroy along with Mr. Gandhi, I believe that that was the worst shock the Congress High Command ever received, because it challenged the sole authority of Congress to speak on behalf of India.... I am sure from what I can see and hear that Muslim India is now conscious and now awake and the Muslim League has now grown into such a strong institution that it cannot be destroyed by anybody.

Highlighting the differences between Hinduism and Islam he said:

> ... it is dream that Hindus and Muslims can never evolve a common nationality and this misconception of one Indian nation has gone far beyond the limits and is the cause of most of your troubles and will lead India to destruction if we fail to revive our nations in time. Hindus and Muslims belong to two different religious philosophies, social customs and literatures. Belong to two different civilizations which are based mainly on conflicting idea and conceptions (Yusufi 1996: 1166-81).

On 23 March 1940, the Muslim League resolved for a separate and sovereign Muslim country named Pakistan, expressed in the Lahore session. The League became further aggressive in its plan for division of the country to acquire the autonomous and sovereign status for the Muslims in its majority dominated areas. The claim for the sovereign nation was made in the name of religion and religious communalism. However to Ayesha Jalal, (2014) it was Jinnah's manipulation 'not of religion, but of politics that enables Jinnah to steer course for the League. By scrutinizing every word of Lahore resolution he managed to create semblance of support for the Muslim league… Pakistan for them was security not just against the Congress dominated center but much more. It epitomized their aspiration for regional self-determination even if cast in the mold of religious communitarianism' (Jalal 2014: 29) Nehru declared Leagues plan as 'mad scheme' and further ruled out the possibility of any settlement or negotiation. Similarly, Gandhi declared the idea of creation of Pakistan as the 'patent of untruth'. He expresses that 'My whole soul rebels against the idea that Hinduism and Islam represent two antagonistic culture and doctrines' (*Harijan,* 13 April 1940, cf. Singh 1989: 59). However, Ambedkar was convinced that a separate and an independent Pakistan scheme; despite all its disadvantages, offered a feasible way out of the political impulse on India (Khalique 2002).

On 20 March 1940, Congress further resolved that it should not be a party to support the Second World War, unless the British gave assurance that a Constituent Assembly would be formed based on universal adult suffrage, and the communal problems would be solved through a Constituent Assembly, where the 'rights of the minorities' would be protected through agreement between the representatives of various communities (ibid.: 55).

The Lahore resolution on Pakistan made the Hindus and Sikhs in the provinces of Punjab feel threatened and vulnerable being the religious minorities there. In April 1940, the Congress Working Committee persuaded Gandhi that the Congress must embark upon the Civil Disobedience movement. Similarly, the Congress Working Committee in July 1940 also offered to join the provincial government, only if the British government would assure that India be granted complete independence after the Second World War and a national government was formed prior to the transfer of power. In August 1940, the British agreed to expand the Executive Council and setting up of a War Advisory Committee, however, it remained silent on other issues. The British government invited both the Congress and the Muslim League to join the War Committee. The Congress turned down the offer. The League initially accepted it; and its Working Committee allowed the League to join the War Committee. However, the League subsequently, withdrew from the War Committee; as the British neither offered them equal membership to that of the Congress, nor considered the League to be the sole representative of Indian Muslims (Singh 1987: 77). The British government also offered the Dominion status and a Constituent Assembly for India at the end and gave assurance that full-weight would be given to the views of the minorities in future in the Constitution and no further 'political development' would be entertained by His Majesty's government, without satisfying the minorities demands (Khalique 2002: 129). On August 14, 1940, His Majesty's Government told the House of Commons that it 'could not contemplate transfer of their present responsibilities for the peace and welfare of India to any system of government whose authority is directly denied by large and powerful elements in India's national life'. Nor could it be a party to the coercion of such elements into submission to such a government (Ahmed 2020).

Towards the end of 1941, Congress leader C. Rajagopalachari proposed to initiate dialogue with the British and offered the solution of cooperation to break the persisting political deadlock with the imperial government. But, Jinnah aggressively demanded an independent status to Pakistan. The British, in turn, got the much-needed opportunity to ignore the demands of Congress through the turn of events of the following months (Singh 1987: 77).

In March 1942, the Cripps Mission came to India to make provisions for granting Dominion status to India, along with an election for the constituent assembly with the condition that, 'any province would be free to keep itself out of the proposed Indian Union, and they could have separate union alongside the Indian Union' (Khalique 2002). However, the Congress rejected the Cripps proposal in April 1942. In the wake of the failure of Cripps Mission, and the increasing communal tensions in the country, Gandhi renewed talks of reinstating the Civil Disobedience movement. Congress

Working Committee resolved in favour of Civil Disobedience and on 8 August 1942, Gandhi officially launched the famous Quit India movement.

Jinnah, on 10 August 1942, described the Quit India movement to be dangerous, as it intended that Congress demands were at a 'point of a bayonet'. On 21 August 1942, Jinnah called on the British to grant the 'right to self-determination' (*Statesman*, 21 August 1942; ibid.: 87). He also instructed Muslims to keep completely aloof from the movement. Likewise to Muslim League's position, the Hindu Mahasabha too opposed the Quit India Movement and boycotted it officially. The British Government also resolved to take firm action against the Congress and its leadership for defying the government. However, despite the British attempts to imprison the prominent Congress leaders and coercive measures, people from all walks of life participated in the Quit India movement in many parts of the country and turned it into a mass movement (*Statesman*, 10 August 1942, cf. Singh 1987: 87).

There were uncertainties in the provincial government because of mass resignation by the elected Congress members. However, Savarkar suggested that where the formation of Muslim League ministry was inevitable, Hindus and Sikhs might enter into a coalition with the League to further assert their interest. The Akali Dal allowed a limited number of its leaders to join the Quit India movement, but Tara Singh's followers organized to support the British. The Akalis debated whether their interest would be served better by cooperation with the League or by joining the 'nationalist' elements (ibid.: 89).

In view of sharpening differences between the Congress and the Muslim League and increasing communal tension across the nation, C. Rajagopalachari, in March 1943, told to Gandhi that an agreement with Jinnah was essential to establish a national government. In April 1944, Rajagopalachari put his formula to Jinnah, which stipulated that when the war ended, a commission would demarcate the contiguous districts in North West Frontier Region and North East India having an absolute majority of a particular community. In the areas thus demarcated, a plebiscite of the adult population would be taken. If the majority voted for a separate sovereign state, it would be given effect to, but the border districts would have the option to join one of the new states. In the event of separation, mutual agreement would be entered in order to safeguard defence, commerce and communication sectors. These terms would be implemented when the British transferred full power to India (Jinnah to Gandhi, 10 September 1944, Gandhi to Jinnah, 11 September 1944, *IAR* 1944, vol. 2: 135-7, cf. Singh 1987: 109).

The Muslim League became jubilant that Gandhi had conceded the formation of Pakistan in principle. Congressmen too were surprised at Gandhi's attitude. Like the Congress, the Akalis, and the Hindu Mahasabha also got alarmed by Gandhi's move. Gandhi had further correspondence that the constitution would be framed immediately by the provisional government following the withdrawal of the British; and independence was contemplated for the whole of India as it was; that the boundary commission would be appointed by the provisional government; where absolute majority meant a clear majority over the non-Muslim population in the Muslim majority province following the transfer of power. For Gandhi, 'Muslim can't be a separate nation by reason of acceptance of Islam. Majority of Muslims in India were converts after all' (Gandhi to Jinnah, 15 September 1944; *IAR* 1944, vol. 2: 141; Jinnah to Gandhi, 25 September 1944; cf. Singh 1987: 110). The Gandhi-Jinnah negotiation failed as Gandhi firmly declined Jinnah's proposal for demand of Pakistan consisting of Sindh, Baluchistan, the NWFP, Punjab, Bengal and Assam; and that the question of their sovereignty was to be decided by the Muslim residents without reference to the wishes of other inhabitants (Note by Jenkins, 23 July 1945, R/3/1/105 pp. 34-5 cf. Singh 1987: 111).

In July 1945, the Labour Party came into power in Britain and expressed its commitment to transfer of power, the formation of newly elected representatives in the provincial legislatures through election and finally, setting up a Constituent Assembly to frame a new constitution. Though the exact date was not fixed, the departure of the British government became widely obvious. The released Congress leaders started giving inflammatory speeches against the British representatives and its bureaucracy. The enthusiastic crowd started greeting the released political leaders. Thus, the question of loyalty of Indian armed forces and the civil servants concerned the British government (Singh 1987: 123-5).

On 21 August 1945, elections were announced. In December 1945 and in January 1946, elections were held at the Central Legislature and the Provincial Legislatures level respectively along with a negotiation between the Indian leaders and the members of British administration, especially the members of the Cabinet Mission. These elections were crucial as these paved the way for the formation of provincial governments and the election of the members of the Constituent Assembly to frame constitution for independent India. As largely expected, fierce campaigns started for these elections. While the Congress manifesto envisaged representation of all Indians, and campaigned for a united India inclusive of all population, the Muslim League targeted the Muslim population with the slogan for independent Pakistan for the Muslims. The Congress won 59 of the 102 seats and the Muslim League won 30 seats, Europeans won eight, independents won three, Akali only two seats in the Sikh constituencies of Punjab for the Central Legislature. In the Provincial Elections, the Congress won 923 (58.23 per cent), Muslim League 425 (26.81 per cent) of the 1585 seats. The remaining were won by the Europeans, Akalis, Unionist Party, Communist Party, independent parties and others. Significantly, while the Congress won most of the non-Muslim seats proving its claim to represent India, the Muslim League won most of the Muslim Seats. While the Congress formed its provincial governments in Assam, Bihar, Bombay Presidency, Central Provinces, Madras, NWFP, Orissa and United Provinces, the Muslim League formed its government in Bengal and in Sind.[4] In Punjab, a coalition government was formed with the Congress, Unionist Party and the Akalis. These election results though showed the electoral victory of the secular forces over the communal one at the all India level, but it also showed the gradual spread of the communal forces in some parts of the country that brought long lasting impact on the Indian society and politics.

[4] *Source:* http//icwu.edu.pk. Accessed on March 2020.

In March 1946, the Cabinet Mission arrived in India to make an arrangement for framing the constitutional structure and formation of a new interim government. When the Mission arrived in India, there were reports of rising communal tensions from all provinces. Even as the League negotiated with the British and the Congress, Liaquat Ali Khan talked of 'Pakistan' or 'death' (*Civil and Military Gazette*, 26 March 1946, cf. Singh 1987: 152-3). The RSS declared that 'Hindustan would be only for Hindus' (cf. ibid.: 152-3).

Jinnah reiterated that Muslim League would not accept anything short of a sovereign Pakistan, and emphasized parity which underlined Muslim nationhood. He declined to be part of any coalition government that would undermine the demand for Pakistan. The Congress demanded independence, assented for Constitution to be framed by the constitution making body, and that there should be an interim government before the formation of the constitution making body to look after the administration of the country (Singh 1987: 156).

For the Mission, there could be no interim government, unless a broad agreement on question regarding one India or more than one India. A degree of uncertainty followed whether India would survive as one country or cut into two or more countries, whether Punjab and Bengal would be divided, whether Princely States would be integrated into Indian federation or become independent kingdoms. On 6th June 1946, Jinnah persuaded a close session of the Muslim League to reject sovereign proposal and to accept the cabinet mission proposal for federal India. To Jalal, Jinnah sanctioned efforts to keep Bengal united and independent noting that it would be in good relation with Pakistan. Towards that end, he demanded a corridor linking two independent Muslim majority states. The Congress high command rejected the plan for a united and independent Bengal, however, Jinnah kept on insisting for undivided Punjab and Bengal from the British (Jalal 2014: 36). In October 1946, India witnessed the'Great Calcutta Killing' or the most infamous Calcutta Riots. Gandhi found the atmosphere in East Bengal charged with suspicion and fear. On his way to eastern Bengal, he crossed the Muslim majority district of Noakhali, where the local hooligans encouraged by fanatical *mullahs* and radical politicians had burnt the properties of Hindus, looted their crops, desecrated their temples, abducted Hindu women and forcibly converted many to Islam. Thousands of Hindus fled their homes. The massacre and riots escalated from Calcutta and other parts of East Bengal, Bihar and West Punjab. Many perceived the riots as the fall out of the gravest political crisis in the backdrop of vested interests between the British imperialism, Congress nationalism and League's separatism (Nanda 2002: 43).

In the summer of 1946, Gandhi accepted the Cabinet Mission Plan. The Muslim League, however, withdrew its acceptance of the Plan and refused to join the Constituent Assembly. When the Viceroy Lord Wavell formed an Interim Government headed by Jawaharlal Nehru, the League announced the Direct Action Day on 16 August 1946. Rattled by the holocaust of communal riots, the Viceroy inducted the Muslim league in the interim government. The Muslim League, however, never deviated from their separationist and obstructionist policies. On 20 February 1947, British government announced the transfer of power by a date no later than June 1948. On 8 March 1947, Congress led by Nehru formally called for partition of Punjab and indicated that the similar fate may wait for Bengal. 'As Jinnah kept on insisting on his demand and not to equate the principle of Pakistan with the partition of Punjab and Bengal, Mountbatten accused Jinnah of megalomania bordering on lunacy (Jalal 2014: 37). Despite all odds, however, Gandhi was trying to stop the process of Partition. Gandhi's proposition that the British had no right to divide India; but should leave India to her fate. But this was neither acceptable to Muslim League, nor to the British. However, Gandhi was prioritizing unity over communal harmony and Partition over short-term madness and hatred. He started touring various riot-effected areas of Bengal and Bihar. No matter how deplorable the communal violence was, it became Jinnah's strongest argument for Pakistan. When the riots broke out, the League leaders were reluctant to condemn the misdeeds of their co-religionists, and heaped all blame collectively on the Hindus, Congress and the British' (Nanda 2002: 47).

In the midst of such communal divides and political uncertainties India was experiencing two contradictory efforts: efforts to

Balkanise India and efforts to keep Bengal undivided by giving it a separate independent status. Jinnah argued for the inclusion of Punjab and Bengal in Pakistan as Muslims were in majority in these provinces. However, for the Congress only the parts of the provinces with Muslims majority should go to Pakistan (Ahmed 1996). For Jinnah, such proposal for partition of Punjab and Bengal was a sinister move to ensure that Muslim will get only truncated or mutilated, and moth-eaten Pakistan. In Jinnah's argument such partition, if executed, logically, that all other provinces will have to be partitioned in a similar way (Godbole 2006: 456) Jinnah insisted that there should be Muslim enclave in every province of India (Jaffrelot, 2002). 'Mountbatten was not thinking the likely creation of just two nations of India and Pakistan, but also inevitability of more than two nations. The British Cabinet Committee on India and Burma 'did not like the idea to reduce the number of choices from three to two, ie they felt that they were pledged to give the provinces the option of remaining independent of either Hindustan or Pakistan if they so desired. The British game was much deeper than partitioning country between India and Pakistan. Nehru during his discussion with Mountbatten objected so strongly the proposal of giving choice to all provinces' (Godbole 2006: 456)

The Partition politics saw a new dynamics in 1947 with Huseyn Shaheed Suhrawardy, the premier of Bengal demanding an independent undivided sovereign Bengal in a divided India as a separate dominion. While one section of the Bengal Pradesh Congress Committee supported the proposal, its dominant section and the Hindu Mahasabha under the leadership Syama Prasad Mukherjee vehemently oppose this proposal. However, despite persuasive argument, the Congress high command never accepted the scheme because according to them independence of Bengal would really mean the domination of Muslim league under that circumstance and that the whole of Bengal would be joining the Pakistan area. Patel consider the cry of Suhrawardy for an independent united Bengal was a trap to incorporate Hindu dominated Bengal into Pakistan. For the Hindu Mahasabha, it was a poly to force the Hindus to live under Muslim domination (Chakrabarty 2012: 176) However, Gandhiji sensed an opportunity and gave his assessment to Mukherjee on 13th

May 'an admission that Bengali Hindus and Bengali Musssulmans were one would be a severe blow against the two-nation theory of the League' (Bose 1953: 253 op. cit., Noorani, 2000: 247).

Meanwhile, highlighting the consequence of Direct Action Plan of Muslim league that resulted into Great Calcutta Killing and Noakhali riots in 1946, the Hindu Mahasabha by mobilizing the Hindus at large launched a fierce campaign for partition of Bengal (Chakrabarty 2012: 178). By March-April 1947 public opinion had hardened behind the demand for a separate province of West Bengal that would be part of India and not Pakistan (Mahajan 2000: 222). As the partition plan was announced on 3 June 1947, the united Bengal campaign came to an end. Ultimately, the Bengal legislative assembly accepted the partition plan by majority votes.

Law and order situation got speedily deteriorated in view of imminent departure of the British. The senior administrative officers had neither the will nor the capacity to deal with large-scale break-down of the ongoing violence. In many places, the police was also becoming radicalized. At this point, both the Congress and the British were driven to the conclusion that Partition was the only alternative to chaos. Ultimately, the Congress Working Committee accepted the Partition plan. Congress change of heart required abandoning two of its oldest and sacred principles of unity of India and full independence (Jalal 2014: 38). However, there was a strong dissenting voice against this Partition plan from the Pashtun leader Khan Abdul Ghaffar Khan (popularly known as the 'Frontier Gandhi'). Gandhi also accepted it with a heavy heart and lamented that, 'Everybody is today impertinent for India's Independence. Therefore, there is no other help' (Kripalani 1976).

Prominent leaders like Nehru, Sardar Vallabhbhai Patel, C. Rajagopalachari, Rajendra Prasad and other Congress leaders were not the only ones, who were persuaded that though the Partition was an exorbitant price, it was worth paying for a lasting peace on the subcontinent. Even as the Muslim League was celebrating getting a homeland; the British were relieved with the prospect of an orderly transfer of power. It was against such a situation that made the Congress leaders accept the Partition plan (Nanda 2002: 48-9).

Sad at heart, Gandhi did not participate in the celebration at

Delhi on 15 August 1947. He spent that day in Calcutta fasting and praying. His presence provided an immediate healing touch to the Great Calcutta Killings of the previous year. His worse fears were confirmed when a fortnight later a Hindu mob inflamed by the news of massacres and migration from West Pakistan went on rampage. Gandhi too escaped a murderous assault, while trying to pacify the rioters. He again went on a fast. He broke his fast only after representatives of both communities gave pledge that they would ensure that Calcutta remained peaceful. The fast had an immediate effect in restoring peace and stability in Bengal (ibid.: 50).

Whether emotionally acceptable or not, India finally achieved its independent nationhood in 1947, but through the division of the country that created a separate Muslim nation of Pakistan with two units – West and East Pakistan, and a secular nation of India. The whole society and the country got shaken. The Partition of India created a sea of hapless migration of people across the border. Though the exact figure is not officially known, for Butalia (1996), about twelve million people moved between the new, truncated India and the two wings, East and West, of the newly created Pakistan, and about 75,000 women are thought to have been abducted and raped by men of different religions. Thousands of families were divided, homes destroyed, crops left to rot, villages abandoned (Butalia 1996). To Anita Inder Singh (2006) anything between two to three million lost their lives between 1946 to 1951, some nine million Hindus and Sikhs crossed the border into India from Pakistan and about six million Muslims went to Pakistan from India. Ahmed (2011) estimates between 500,000 to 800,000 people were killed in Punjab alone; 75,000 women were raped, many women were killed by Hindus and Sikhs to save the family and community honour, many of the raped women were either killed by the rapists or by their family members, or the victim themselves committed suicide. Many women committed suicide to save the 'honour' of their family and community. It is also estimated that after Partition, there was a total migratory inflows of 14.49 million and outflows of 16.7 million on both the sides, and 2.2 million 'missing' people (Bharadwaj, Khwaja and Mian 2008). Many people; besides facing problems of uncertainty, hopelessness, cultural uprootedness and spatial displacement, underwent the tragic and traumatic experiences of riots, looting and destruction of their properties, threat, violence, murder, and physical harassment of both women and children. Though Partition was planned, migration was not expected by masses. Though, many of the leaders fulfilled their aspiration and secured their destiny and future in politics, the destiny of vast sections of the people who became either refugee or alien on either side of the border emerged as vulnerable in all possible terms.

CHAPTER 3

Partition and Persecution
Fakir and his Family as Minority in East Pakistan

Hindu-Muslim Friendship and the 1947 Partition

Traditional Friendship, Spread of Communalism, Division of Country, and Migration

During the anti-colonial struggles, India witnessed waves of uneasy tensions between the formation and the arousal of national identity, on the one hand, and the articulation of religio-communal identities, on the other. These produced in one way or the other long-lasting communal divides, hatred, and violence in many parts of the country. Largely, these also consolidated binaries both in the thoughts and actions at all levels among section of social groups. All through the independence struggle the communal identities and tensions, which were getting intensified at the regional and pan-India level, started being consolidated and spreading at the local level, though with diverse intensity. Villagers who had been living in their peaceful surroundings with age-old communal harmony in many places gradually started becoming conscious and assertive of their respective religious identities. Many social practices, those which were considered natural and non-oppositional, started becoming subject of social acrimony, contradiction, and conflict across the space. At times, the spread of disinformation, rumour, and misdirection of political leaders of communal pursuits aggravated the peaceful social setting even of rural areas. Tacit contradictions also started becoming explicit in their attempt to consolidate their community identity vis-à-vis the formative national identities. Many a times, these added more confusion than clarity for the patriotic common man as to whether to associate with the national identity over the religio-communal identity, or vice-versa. Many people living in the eastern part of undivided Bengal became increasingly subject to such unprecedented confusions and tensions in the latter days of independence struggle and the subsequent division of the country, thereafter.

A cluster of Hindu families of a remote village of Nadia district of undivided Bengal started getting a feel of such communal tensions starting from late 1930s. Such tensions became visible among the members of Muslim family living in adjacent clusters of the same village. Those who chanted the slogans like *Swadhinata chahiye!* (we want freedom), *British Bharat choro!*; *Congress zindabad!; Mahatma Gandhi zindabad!; Hindustan zindabad!*' (British, quit India!; long live the Congress!; long live Mahatma Gandhi!; long-live India!) also started becoming parts of various communal slogans like, '*Hindustan for Hindus*', *Jinnah zindabad, Pakistan zindabad, Larke lengye Pakistan*! (long-live Jinnah, long-live Pakistan, achieve Pakistan through struggle) and so forth. Though, members of most of these communities tried to maintain peaceful coexistence in these villages and hamlets, tensions and uncertainties started brewing in the social fabric of this area. Undeterred by these tensions, communal divides, and social uncertainties, two teenaged boys from rural areas, Fakir from a Hindu family and Jamal from a Muslim family developed an intense friendship and became bosom friends. Even though Fakir was from an orthodox Hindu family, he acquired his Muslim nickname at his birth. Some belief systems, family incidence and localized cultural practices were behind getting such interfaith nicknames.

Fakir's father was a local landlord belonging to a Rajput clan, whose forefathers came to Bengal from Rajasthan as part of the contingents of a Mughal army during the rule of Emperor Akbar. Gradually, they were naturalized with the cultural traditions and practices of Bengal. Fakir's father got married at an early age and entered into a happy married life. However, Fakir's mother was unable to bear a child. Initially, she gave birth to two stillborn babies and another baby died immediately after he was born. The couple went to a local *pir* (a Muslim ascetic) following the advice of neighbours and relatives for his intercession, as his blessings were free from religious affiliations. While giving the blessings, the *pir* advised the couple to donate the newborn baby to a *fakir* (an ascetic, who lives solely on alms) and further to purchase that baby back from the *fakir* by giving him some alms. After a few years, the new baby was born to this couple, a *fakir* was called within few hours, and the baby was donated to him. When the couple wanted to get the baby back, the *fakir* returned the baby to them with the condition that the newborn be named as 'Fakir' as part of his alms. The couple happily agreed and so named the newborn, as per the advice of the Muslim ascetic. Though a loosely framed Muslim name was a matter of contradiction in an orthodox Hindu family, it was a matter of inter-faith coexistence for the wider society. So Fakir grew up with this name. However, his formal name was different. His formal name was given in a traditional Hindu *namkaran sanskar* (child naming ritual). As he grew up he also underwent an elaborate *upnayana sanskar* (sacred thread ceremony) according to the traditional Hindu opractice.

Fakir had many friends from both the religious communities. However, his friendship with Jamal was different from the rest. Jamal's father was also a landlord and was an enlightened person in the locality. Jamal's father's gramophone and radio and Fakir's father's bicycle, which were the rarest commodities in those days, were the prime matter of attraction to both of them. Though the houses of Fakir and Jamal were around two kms away from that of each other, they would make it a point to visit each other's house regularly, whoever wanted. Parents of both these children were also friendly to each other and traditionally, they participated in each other's religious and family rituals and functions. Religious distinctiveness and divisions had seldom been a matter of social differences and conflicts in the neighbourhood.

Both Fakir and Jamal studied in the same school that was located around six kms away from their home. They shared the same bicycle, food, books, stories; they experienced growing -up together despite having different religious backgrounds. Friendship of these two adolescent children grew in their natural habitat against the backdrop of independence struggle in the surrounding. As they grew up, Jamal started managing his parental property and business, while Fakir besides managing their own landed property, also started practicing allopathy in the village after taking the necessary training.

Fakir got married at an early age of seventeen years to a beautiful girl named Revati from his own clan from northern part of Bengal. Similarly, Jamal also married to a local Muslim girl. These marriages, however, had not taken place in isolated situations. The family members of both of these friends were deeply engaged in identifying suitable brides for these prospective eligible bachelors and participated, with all enthusiasm and sincerity, in solemnizing those marriages following their own religious rituals and customs. Jamal's uncle, who was living in the northern part of Bengal identified Revati as a prospective bride for Fakir. Fakir and Jamal's families gradually developed a deeper connect. Fakir's family had elaborate ceremonies related to marriage, pregnancy, child birth and *namkaran* ceremony (naming) and death. The Muslim family was always beside the Hindu family, may it be the matter of joy or grief. Exchanging and sharing several fruits and vegetables was, but a normal practice. In fact, their lives were incomplete without the regular reciprocity and cooperation from each other.

Fakir had several setbacks in his life for a few years immediately after his marriage. Fakir's only sister Falguni, who was six-years younger to him got married, when she was only nine-years-old, with a man triple her age. Unfortunately, she became a widow a year after her marriage. The child widow was, therefore, abandoned and sent back to stay permanently with her parents by her cruel in-laws describing her as *kulakshana* (baneful character). Both, the shocked parents of Fakir and this innocent child widow herself, had no option but to accept it as a matter of destiny. Though Fakir tried to revolt against social injustice, the decision of the elders only conditioned him to accept this as a tragic reality of his life.

Fakir's father was unable to bear the pain of widowhood of his daughter and the painful lifestyle imposed on her by the traditional Hindu orthodox system. Falguni was compelled to wear cheap white cloth, shaved her head by looking at a broken mirror, to boil her food herself and to eat only that boiled food once in day, to remain confined within the house only and so on and so forth. Fakir's father suddenly died after six months of the widowhood of his daughter. From the deathbed, he asked Fakir to promise that he would never abandon his widowed sister throughout his life and protect her from all situations and to keep her happy. Fakir promised to live up to the expectation of his father.

Fakir got engulfed with pain, sorrows and uncertainties. After the sudden death of Fakir's father, the whole responsibility of looking after the landed property fell on him. He was not much aware of the papers and possessions of the land. Taking advantage of his innocence and ignorance, large parts of their traditional land were encroached upon by the relatives and others. Young Fakir and his widowed mother were left in despair. They started getting repeated notice from the government about the rent. However, the receipts from their land were disproportionately lower than the rent demand from the government. The mother-son duo started identifying the areas of their land possession. As expected, little help came from the relatives. However, Fakir's friend Jamal and his father stood firmly with them to recover their lost properties. With their intervention, they quickly got possession of their whole property and all dues were timely settled. Friendship between Jamal and Fakir's family gradually got further strengthened and normalcy returned in the life of young Fakir and his family.

The small family of Fakir, consisting of his widowed mother, widowed sister and his wife, now started getting a new life. With the passage of time, Fakir became a parent to a daughter. Around the same time, Jamal became a parent to a daughter too. Both Fakir and Jamal's daughters grew up together and were good friends to each other. As a mark of enduring and close relationship between these families, they solemnized the friendship ceremony for their daughters. These young girls became *soi* (traditionally, solemnized friends) of each other. Through this ceremony those girls promised that they would remain friends to each other all through their lives. It also sealed the bond of friendship between these two families for long.

Besides, both Fakir and Jamal were patriotic Indians by heart. Notwithstanding their distinctive religious identities, they experienced the era of colonization together. When they were addressed by the freedom fighters in school and in neighbourhood, these young men felt their national identities intensified against the British. They also participated collectively in the protest march, rail obstruction, and various public gatherings, which were organized by the freedom fighters of that area. Despite the increasing sense of communal divides that started engulfing this area from the mid-1930s, they strengthened their commitment for a communal unity. These families, along with the neighbours and villagers started dreaming of an independent India together where everybody would be happy and free and would get the space for a dignified existence. However, their thoughts and dreams started getting unexpected jolts since late 1930s. Listening to these aggressive speeches by the communal leaders, in turn, made their neighbours to identify each other in terms of the religious differences rather than their age-old commonalities.

The political happenings of that time in the country put enormous pressure on lives of these families. Since Jinnah aggressively demanded for a separate sovereign state of Pakistan in 1940s, it started encouraging the local communalist leaders to assert their identity in communal term. Simultaneously, the emotional appeal of Gandhiji for mass participation in the Quit India movement and the news of Netaji Subhas Chandra Bose's heroic act of organizing Indian National Army against the British engulfed the villagers despite communal tension and uncertainties.

Three contrasting images of independence struggle started appearing before them, the struggle for united independent India, and struggle for a Muslim Pakistan and struggle for a Hindu India. These villagers became very confused and concerned about their association with the first two images of independence struggle. Furthermore, in the mid 1940s, the disastrous idea of Partition started becoming obvious to them, and they increasingly became uncertain as to whether they would live in Hindustan or in the likely carved out Pakistan, as to which side of the country or border they would choose to live and who would be the natives, and the refugees? They could also realize that such decisions would only come from above and they would have a limited choice. Tensions and rumours started spreading rapidly everywhere. While the local Muslim League leaders became engaged in uniting Muslims to press their demand for a Pakistan, the secular nationalist activists had a very minute presence and the Hindu nationalist leaders were conspicuously absent in this area. Most Hindu families started feeling insecure because of sudden spouting of Muslim communalism and exclusivist nationalism in this Muslim dominated area. Significantly, most of these communal uncertainties got injected from outside by the ultra-nationalist communal leaders.

Both Fakir and Jamal's families also got affected by these communal tensions. Though the rise of communalism and exclusivist nationalism brought uncertainties, emotional threats, and the fear of dislocation for these families, these also brought them further closer to each other in these difficult times. They also firmly decided not to migrate anywhere, or to cross the other side of the border of the newly carved India or Pakistan, notwithstanding the outcomes of Partition. They emotionally vowed to help and safeguard each other's family. Within these heightening tensions and uncertainties, they were indeed wondering as to whether they fought for independence or for the partition of the country. They indeed earnestly prayed for independence of the country, but not for the partition of the country.

By this time, the family structure of Fakir has changed and he had acquired added responsibilities and recognition in this area as a reputed medical practitioner and a social worker. His widowed mother, who was giving directions to Fakir on the matters of property and family affairs, passed away. Now, Fakir was to look after his family members of six people, all of whom were dependent on him. In his family, besides a six-year-old daughter, he had another two sons of four and three years of age respectively. His widowed sister was now an adult. His wife Revati always gave her special care and protection. Among the social circles, he got wide social recognition as *doctor babu*, because of his good command over medical knowledge.

As the country, unfortunately, got divided on 15 August 1947, as the reflection of victory of communalism and exclusivist nationalism over patriotism and civic-secular nationalism, this village became a part of East Pakistan. Binaries such as 'we' and 'they' and 'otherness' came into play in a big way in this newly created independent country of East Pakistan. Though, there were celebrations for both the attainment of independence and for the creation of Pakistan by the large section of local Muslim population of this area, it became a life threatening and traumatized reality and experience for all the Hindus there. Overnight, all the Hindu families became the religious minorities and alien in their own habitat. Radio broadcasting and newspaper reports on the celebration of independence, along with creation of Pakistan and the outburst of communal riots in the region further added agony and uncertainty among the Hindus. It started appearing as if the whole independence struggle was entirely against the Hindus and they had lost the battle there. Chaos and uncertainty started looming large on the Hindu families on hearing the news of massacre of Hindu population elsewhere in the country. Most of the Hindu families of this village became very suspicious of the 'others' (i.e. the Muslim community). Altogether, it became a question of life and death overnight. Recurring incidents of looting of property, communal threats, arson started spreading very rapidly there. Communal threats, which were once only a part of imagination, emerged to be a hard reality for the Hindu families. Unable to bear any further threats, most of these, over night designated the 'Hindu minority' families of this area started departing for India undertaking arduous and painful journey to unknown destinations as 'refugees'.

Was it that struggle, which they fought?
Was it that independence that they sought?
Why they got threats for days and nights?
Why friend became enemy and joined street fight?
Why the helpless father running in haste?
With crying babies hang on mother's chest?
They run around for life and safety
Get confined as criminal and guilty
They leave the place where they were born
All became alien in the land of their own,
They left the place in the dark,
Becoming afraid of disguised shark,
With heavy heart and teary eye
Pain sobbing chocking voice and deep sigh
The salute the motherland and say a good bye.
Was it a war, that they fought?
Was it the independence that was sought?

The Stayed Back Lonely Hindu Family

Partition of the country was not only shocking, but also unbelievable to the family members of Fakir. It was difficult for them to believe that everything had changed overnight, and that the country was divided and they had become alien in this new land. For this orthodox Hindu family, their house was not only a piece of land, but it was their ancestral land (*janmabhumi*) and the motherland, their birth place. The souls of their ancestors are attached with its land, river, air, sky, tree, birds and animals of this area. Both emotionally and socially, they were not convinced with the Partition of the country. Rather, they started considering that the Partition was a temporary phenomenon, and that the country would be united again, and each one would be coming back to this beautiful village. Fakir's family started convincing the leaving Hindu families to stay back in the newly created East Pakistan. The slogan 'India will be united again' was the repeated sentence of both Fakir and Jamal.

Over the course of time, Fakir started shockingly and saliently observing the immediate desertion of the village by the Hindu people, and arrival of huge number of Muslim refugees mostly from the newly independent Indian state of Bihar to this village. These refugees quickly started occupying the houses and the properties left behind by the Hindus and started presuming that the remaining Hindu families would leave the village quickly. The migrating Hindu families tried to persuade Fakir's family to migrate to India along with them, and some blood relatives in India also asked them to go over to them in India and to get settled there. Revati was not in favour of staying back in East Pakistan as a religious minority. She repeatedly requested Fakir to take a decision to migrate to India and join her brothers, who had also migrated to India. Additionally, she was in an advanced stage of her pregnancy. The aggressive hostile attitude of the refugees and a section of neighbours made her more insecure about her children and her adolescent widowed sister-in-law Falguni. However, both Fakir and Falguni's deep attachment to their native land (*janmabhumi*) overshadowed the threats of the ongoing communal tensions. Jamal was persistent in his efforts to invoke the pre-Partition days promising that notwithstanding the result of Partition of the country, none of them would leave the village; and they would stand for each other. Jamal and many Muslim families from their neighbourhood came forward to assure them of help in the event of any threat to their lives. They came forward with open arms to provide this lonely, insecure and disturbed Hindu family all kinds of safety and security. Ultimately, the love, affection for the motherland and cherished friendship with the neighbours and family friends, on the one hand, and a sense of insecurity of unknowingness with the wider world in newly independent India on the other, prevailed over this small Hindu family (consisting of Fakir, his wife, his sixteen-year-old widowed sister, six-year-old eldest daughter, and two sons of three and two-year-old) to stay back in East Pakistan. Nevertheless, as the new history got unfolded the destiny took a new turn to test the depth of the bondage of Hindu-Muslim friendship within a few months.

Despite the fact that Jamal's family and Fakir's neighbourhood stood with them, this family was made to realize within a short period that political partition had been enforced and institutionalized at the village level. It was also made obvious to them that the social division had acquired a political meaning, where enemies were created out of old friends, community of refugees and natives, and majority and minority were made conspicuous in the name of religion. The imagination of communal threats and identity became such a reality for this Hindu family, that they started observing other community's behaviour with more suspicion than with trustworthiness. They gradually started encountering an unexpected experience of humiliation and alienness on an everyday basis, despite the overwhelming support and sympathy for them by their few Muslim friends and neighbours. Not willingly, they had to re-socialize in a new political culture as a religious minority. For them, it had remained a lifelong experience of alienness, on the one hand, and relocation in the 'unimagined' nationhood, on the other.

Sudden Communal Attack and Friend's Protection

With the arrival of Muslim refugees from India and exodus of Hindu population, the demographic composition of this area changed substantially. They found that with the partition of the country, it not only emerged as a religious minority, but also became an eyesore for the communal politicians and few neighbours. The refugees also became aggressive and hostile in their behaviour in their public resentment against this Hindu family. All of a sudden, the inherited mutual trust and traditional sense of multireligious bondings and belongings in the neighbourhood started waning. Therefore, an uneasy coexistence developed in the locality.

However, as a local doctor, Fakir kept on treating the patients and started getting adjusted in this new communal environment. Around late October 1947, one morning, as Fakir was about to attend patients in his dispensary, a huge crowd of Muslim refugees led by a few local leaders gathered in front of their house. They became abusive, aggressive and hostile and started chanting anti-Hindu slogans. They created chaos, drove the Muslim *lathel* (regular farm servant-cum-security guard) of Fakir's dispensary, set the waiting room of the dispensary on fire, and told him to vacate the house and leave for India immediately, or else all would be burnt to death. Fakir was shocked and surprised and got shaken from within. After recovering from this immediate shock, he somehow tried to resist and reason with the attackers. Few patients and neighbours also came forward to reason and resist the attackers, but of no avail. The crowd overpowered everybody and pushed all the neighbours and patients outside the dispensary. They started shouting perojative slogans like *nara-e-takbir!* (slogan of magnification), *allah hu akbar!* (God is great), 'drive the *malauns* (accursed) and *kafirs* (infidels) out of the country!' Fakir became more and nore nervous. There was nobody around to stand for him or speak for him as all were driven away. His own *lathel* was physically pushed back alleging him to be a *namak haram* (unfaithful), as he was serving a *malaun*. Fakir requested the crowd to give him time for at least six to seven days to vacate the house as his wife was in an advanced stage of pregnancy. But, the mobs were, as usual, non-compromising, and allowed only a few hours to vacate, and sat in front of the house for getting its possession within the prescribed hours. The attackers also put fire to one part of the outhouse and started pelting stones inside the house.

As the noise of the crowd entered the house, all the family members became nervous and tensed. Unable to bear such tension, Revati got the labour pain and collapsed. Fakir's sister started taking care of his wife and of the screaming helpless children, as much as, she could do. Disregarding all the perils and tensions, few Muslim women from the neighbourhood came to the house from the backyard to take care of pregnant Revati and their shocked toddlers. They stood firmly in front of the main gate of the house and quickly developed a barricade against the entry of any outsiders there.

Fakir constantly went in front of the aggressor and kept on repeatedly pleading and requesting for more time from them, but in vain. This continued for around an hour or so which only produced amusement and encouragement for the attackers, and developed frustration, pain and helplessness in him. His repeated pleas for time was of no meaning to the crowd. Now, he could realise that he and his family members were standing between life and death with a little difference. As the crowd was becoming more and more aggressive, and started advancing towards the inner part of the house, he decided to give up and getting immediately ready to vacate the house to save at least lives of family members at all cost. The aggression of the attackers started getting intensified.

Frustrated, Fakir rushed inside the house and got internally shaken by looking at the pale, insecure, grim, shocked, and helpless still faces of his kinsfolk at home mercifully waiting for their protection and help. Despite the support from few women from their neighbourhood, he felt he was helpless, waiting for the genocide of the family by the furious attackers. He brought everybody closer to his arm and looking at the heaven and started remembering his ancestors and the God. Some neighbours also tried to come inside the house to protect them; but they could not do much as they were outnumbered by the crowd.

Meanwhile, he saw a large convoy of bullock carts with hundreds of club-wielding people rushing towards his house. They were shouting *maro, maro, bhagao* (kill them, kill them, drive them away). Fakir became highly despaired and tried to close the main gate of the house to protect his family from an immediate assault. The crowd disallowed Fakir to close the main gate. Some from the mob started banging the main gate and entered the house forcefully and threw away the household belongings. He was extremely puzzled and threatened and was at a loss of how to protect these innocent lives. He picked up a club as his last resort to protect the family and breathlessly started waiting to face the attack and started shouting 'don't enter the house, don't enter the house…'.

However, he was surprised to see that these people on bullock carts were his neighbours from neighbouring villages, friends and well-wishers led by his friend Jamal and his reliable *lathel* who was pushed away by the attackers. As they inched more closely towards the house, they started shouting, '*Doctor babu*! We have come, please open the gate and come out. Do not be afraid of these scoundrels'. '… *naya bhabhijan*, you are our sister'. 'We will give our lives for you…' His Muslim neighbours also came out wielding clubs in their hands and jointly surrounded the house to overpower the aggressively attacking refugees. After a small spell of fight, they captured the mob leaders and drove away the rest to restore the safety and security of this lonely Hindu family. They started throwing water on the burning house to keep the fire under control. Jamal stood firmly in front of the main gate of the house to ensure that nobody could enter the house for any further damage. Shaken Fakir came out of the house; he was greeted with open arms by Jamal, neighbours and the *lathel*. Jamal held him tight to his chest and both started weeping profusely. Fakir stood in front of the house speechless and emotionally broken with much gratitude for his friend, neighbours and his *lathel*. There was silence everywhere; only sobbing and tears were expressed the intensity of the trauma both of them had undergone.

The whole family and the neighbours were moved and surprised by the turn of the events. It appeared to Fakir that he had a new lease of life not only for himself, but also for his entire vulnerable family. The whole family got back their dignity and faith due to the commitment of their neighbours and especially of Jamal and the *lathel*. This move for the protection of this Hindu family was indeed taken by the *lathel*, who despite receiving threats by the attackers, rushed to Jamal for help without informing anything to Fakir at that moment.

Meanwhile, the rest of the attackers and their leaders were rounded up by the agitated neighbours and the *lathel*. The attackers were publicly thrashed. Quickly a meeting of village elders was held. The captured attackers were placed in the village court. The attackers started pleading that they should not be handed over to the police. They were publicly rebuked, and made to beg apology and to give a written undertaking that they would not enter the premise of this Hindu house any more. As the law and administration was very shaky at that point of time, collective pressure and public scrutiny was the only option. The neighbours and Jamal again assured Fakir and his family of all support and arranged round the clock village security for their family.

It was, indeed, an emotional reunion of Hindu and Muslim neighbours and reposing of trust and sympathies for each other in times of need. Jamal felt very sorry that he was unable to pre-judge the situation and pre-empt such events of communal violence. However, Jamal again appealed Fakir to stay in this village only and not to leave for India. The neighbours also repeated the same appeal. Also, he publicly announced that he would sacrifice his life to give protection to his friend and his family here in East Pakistan. He again reminded Fakir of their promise that, as long as they would remain alive, they would not leave this country. The utterances of Jamal started echoing everywhere. Fakir was overwhelmed with the timely support and help of his friend and the neighbours. He publicly accepted that appeal and promised to live there with his friends and the neighbours till he was alive. He caught the hand of Jamal on the one hand, and *lathel* on the other, and promised to stay back there.

As Fakir, Jamal and the *lathel* entered the house, they found the house was occupied with women from the neighbouring families and the villages. Wives, sisters, daughters and mothers of many of his Muslim patients had gathered there to protect the women and children of this vulnerable family. They themselves had already brought a mid-wife to take care of Revati. All were anxious to secure the life and safety of this lonely Hindu family. As Revati regained her consciousness, she had very little to utter except to hug her little susceptible children, widowed sister-in-law and all the other women neighbours with tears. Perhaps, she was only trying to say that 'I am grateful to you for saving the lives of my innocent family members…I will remain grateful forever'.

This episode of 1947, though, reposed the strong bond of communal unity among Hindu-Muslim neighbours, it also brought a deep sense of threat and persecution not only to the members of this lonely family who experienced it, but also to successive generations. A mixed feeling of threat and cooperation had remained integral part of their existence there. This episode and many such incidences created a feeling of insecurity in the family members, on the one hand, and love for their Muslim neighbourhood friends, on the other.

Indo-Pak War 1947-8 and Encountering New Tensions

Living as a religious minority in a theocratic state had several political connotations. The relationship with the neighbours and the wider society was linked to political dynamics of the state against the backdrop of Indo-Pakistan relationship. In the wake of heightening tensions between India and Pakistan, Fakir's family had always been the immediate target of communal attack. In October 1947, Indo-Pakistan War began as armed tribal men and irregular military forces of Pakistan invaded the Princely State of Jammu and Kashmir. Maharaja Hari Singh requested India for help. The instrument of accession to India was signed, and Jammu and Kashmir became an integral part of India. The ceasefire was signed on 1 January 1949 and the Line of Control was established. The ongoing Indo-Pakistan conflicts and the accession of Jammu and Kashmir to India became a matter of dispute in the neighbourhood and this lonely Hindu family once again became the immediate target.

Fakir inherited a big house from his parents. It was surrounded by around five acres of land. Their house was separated from the River Ganga, along with a broad gauged railway track, which is another 500 meters away. Significantly, the railway track was used more for variety of social purposes other than for running the train. There were only two passenger trains running daily on the track, one in the early morning; and other in the late evening. This village was so remote and peaceful that the sound of passing trains was heard even several kilometres away. Waters of River Ganga nearly touched the railway track during the rainy season and withered away in the dry seasons. Notwithstanding these seasonal variations, the River

Ganga was always full and the other extreme of the river bank could hardly be seen from this side of the river. Their big house was as much a sense of pride, cultural rooting and practices for Fakir and his family, as much as the matter of growing security concerns in the wake of increasing communal tensions in the country.

Abusive Attacks and Attempt to Abduct Falguni

As the border tension increased, Fakir's family marked that more and more people started using the road connected to his house during the night-time and they started using cuss words against the family members. Some even chanted, 'Go to *Hindustan*!, or else, you will be butchered here!'. Someone would indulge in stone pelting and run away once chased by the *lathel*. Though the family members would be disturbed and would feel insecure, Fakir was firm in his conviction: 'These are cowards and disturbed people … things would be alright'. Jamal and few neighbours were always reported about these incidences. Gradually, the stone pelting became a regular phenomenon at night. Meanwhile, Fakir's three children (eldest daughter Juhi, eldest son Pontu and younger son Bulbul) started attending a local primary school. Falguni too was grown up. She emerged as very beautiful and caring *pishima* (father's sister) for her nephews and niece. She would roam around freely all around the village with her brother's children, play with them and socialise with them. As part of her regular practice, she would go to River Ganga to take bath and fetch water in the noon. This adolescent widow was un-disturbed by the ongoing tensions going around the village surrounded by the religious orientations of her family.

Once she was late for a couple of hours in returning from the river after bath, it became a matter of concern. Revati too was highly tensed about her. Fakir was away to attend his patients in a far-off village. She sent the *lathel* to go to the river and report immediately. He came back without any trace of her exact location. Fakir also came back from his medical cell and became highly disturbed to see that his sister was missing. As he was about to head towards his house, he found that she was coming back home accompanied by Jamal's wife. All were puzzled as to what had happened. She started weeping and rushed inside the house. Meanwhile, Jamal arrived on his bicycle. He took everybody inside the home and narrated to them the entire incident. There was a plot to kidnap Fakir's sister and forcefully marry her to a Muslim man and to convert her to Islam. Jamal came to know about this plot a few days back and he was sending his wife and few other women daily to the bathing place area in the river to ensure the security of Fakir's sister and to identify the kidnappers. Despite perils and risks involved, the kidnappers executed their plan to abduct Falguni. Some came on the boat from the other bank of the river and some from the river-bed side. But Jamal's persons chased them and they ran away. Eventually, their plan was foiled before they could do any harm to Falguni. These kidnappers were identified and impounded and they would be punished as per the desire of Fakir. Though the safe return of Falguni gave Fakir and Revati some relief, they felt threatened and shaken from inside. Against the backdrop of prevailing political tensions and the possible abduction of his sister, Fakir decided not to go far with any legal or village-level action. However, Jamal threatened the attempted kidnappers of harsh action and took assurance from them that if any such thing happens to this Hindu family, the kidnappers would be responsible.

Though this episode ended peacefully, and Jamal reassured all his help and support for Fakir's family, this altered the lifestyle of widowed Falguni drastically. As per the orthodox Hindu tradition, a widow can't be remarried. The proposal for her remarriage was never discussed in the family as it was tabooed. Her life became further circumscribed as a widow with varieties of denial.

In view of these adverse situations, the issue of migration to India always came forth in the regular discussions in the family. However, the decision from Fakir's side was always negative. As Fakir's family stayed back, the status and identity of a religious minority got transmitted to the next generation eventually. Fakir also developed a compartmentalized life that was full of dedication towards his patients, social service and maintenance of landed property on one side, and orthodox disciplined lifestyle of his family, on the other. Decades went by and the size of the family and responsibilities increased amid the contradictory situations.

Generations Getting Rooted for Uprooting

Around a decade-and-half had passed by now. Fakir, is now a middle-aged person, with a host of responsibilities. Several new families had joined the village and the number of the native families had also increased. Fakir's family was now surrounded by a numerically dominant friendly group of native Muslim families, but also with a sizeable number of hostile and aggressive Muslim refugee families, especially from Bihar. These migrant families had their culturally distinctive rituals, religious practices, clothes, languages, and mentalities. The size of Fakir's family had now increased. All the members of this family grew up under the shadow of communal tension in late 1950s and early 1960s. Notwithstanding the shadow of communalism, Fakir's children were engaged with their surroundings in the process of their growing up.

The Family, Familial Practices, and the Surroundings

Over the years, Fakir had emerged to be a strong disciplinarian, protective and a distinctive personality from the rest in the area. He was engaged in maintaining this distinctiveness by preserving his religious identity and giving good education and upbringing to his children. By now, Fakir had eight children – eldest daughter Juhi (19), eldest son Pontu (18), Bulbul (16), second daughter Kajal (14), third son Bisnu, fourth son Sadhu, fifth son Laltu and the sixth son Som were of twelve, ten, five and two years of age respectively. Among all these children, Laltu was very active and talkative in nature and he was always dealt with special care. His eldest daughter Juhi got married in Rangpur, another district of East Pakistan, and his second eldest son was sent to India to stay with his maternal uncle to study. Except Laltu and Som, all other children were studying in the local junior schools at different levels. Fakir, Revati and Falguni were deeply engaged in imbibing the children with Hindu orthodox cultural practices. It was quite visible that more the communal tension increased in the neighbourhood, the more they became insecure, and the tendency to control the children to keep inside the house increased through religious orthodox practices.

At home, the children were made to follow and practice the orthodox Hindu culture which was regularly reflected in the performance of various rituals, worshipping and behavioural patterns, choice of food and clothes and the usage of language. All children were to follow instructions of the elders religiously and to speak only pure Bengali language (*bhadra bhasha*) against the colloquial language (*chalti bhasha*) spoken by the other children in the neighbourhood.

With times, Revati had now emerged to be the true homemaker and performed all rituals as per the Hindu traditions. Like a conventional Bengali Hindu wife, she was fond of wearing a red border white *saris*, with deep red (*poula*) and white bangles (*shankha*), putting a red tip of vermilion on her forehead, a thin ring on her nose and bright hanging rings on her ears. She was not so fair in complexion, but always had a refreshing glow on her face. From her practices, gestures, attires and behaviour, she appeared to be the most divine woman on earth to the imagination of the children and of the neighbours. She started her day with a salutation and offering water to the *tulsivedi* (a raised platform with *tulsi* plant on it) located at the centre of the house and ending the day by blowing a conch shell and lighting a lamp in front of a *tulsi* shrub as a mark of her devotion to various Hindu deities. She also leisurely narrated the stories of *Ramayana, Mahabharata*, and other Hindu mythological tales to the children. For all the children, their hero of all these stories were their parents.

Falguni, who was known as the caring *Pishima* to all the children, was the best friend to all the children at home and was the best storyteller for the children during night-time. As per the practice of a traditional Hindu widow, she always wore a white cloth and did not adorn ornaments. She was a friendly saint to all the children, as she was always ready to take care of them. Fakir was, however, a disciplined patriarch; speaking very minimally and a 'no-nonsense' type of personality. Despite having a huge property and being a good medical practitioner, he had a good rapport with all the communities in and around the village. However, his public life was highly compartmentalized from his private one. He adhered to traditional Hindu rituals, wearing a sacred thread on his body, wearing only *dhoti-kurta*, maintaining a Hindu calendar for various rituals and ceremonies, daily worshipping Hindu deities, including the worship of nature. Throughout the day, he remained busy with his patients, land tenants and his regular friends (mostly Muslim), and also had dedicated time with his family members.

Fakir was always well-dressed, starting from early morning as a part of his Hindu tradition of purity and cleanliness. After shaving and taking regular bath and performing his daily *puja*, he would wear a pair of spotless white *dhoti*, *kurta* and a pair of shoes. While going out of the house to attend medical call, he wore a doctor's hat, an overcoat and a red stethoscope hanging around his neck. He was fond of his old, but well-maintained bicycle that was gifted to him long ago by an admirer. He took an absolute care of it to give it a new and glossy look always. Before leaving home, he always cleaned the bicycle and checked the air-pressure of its tyres.

Apart from these, Fakir was fond of teaching English and mathematics to his children, and liked sharing news of his choice from various Bengali newspapers and inspired them with the stories of several freedom fighters. Under his tutelage, his children were not allowed to take food from the neighbour's house, nor were they allowed to play with children in the neighbourhood, except select native Muslim families. There was a *lathel* in their house, who always kept a watch on the children, once they went out of the house to play. The daily lives of the children were conditioned with several restrictions. For the children, however, it was an emotionally ensured close-knit family that was pleasantly and emotionally engaged with each other but with a conditioned lifestyle.

Within these boundary walls, a distinctive variety of daily routine, socialization, cultures, rituals, values, and worldviews were articulated and practiced. The children, overall, had seen from their early years that there were certain unforeseen fears and anxieties amongst the elderly members of the family. Many a times, these fears and anxieties were, knowingly or unknowingly, passed on to the growing toddlers and other children. Most importantly, more the communal tensions in the neighbourhood, greater the restrictions and the quantum of imposition of Hindu orthodoxy were on them. All these created a barrier with the outside world. However, despite the segregation tendencies and severity, there was also a deep tendency among the children to mix with the outside world.

The Conditioned Start of the Day: Imbibing Discipline and Social Codes

Within the disciplined and conditioned atmosphere at home, the children had a programmed lifestyle. The start of the day was very hectic and unpleasant for the children, as per the daily routine, they were to get up from bed before sunrise. The day started with the father rising from his bed at dawn, especially with a long and loud throat clearing sound and chanting popular hymns like '*hare krishna-hare krishna … jai-guru, jai-guru, jai durga, jai durga….*' Thereafter, Fakir would start walking in the courtyard of the house wearing a pair of wooden sandal (*kharam*). The combined sound of religious chanting and frequent sound of wooden sandals were like alarm bells for everybody in the house. Revati, thereafter, would gently wake up all the children. Falguni used to get up much earlier than anybody else, however very silently by ensuring that nobody was disturbed by her movements. The courtyard of the house was cleaned and mopped with water and cow dung before it dried up. The mopping of the house with cow dung was a part of the ritualistic practice pertaining to purity of home. These were done under the strict supervision of Falguni, who herself was a strict disciplinarian. When the courtyard became wet and slippery, Falguni took special care about the movements of children within the house.

As a part of their daily routine, children of the house visited the *koltala* (open bathing place surrounding the dug well), where their *pishima* (Falguni) waited with a bucket full of water to clean their face and teeth. At one side of this dug well was a brick-built open platform for bathing the boys and men. And on the other side was a small covered bathroom for women. There was a bamboo shaft fixed with a long rope and a bucket to fetch water from the well. For all the children, the shaft was a source of attraction. Invariably, all would try to fetch water from the well with the help of this bamboo shaft taking advantage of any oversight of the elders at home. Though, it was difficult for their *pishima* to control all the children, somehow, she reasoned with everybody by showing the threat of punishment. Laltu was always the first to fall in line as per the practice of discipline at home. All were to brush their teeth, wash mouth and face with water from the bucket in front of their *pishima* and were to be ready for the regular morning walk with their father.

Fakir was very passionate about seeing the sunrise early in the mornings. He had made it a point to see the sunrise everyday with his children and to have fresh air in the river bed of the mighty river the Ganga, that was located a little away from the railway tract. The sunrise could easily be seen by walking up to the railway track located at the northern side of house.

Getting the Feel of Nature and Motherland in Early Morning

Fakir marched towards the high-raised railway track running along the river Ganga in the faint light of the daybreak as a ritual to have a glimpse of the rising sun. He would be followed by all the children from the house. They regularly saw the rising of a big red sun on the eastern horizon of the village with a unique combination of glittering red and yellow colours gradually spreading all over the village, cutting the silence of all lashing green mysterious trees. As the sun started rising, thousands of birds would chirp and would fly all over the trees, riverbeds and the sky. As others silently observe the rising of the sun from the eastern horizon, Fakir would always engage himself in constructing a new meaning out of the play of the slow-moving red sun, white cloud, and the blue sky.

A tender ball of fire above the ground
Raises towards heaven without sound.
So gentle and majestic with colour of play
Red, yellow, pink and blue to paint the day.
The mountains of cloud touches its feet
The sun god smiles showing his glittering teeth
On the drop of dew on the grass
Sun-god comes with paint and brush

I always try to catch it in my hand
Jumping all around on the dew and sand!

These words were mysterious and pleasant even for the children. They got an intense sense of joy to see the colourful sunrays to be fragmented on the ground with the touch of the leaves and dews. For Laltu, it was as if the sunrays were trying to touch the earth while the green leaves and brown branches of the tree were trying to hold the yellow sun beams with their tender green long hands. The glittering of the dews, smaller waves of the river water, and the appearances of red, yellowish and white cloud on the sky made children restless. Laltu was not ready to close his eyes even for a second, and would become crazy and adamant often to climb down from the lap of Fakir with the intention to catch those glittering rays in his hands, but in vain. Fakir would also try repeatedly to persuade him to stop this madness and return home, but Laltu repeatedly tried this stunt along with other children. For them, these failed attempts were also success. When they failed in all attempts to catch the sun rays, they would go to catch the sun itself in the glittering dew spread all over the grass. After a while, when everybody was in hurry to return home, little Laltu and other children engaged themselves in catching the sunrays and sun itself within the fold of their small tender palms. However, they would ultimately be dragged by their elder siblings to return home. On several occasions, Fakir would come closer to these children and say very calmly, 'These are the natural gifts of mother earth. We are also part of this nature. Will not be able to catch it; be part of it.' Laltu repeated his innocence every day; and listened to the message of Fakir, but without knowing much of its meaning. In the undifferentiated world of his senses, he was only engaged with the play of nature as part of nature.

Life was, in fact, very easy and relaxing in the morning hours. After watching the sunrise and performing the *surya pranama* (traditional Hindu salutation to Sun God) Fakir would strictly instruct the children to go back home, and to get ready for study hours. Thereafter, Fakir himself would take a long walk along the bank of river Ganga leaving everybody behind him. While returning home, at times the children would go close to the river Ganga. They would always try to touch the waves and water of River Ganga. In those days, Ganga was full of water and there was regular traffic of commercial colourful boats on it, creating millions of glittering waves of water on the river. This was another early morning attraction for the children, especially for Laltu. Along with other children, he would raise his hand to allow the fresh wind from the river to blow all over his body, as if the mighty river with a unique fragrance was throwing all its attention towards them. However, the morning plays and pleasures were momentous yet short-lived, and were passing by so quickly for children like Laltu that the thirst for watching the early morning sun, river flowing and moving boats uninterrupted always remained unfulfilled. Laltu often remained emotionally charged and unsatisfied very often while returning home with other children. However, he would eventually wait for the next day. Fakir would always console Laltu to remain patient till the next morning.

Laltu's and Other Children's Confusion with Undefined Motherland

While returning home at time, Laltu had seen Fakir take elaborate dip in mighty flowing Ganga. It was a regular practice for Fakir to take bath in this river and to chant loudly some Sanskrit hymns. Laltu could neither recollect the full lines, nor the meaning of the same. However, he never failed to imitate Fakir, though incorrectly. Later, Laltu was corrected by Fakir by chanting *janani janmabhoomischa svargadapi gariyasi* (mother and motherland are more glorified than the heaven). He, however, wondered as to what is motherland? He kept on asking the elders about motherland. Mostly, they replied that it was the place where we were born. His next question was, 'please show me where was I born'? Some showed him the corner of the house. Some showed a secluded place adjacent to the house. He asked the following question, 'If I was born there, then why we go to the river and to other places to salute it as birth place'? 'Why are you telling natural surroundings to be our mother and what is the need of saluting another mother?' He was, however, told by elders like his *pishima* that he himself would know of its meaning, as he would grow up. He would simply murmur, 'When will I grow up?'

Practice of Purity and Pollution at Home

Though the early morning was full of fun, there were equally full restrictions too for the children. They were not supposed to enter any room of the house or to touch anything before changing the cloth and wearing fresh clothes. They were to wash themselves from feet to neck with water. Near the main entrance of the house there was a small changing room. The room was marked from others by a thick rope to hang *akacha* (unclean/impure) clothes there. The notion was that the clothes used for outside purpose became unclean and not to be taken inside the house without washing them. Following this principle, the uncleaned clothes were thrown on a tight hanging rope or in a big bamboo basket that was kept in one corner of this room. It was a usual practice at home that before going out of the house, all the members were supposed to wear a wet *gamcha* (thin cotton towel) and remove their *kacha* (clean clothes) in their respective rooms. The wet *gamcha* was ever pure and it was never soiled, if it was wet. After wearing their wet towels, they headed to the changing rooms. They were to take off the wet towel and wear another set of *akacha* (soiled clothes), while going out of the house. This was applied to all and was observed religiously while going to visit somebody's place, to play with others, to go to school and so on and so forth. The same process was followed while returning home in the reverse order. This discipline was strictly followed under the careful vigil of their *pishima*. No logical explanations, and no argumentative conversations were allowed on this practice. If someone violated this discipline, it was immediately reported to *pishima*. She would give not only a good bundle of advice, but also sprinkle Ganga water all over the house to purify the house again. Often, punishment was also given by her in the form of rebuking or mild ear and hand twisting of the children. Again, for *pishima* the intended or unintended act of looking at each other's body especially the private parts while changing clothes, was an immoral act and sinful in nature. The offenders were severely criticized and punished publically by severely pulling their ears. In fact, all the children would silently pretend not to have seen each other or anything. Irrespective of summer or winter, rain or spring, children were to be part of that practice. Thus, the tender lives of these small toddlers were conditioned with more than dos and don'ts.

After changing their clothes, the toddlers entered the main part of house with bare bodies wearing wet *gamchas* only. They invariably found their *pishima* to waiting for them in the *kaltala* with a bucket full of water. Under her strict supervision, they were to get their hand, face and feet washed with simple water and then to wear clean cloth. As per the disciplinary practice of the house, after wearing clean clothes they were to sit for study. Breakfast was served only after the early morning study guidance and disciplinary inspections under Fakir was over. Most children would saliently feel a sense of emotional torture and immense burden of disciplinary practices at home.

Daily Routine in the Life of the Children: Morning Study Hours

While the children went for a morning walk along with their father, their mother would remain busy in plucking flowers from the garden, sweeping the rooms, and getting the house mopped up with cow dung, and taking care of all other household chores. By the time the children returned home, their mother performed her *surya-namaskar* and offered water to the *tulsi* plant after taking her bath. After receiving the children, she prepared them for study.

They were made to sit for study in the veranda of their bedroom that was facing the kitchen, which was located on the other side of the house. They would sit in one row and start reading their lessons with loud voice. Revising lessons was their art of learning at that stage by rote, repeating the same lines until it was fully memorized. These were so repetitive that most of the regular passers-by and the domestic helps of the house knew most of the rhymes and lines memorized by these children.

Meanwhile, Fakir would also return home from his morning walk. After taking his regular bath, chanting the *gayatri mantra* several times and performing his *puja* with dedication, he would wear a spotless white *dhoti* and *kurta*. Thereafter, he would sit in a chair in front of the children to guide them in their studies. Fakir would ask each child about the subject they were reading, asking questions to answer, correcting their mistakes in his authoritative loud voice.

In case of good performance, he would be appreciative; and if any mistakes occurred or performance was poor, they were given time to improve till evening or another day, whichever was convenient. No excuse for lagging behind in studies were allowed. He checked regularly everybody's nails, teeth, and length of their hair. A traditional barber was employed to visit their house every week to cut their nails and every month to give them a haircut.

Children were more interested in looking at the kitchen than at their books. They would look at the gate of the kitchen with an angular eye hiding from each other. Similarly, Laltu's immediate elder brother, Sadhu was always fond of food. He would frequently expressing his eagerness for the same by complaining against other siblings just saying that: '*Ma*! see he is not reading and always looking at the kitchen'. At times, these uneasy complaints caused unnecessary fights among the young siblings during the study hours. However, the result was positive at times, since such complaints compelled their mother to keep the breakfast ready, despite several engagements. However, the breakfast was served only after the first round of the study was over. Once the breakfast was over, Fakir would head to his dispensary located adjacent to his house.

Children were to switch over from reading to writing activities, which were usually looked after by their mother. In those days, fountain or ball pens used to be luxury items for the children. Pens (*kalom*) were made out of a tender bamboo stick by sharpening one of its edges with a knife. Ink powder was made available to the children. It was mixed with warm water in small bottle. The intensive use of these pens repeatedly by soaking them in the bottled ink not only made the hand and lips dark blue, but also the papers and clothes very untidy. *Pishima* always made an effort to clean them while giving them baths. *Pishima* had a poetic satire for children: '*or hate kali, mukhe kali, ma bole toi pare eli*' (looking at the ink spots on the hand and mouth; mother becomes satisfied that that you have studied).

Children had little time to relax or play in the morning as study hour was over by around nine in the morning and it was marked by the passing of a passenger train through their village. However, if the train was delayed, the study-hours were prolonged. However, at times, their father became lenient. After he came back to his house from dispensary, he would instruct his children to get up from the study and to get ready for the school. Except for Laltu and his little brother, all children were given full bath and readied for their school.

All children were to go to school after having *seddhabhat* (boiled rice with boiled potatoes, seasonal vegetables, and ghee). The *seddhabhat* was cooked in an open hearth by their *pishima.* They would go to the school following the same process on a daily basis.

Laltu's World: Lonely Noon, the Surroundings and Imagining of the Desh (Own Country)—Fantasy and Reality

Once all his elder siblings left for the school, Laltu would find the house too big a place to roam around, with his toddler younger brother, but usually alone. If Kajal stayed back at home or had returned from the school early, he would get an opportunity to play with her. Otherwise, he would be left to play with his wooden or clay toys. As Laltu was not allowed to go outside the house alone, he found himself as a brave discoverer. He discovered small things of the house to his best of knowledge and excitement.

Laltu would invariably find his *pishima* in the early mornings in wet clothes and usually unkempt hair. At times, she would come from outside with a pot of water in the curve of her waist. He frequently asked her as to where was she coming from? Her ever-smiling reply was:

'To collect stories from a beautiful prince who lives in his beautiful *desh* filled with forest, river, birds, butterflies and greens, etc. The prince whispers many stories for you. The prince has gone back to deep forest in his *desh* and I am back'. He would put several questions to *Pishima* that

'What is a *desh*?'; 'How many Princes are there?'; 'And, tell me the stories, which were whispered to you by the prince'. But she remained firm and consistent on her utterance, 'No! Not now, but in the late evening only. If I tell you the story now, the prince will never come back to this *desh* to whisper any new story to me. Furthermore, the prince will curse you to get a blind, ugly and deaf wife, if you listen to the story in day time'. This little boy would become fearful of getting an ugly wife, as he contemplated a beautiful wife to be his playmate. Looking at his grim face, his *pishima* would say, 'I will request the prince to identify the most beautiful girl of our *desh* to be your wife'. The pleased and shy Laltu would ask again,

'What does he look like? When will he come back?' *Pishima* replied looking at the sky:

'He lives in the forest. He is as fast as wind, as bright as light, he is as fresh and beautiful as a lotus. He has gone too far and will be back tomorrow early morning....' Her replies were highly insufficient for this boy to be reasoned with. He kept on asking about Prince's look, height, colour, hair, ornaments, shoes, flying horse, wing and everything.

However, *pishima's* replies were quite authoritative, 'I will tell you everything in the late evening after the dinner is served. Now will you stop questioning me. Okay! Just listen to me like a *bholochely* (good boy)'. *Pishima* was usually busy with her household chores, cattle and with the children. Though this boy remained unsatisfied, his fear of not getting new stories and fear of getting a blind, deaf wife with the curse of the unseen prince often prevailed over his lust for new stories. Laltu, however, developed a deep fascination for the prince.

Ma, Pishima and the Noon: In Search of Prince and Fantasy

Laltu was dreaming, thinking, and aspiring to meet the prince. As per his daily routine, he always waited every noon to follow his *pishima* to reach out to the prince. In fact, his feeling for the unseen prince was very intense. He was at time dreaming of him:

As I was asleep with his sweet dream
I found the Prince to float in the cloud of steam
Flying high with a glittering white swan
Touching tender hand as raised by every one
With bright glow on his face
Moving gently from ground to space

Whistling slowly to make me his friend
I was waving my hand to pave the Prince's descend.
The Prince touched me with twinkle in his eye
Planted new stories on earth and say goodbye.
I lived in dream for day and night
To imitate Prince's glory, courage and might.

At the noon time of the day, little Laltu always found his mother taking her breakfast, relaxing a little bit sitting on the verandah of the bedroom preparing *paan* (traditional mouth freshener) with betel leaves, nuts and other condiments from a container and, thereafter, chewing it for few minutes silently. Simultaneously, he also saw his *pishima* sitting on the opposite side on the veranda of her room to eat her breakfast.

Generally, *pishima* never dared to share her breakfast, lunch or any food with anyone, including the children. But Laltu always tried to sneak into *pishima's* plate, while she was having her food. At such times she was very harsh towards Laltu. He would see *pishima* hide her face and food with one edge of her white sari. He had also seen teardrops falling to the ground from the eyes of his *pishima* while taking food. This increased his inquisitiveness about his *pishima* more and more. Despite several disappointments, Laltu had always tried to see the cooking, eating and household chores of his *pishima* hiding himself from the eyes of others. In case, he had an eye contact with his *pishima,* he pretended to show as if he had neither seen her nor was interested to go there either. His *pishima* had a similar reaction as that of Laltu. However, these pretentions were enough to express the sense of affection, care and anxiety for each others. He was always curious to know the reason of contrasting behaviours of his *pishima.* He was eager to see her always smiling, and to get back the same affection and behaviour from her as seen in her every early morning or late evening.

Laltu had seen his *pishima* to cut her hair by herself keeping a broken mirror in front of her. She wore only a white cloth, and wore no ornaments, and did not chew pan at all. She kept aloof from the guests, cooked and ate her dish alone in an earthen hearth located at one side of the courtyard, which was covered with old jute mats. She made special efforts to lit the fire on the hearth. She cooked her meal only once in a day and after completing it, she put water on that hearth to ensure that it remained beyond the reach of the children. The unhappy appearance of *pishima* always bothered this boy and provoked him to know more of his *pishima* by putting several questions to her, some of which were avoided and for some he was rebuked. His *pishima*, however, answered some of these innocent questions. His inquisitiveness and questioning continued, as his *pishima* was his best friend and she entertained his questions. He would only silently follow her with a mixed feeling.

Clarifying Sessions with Pishima and Baba

Laltu's *pishima* was all alone during the noon. After taking her bath and offering her *pranama* (salutations) to the Sun God, she uttered the hymn, *janani janmabhoomischa svargadapi gariyasi*. After taking her food, *pishima* would finally sit on an old mat on the floor of her veranda to relax. Laltu once gently came closer to her and asked her politely: '*Pishima*, Why do you put water to the trees after having bath?' She replied: 'Our parents, our grandparents, our great grandparents, and all the Gods and Goddesses regularly come over and sit on this tree to bless us'. He again asked: 'What is the meaning of the hymn that you recited after the bath?' She busted out with laughter after listening to his questions, and replied: '*janmabhoomi* means *desh* (country) where we are born'. This boy was quick to throw another question: '*Pishima,* how big is our *desh*?' *Pishima* was very clear in her imagination. She replied: 'It extends as far as your eye goes. It covers the river, land, air, forest and everything in it. It is your own'. The boy was confused, but was amazed to link himself with everything as far his eyes went. The boy went one step further in his question: 'Then the moon, the sun, the star also belong to me? I can see the train in the land, aeroplane in the sky, boat and steamer in the river. Do they belong to me and to my *desh? Pishima* corrected him: 'Not only you, but to all of us.' The boy quickly asked: 'Then, who are we?'. She replied: 'Everyone, who you could see here – our family, our neighbours, all people whom you could you see through your eyes around here'. The boy was further amazed with linking himself with the variety of people to be a part of the newly found 'we'. But again he got confused. He again asked: 'As everybody lives in one's own house and we don't play with everybody, how can we be part of them and they be us?' The enlightened *pishima* said: 'It is through sharing each other's *dukkha o bhalobasha* (pain and love). You need not go to everybody's house, every day. But you and everyone else are part of this *desh*.' The boy was amazed with such description of this *desh*. Laltu would keep on asking an array of questions on her imagination of a *desh*. However, his *pishima*, vexed by all such questions would call his mother to take this boy away so that she can relax for a while.

Once Fakir was back home, this boy would pretend to be disciplined. Fakir would ask this boy very laughingly whether his questioning rounds with his *pishima* were over or not. Many a times, the boy repeated many of his old questions to Fakir also, where the beginning and the end point revolved around *janmabhoomi* and the *desh*. Similarly, Laltu was equally amazed and confused in getting the utterances of his *pishima* in the reinforcing voice of Fakir. The latter asserted that, 'Whomsoever you could see here, belongs to this *desh*. You are equally part of this *desh*'. In fact, he was finding a conviction from Fakir that he was a part of a larger identity that was extended far beyond their family and was part of an integrated larger society.

The Afternoon

Despite having a busy time, Fakir had always nurtured some hobbies. Gardening, kite flying, basketmaking with bamboo sticks, and watching local games were his most favourite pasttimes. He himself did most of gardening along with the farm workers. He gathered most of the children of the house and neighbourhood for kite flying. He used to make big (at time 4′ × 6′ size) colourful kites, by using old clothes and strong bamboo sticks. On other days, he took his children to watch local football and volleyball matches, bullock cart racing, local boat racing, etc. He, however, allowed his children to play with selected neighborhood boys under his watchful supervision and strict conditions.

The Evening Study Hours

It was a very close-knit family in the evening where everybody was active. Despite having a family reunion, it was also a time for practicing strict discipline. After returning from home at sunset, they were to wash their legs up till the knee, and hands till elbow and whole face very neatly under the close supervision of their *pishima* and change their clothes. Revati sprinkled Ganga water all over the house, lit an oil lamp and placed it before the *tulsivedi*, blew conch shell thrice and recited the name of her favourite deities for several minutes. Fakir, by this time, would also return home after closing his dispensary. After freshening up, and having very light refreshments, and making the children drink their milk, he would make every child sit properly to start reading and to complete their study with all dedication and discipline.

In those days, kerosene lantern was the only available source of light to study at night. In the evenings, there would be pin-drop silence all around except the occasional sounds of birds and foxes and other small wild animals in the forest. *Pishima* would have a dim lamp in her part of the house. She remained engaged in knitting *kantha* (cotton blanket made out of old cotton clothes), or make fine rope out of jute, using a wooden cross. Revati would remain busy in the kitchen in cooking food for all. Fakir would sit on a mat with a bright lantern in front of him. He would also keep a torch light and read a Bengali newspaper in front of him. He would call all of them one-by-one to come in front of him and to get the homework, oral or written whichever, to be checked by him. The children would sit on another two mats with two separate lanterns.

The study began with a salutation to Goddess Saraswati and to their books, copies, pens and pencils. It was ensured that legs did not touch the study materials. If, by mistake, these items were touched by leg, they were to be saluted again for asking forgiveness. Children were to study loudly and clearly. But, as study progressed with time, many of the children would feel lethargic and hungry. Fakir would shout if anybody would feel sleepy. For him, distractions were not allowed. If sleepiness did not stop, he made his children get up and sprinkle water and apply oil on their face and shoulder, to ward of sleep. Even for going to toilet while studying, they were to take permission from Fakir. Once cooking of dinner was over, Revati would silently close the door of the kitchen and sit around the mat to help the children in completing their study. Though the spices from the food tempted children, there was no escape from the discipline. It was very frustrating for the children to see that their mother completed her cooking, but would not serve the food, until the train crossed the village. The study and practice of homework were continued for two to three hours in the evening. His *pishima* would also wait till their study was over and dinner was completed to tell them stories.

These impatient children would let out a sigh of relief, once the sound of the moving train approached their village. As the mighty train passed the village with a loud sound, they would look at each other's faces with a smile and joy and wait for the permission of their father to conclude their session. Before Fakir would say anything, Revati would sort out their books, slate and pencils, etc., indicating that now it was time for dinner.

Before the food was served, Fakir would highlight the mistakes made by any child during the day time. It was time for huge tension for the children. There would be absolute silence in the house. The children would look at each other. Fakir reprimanded them for their behavioural mistakes, if any, and cautioning them against committing any such mistake in future. The word 'sorry' was never used those days. In case of minor mistake, the children were made to sit and stand for five to ten times. In case of a major one, either kneel down or stand-up position, or sit down by lightly pulling their ear was a standard punishment. In case of any attempt for argument by the children, Fakir would simply shout them down.

After their dinner was over, all children would rush to their *pishima* to listen to her story, *pishima* would also wait for the children to narrate stories. They would sit on a mat making a half-circle around their *pishima* keeping a dim lantern at the centre. There would be pin drop silence all around, except for occasional sound of utensils from the kitchen as their mother was busy putting the kitchen in order. Crying of owls, howling of foxes and other small wild animals from distance added further suspense to *pishima's* story.

Pishima would start narrating the stories – one after another. The first one would be short and the second one would be very long. Her favourite stories would always start with her signature sentences. 'There was a prince in a deep forest. The prince, however, got lost in the forest. He underwent several hardships. He encountered several wild animals, forest dwellers, etc.' The end of a story was a romantic reunion of the prince with a fascinating and ever beautiful princess. In-between, there were several moral stories. The second long story was never completed, as most of them would fell asleep much before the end of this story. Laltu would also fall asleep on the mat spread in the verandah much before the story was completed. However, in the morning when he got up, he magically found himself and his other siblings in the bed of his mother. Though others said that he was brought to this side of the house while he was asleep, he was not convinced. He was repeatedly told by his *pishima* that the prince had come to meet him last night, but as he was asleep the prince had gone back and that he was shifted by the prince to this part of the house. It was magic feeling for him. He believed in that and his inquisitiveness about the prince increased day-by-day.

Control, Suspicion and Friendship of the Children with Neighbours

Though Fakir sent all his children to the local school to study at an appropriate age, he had not sent Laltu to the school until then because of his extrovert behaviour and asking too much questions. It was decided that up to pre-primary level, he would be studying at home under the supervision of the family members and his sister Kajal. He read from the old books of his elder siblings. Getting a new book was very special for him. Once he got new books, he became very excited. To *pishima*, 'the colour of the book was as bright and attractive as that of the prince, while the pages of the book were those of the wings of the horse of the prince, alphabets were like the eyes of the prince and princess and the fragrance of the lotus from the book was like the breaths of the prince'. He was becoming more enthusiastic to get engaged with the book. At the end of this book, there was a small poem. He was so happy that this was the same poem that was repeatedly recited by his siblings at home. In the afternoon, he rushed to show his playmates from his neighbourhood – Hamid, Salman and Amena, this newly acquired treasure, the new book. Fakir was always watchful of little Laltu because of his restlessness and his habit of breaking the disciplinary boundaries of home. But this enthusiasm for study made Fakir think about the schooling of this boy. Fakir consulted his friend Jamal, and he admitted Laltu in second class to a local school, where the other children were studying.

Laltu's playmates, Hamid, Salman and Amena were also studying in the same school. Their parents requested Revati to help these children in their study. Looking at the good manners of the children, and commonness in their study, Laltu's mother agreed and invited them to come to their house every evening to study along with her children in the house. New vistas of friendship and openness started for this little boy. He got pleasantly surprised with the changing attitude of his parents. A new phase of an organized life now started for him.

Looking at the excitement of Laltu, Fakir bought a new set of clothes, sandals, books, slate and pencils for him for school. Laltu started getting excited on receiving these items. He was getting a new feeling of engagement with himself. He was getting a sense of joy everywhere. He made his mother fix a cover for his book with old newspaper. To him the books, slate and pencil were sacred items and to be handled with all sanctity of his standard. He saluted them as these represented Goddess Sarasvati. His sandals also become a rare item for him. Hamid, Salman and Amena too were enthusiastic about Laltu attending the school. They thoroughly sneaked into his newly-acquired belongings and provided him with all 'serious' tips about the disciplinary procedures of the school. His siblings, especially his elder sister Kajal, were very cautious and careful about his attending school, since this hyperactive child was going to be inducted in a new culture and routine.

Fakir Sends Laltu's to School: Frustrating Sense of Communal Divide

Fakir sent Laltu to school along with his other siblings. In addition, Kajal was given special instruction to take care of him. The school was just one km away from their house across the railway line, near the riverbed. There was a narrow thin white mud road covered by green grass and bushes on both the sides to reach the railway track. Laltu found a new excitement, hope, legitimacy and an unknown pleasure and confidence in going to school. As he started moving towards the classroom, he found several young children, mostly of his age, active in the playground. He suddenly found himself in a big pool of children. Some were jumping on to the ground, holding each other's hand, others were reading books sitting on the ground, some were sitting in the classroom, while some were standing in queue. He started feeling a new emotional attachment with the surroundings of the school and the place around. He suddenly started discovering a bigger space of his association, which was much bigger than his small and conditioned family. Laltu, initially, had a conditioned state of mind about the wider world. He had grown up within familial protection. The fear that the threat of communalism was looming around the entire family in one way or the other had conditioned his mind. They were often isolated from the rest of the world. However, he was inquisitive to know his linkage with the wider world. That's why he developed a curiosity about the notion of the *desh* and his relationship to it.

As the first bell of the school rang with a repeated sound, marking the beginning of the school day, his sister took him to the school assembly to sing the Pakistani national anthem – *pak sarzamin shadbad.* Laltu knew some parts of this anthem, as he learnt it at home from his siblings. He always tried at home to get the meaning of this national anthem, but nobody at home, was able to explain its true meaning. His mother and *pishima* advised him to ask the school teacher about the meaning of this anthem. It was a new experience for him to stand in queue in front of the national flag along with all school teachers and students. After the national anthem was over, his sister took him to his class and before leaving him there, gave the little boy several advices to remain disciplined and contented in the school. He was determined that he would ask his class teacher the meaning of the national anthem in the opening class itself.

As he entered the classroom, Laltu was instantly surrounded by several of his known neighbourhood children and also some unknown faces. He was feeling himself happy at being introduced to a wide number of children and people. He remembered his *pishima,* who narrated that, 'we are in a *desh*, which is larger than family'. For him, it was just an experience of moving out from a well to an ocean. He entered the classroom with a desire to sit in the first row in class along with his playmates in the neighbourhood. As he was trying to occupy a seat, to his surprise and suddenly, he was pushed by a student who rudely instructed him to go to one corner of the classroom and to sit in that corner only. Incidentally, in the class-room most of the students were higher than his age, size and height. He accepted the rude instruction of that boy, occupied a corner seat, and sat there. Though he was shocked, surprised, and puzzled, he accepted it silently.

Laltu had joined the school in the middle of the academic year. There was only one teacher to take care of the whole class, which was also a new experience to him. However, all other students were known to each other and to the teacher. He could easily realize his unfamiliarity with other students and with the school culture. As the teacher came to the class with a duster, attendance register and a long bamboo stick, the noisy room became silent suddenly, and every student stood up and saluted him by saying *adab,* as a mark of respect to him. Laltu also did so as he was told at home for the same. He remained seated in one corner along with another unknown face. The teacher took his name at the end, while doing the roll call. The teacher was very grave and authoritative in appearance and expression. In his imaginary world, he was expecting special attention in the class from the teacher. However, no special attention was given to him. After introducing a new Bengali poem, the teacher asked all the students to recite a memorized paragraph of a poem as a part of the assignment. Laltu was told about this assignment by his playmates at home, who also happened to be students studying in the same class. All the students recited the poem one-by-one. But he was not asked to do so, even though he had memorized the whole poem – '*kumor parar gorur garhi, bojhai kora kolsi handi, hat boseche sukra bare, boxiganjey padda pare* (A bullock cart from a hamlet of potter with full of earthen pot on it is moving towards a weekly Friday market at Boxiganj located on the bank of the river Ganga)'. Though he wasn't nervous, as it would have been for any new student, he got a mixed feeling about not being asked to recite the poem. His innocent mind got a further inkling of a sense of avoidance by the teacher. Moreover, he was unsure, whether he was ignored by the teacher or was given a benefit of doubt for being a new student. He, however, felt that he should have been asked to recite the poem. He was interested to recite that poem in the class, as he knew the poem. He started looking around with despair and become very unhappy, as he didn't get a single chance to ask the teacher the meaning of the national anthem. As the teacher left the class, a fat boy, relatively senior to him by age and size whom he had seen earlier in his neighbourhood, came closer to him and made a very discriminatory remark: 'The Hindu boys are to sit on the corner of the class and they are not be taught by the teacher – you know it. The teachers are here not to teach you *kafir*!'. As soon as Hamid, Salman and Amena came closer to Laltu, that fat boy left the class room. Laltu got very confused, and was unable to know the meaning and intention of such talk.

However, his confusion got overshadowed for a while as he found that several boys and girls were peeping through the window of the classroom and looking at him and whispering. Within this whispering, a loud sentence was coming very clearly to him: 'Look, a small new Hindu boy has joined the school today'. He found that all children were looking at him with a high degree of curiosity. He became shy and curious. His elder sister (*didi*) also came with few of her friends. The other students developed a curiosity about him. They asked his name and touched his cheeks and head and went back. Among all these interactions, the sentence 'a small new Hindu boy' retained a place of prominence in his mind. The first period was followed by Mathematics and English periods by the same teacher. He remained seated in the same corner, learning a bit about the addition and deletion, English words and sentence formation. Again, Laltu was asked no question. On the first day, he watched the surroundings of the school more and learned very little. As he was looking outside from the window of his classroom, he was getting more excited to see how huge number of boys and girls had gathered at one go. The combined voices of the children were making new waves of life in him in every moment. He was trying to be attentive, but in vain.

Laltu's first day in the school was over after a final ringing of the school bell. The primary section of the school was closed by the noon. He returned home with his *didi* and other siblings. His, father, mother and *pishima* were anxiously waiting for him. The housemates appeared to be more curious about the newly school returned boy than the rest of the students in the school. As they started asking about his experience in the school, he simply replied: 'A small new Hindu boy'. Though everybody was laughing at his experience, he was trying to be articulate and making a sense of his uniqueness in the school. He asked himself a question as to why 'a "Hindu" is allowed to sit only in the corner seat of the class room' and why, 'teacher would not ask him to recite poetry', why he himself would lack the courage to ask question to the teacher. These were initially bothering him, though not preventing him from becoming excited about the experience of meeting several students in the school. He had got another important place, besides the family, to be associated with. However, the first day's incidence in the school made him ask more questions to get their answers from his mother and *pishima.* Fakir was satisfied that the first day of the school went off well. However, Fakir was unable to realise that some bothering questions related to communalism in the society had entered the mind of Laltu and other children at home.

Communal Divides, Local Culture and Growing up of a Hindu Boy in East Pakistan

In the afternoon, while his mother was alone, Laltu started asking his mother: '*Ma*, tell me who is a Hindu?' His mother was surprised to hear this question, but replied after taking several pauses. She said: 'Hindus are those who worship *bhagaban* (god) Krishna, Ram, Shiva, Durga, Kali, Lakshmi, Sarasvati.....' Before his mother finished her answers, *pishima* further added that, 'Hindus are the worshipers of sun, moon, stars, plants, rivers, wind, earth, and animals – like cow, and worship the incarnations of god like lion, fish, tortoise...'. This boy again asked another question: 'I don't do anything, then why I am a Hindu'? His mother replied: 'Because you are born in a Hindu family, you are to do all these as you grow-up.' Laltu questioned further: 'Then tell me whether my play mates – Hamid, Salman and Amena – are Hindu or not?' His *pishima* replied: 'No. They are *musalmaans.* They are different. They worship Allah, they do not worship our God. They do not perform *pujas*. They perform *namaz.* They wear a *lungi,* go to a mosque (*masjid*), wear caps and eat beef. We wear a *dhoti*, go to temple, do not wear cap and worship cows'. This boy asked his *pishima* again: 'But that day you told me that we are one. As far my eyes go, it is my *desh.* As we belong to this *desh* we are same.' *Pishima,* however, reiterated, 'No, they are *musalmaan.*'

Laltu though had heard terms like '*musalmaan*', '*namaz*', '*masjid*', and seen people wearing cap and a *lungi*, but he hadn't seen them as different from him and his family. Strict discipline and security had not only prevented him from mixing with other children of the neighbourhood but also knowing about their differences. For him, the Muslim children were different only as they lived in a different family and belonged to different parents. Sense of differences as shown to him in the school was devastating for him. In his own imagination of undifferentiated world, there was no place of difference in his *desh*, except for the fact that each one belonged to their respective family and parents. To him, Hamid, Salman, Amena were all same. At this point, he asked his mother another question and *pishima*: 'Then, tell me – which one is superior and better?' *Pishima* replied that, 'All of them are equal. No one is superior. We are born to different religion, that's why we are different.'

Laltu's mother Revati was very philosophical in her approach. She said: 'All of us are made from mud, and will turn into a mud in this earth on death. Within this mud, the same blood flows in everyone. If you get a cut in your hand, the blood will come. Colour of blood is red for everyone, even though we are different'. She made the thing clearer for him: 'We are like raw milk. Muslims make *shemai* during their festivals, and we use it to make *payesh* (sweet dish made of milk, rice and sugar) during our festivals. Overall, the content is the same only the difference is in the usage.'

Fakir was a salient observer of this discussion that was initiated by his little Laltu at home. He felt amazed, but concerned too. Though Laltu's questioning generated a concern in his parents and *pishima,* they ignored these things simply as a child's curiosity.

For a few days, Laltu's elder sister Kajal and brothers accompanied Laltu to their school. Thereafter, he started returning from the school either alone or with Hamid, Salman and Amena. Laltu gradually started learning the subjects like Bengali, Urdu, English, Mathematics as taught in the class. He also memorized the full national anthem of Pakistan—*pak sarzamin shadbad* … within a week, without knowing its actual meaning and getting the courage to know its meaning from the teacher. However, along the process he also started having regular encounter with a few class and schoolmates who were regularly addressing him as *malaun* and *kafir*, and made him sit only in the back row of the class. The corner of this class was meant for *malaun* and *kafir* students like him. Over and above, he was instructed by those boys not to complain to anybody about them. And in case, he ignored their instruction, he would be beaten with a stick. Laltu did not know the meaning of the terms. Even for a silly mistake in the class or in the playground, he was reprimanded as *malaun* and *kafir* by those boys, and others would laugh at him. Despite several comments – Hamid, Salman and Amena stood always with him. They advised him not to mix with them as these were the *dustu cheley* (rowdy boys) hailing from the refugee families. These boys also started threatening Hamid, Salman and Amena for mingling with Laltu. But Laltu was avoiding informing or complaining to anyone as he would then be meted out with unforeseen consequences.

Fakir observed that Laltu's initial enthusiasm about the school had dampened. During his study hours, Fakir noticed Laltu was giving only replies while checking his homework and asking about his day at school. Though he could sense that there was something wrong about him, he was unable to trace the reason. Fakir requested another of his friend, widely known as the *maulvi master*; who taught Urdu at the school and was a friendly figure among the children, to keep an eye on Laltu and his performance. Though Laltu's changing attitude bothered Fakir and other senior members of the house, they ignored it considering that it was momentary and it might be because of the study pressure on him.

Several months passed, and the aggression of those refugee boys became intense towards Laltu. He gradually started feeling lost, humiliated and lonely in the school. He, however, mustered no courage to inform to his siblings, who were already in that school. Though the *moulavi master* was very friendly towards him, he was unable to express his emotional plights to him either. Because of consistent nagging by those boys, he remained very aloof in the class. For this lonely isolated boy, though school gradually became a very non-attractive site for learning and playing, he had no option but to attend this school due to his parental pressures.

Childhood Friendship and Communal Naming

Away from the sight of Fakir, little Laltu was now growing mentally at a faster rate than his parents thought. He started thinking about the world differently, as he was looking for more and more space for liberation from the strict disciplinary boundary of his family, on the one hand and non-attractiveness of the school, on the other. Though he would go to the school along with his siblings, he would look for the opportunity to come back early with Hamid, Salman and Amena. He indulged in plucking green mangoes, lemons, cucumbers, guava fruits from each garden and trees on the way. Often, he jumped into the pond to pluck colourful lilies or at a fallen tree for fun. While Amena would be on the ground, they would be on the branches of the tree to pluck the fruits. They would run after butterflies, and try to catch baby birds from their nest. Sometimes, they were even caught by the neighbours for making such unexpected ventures and were cautioned afterwards. However, Laltu always used his liberty, while commuting from the school out of the sight of his parents.

Over the years, Fakir had emerged to be an authoritative patriarch. A sense of minority victimhood got rooted in him. Moreover, he was cautious about the security of his own children and their Hindu *bhadralok* (cultured mannerisms associated with the upper-caste Hindus) upbringing. No cuss words, slangs, or even loud noise were allowed any time including the playtime.

In the afternoon, Laltu and his siblings were allowed by Fakir to play with the neighbourhood boys under his own supervision. Despite the disciplinary control, children were taking liberty to make their own innovations. Both football and *gadan* (a non-instrumental game played in a cubically marked courtyard between two groups) were their favourite games. If there was no football, the children would make one with old clothes by giving them a round shape and tightening it with thin rope made of jute. Often, they would pluck a green pomelo or even a green coconut from garden and cover it with old soft clothes to use them as football. If somebody got injured, the parents were never informed in order to avoid being rebuked or being cancelled the game. For children like Laltu, the world itself was a socially different place, but a visible phenomenon of differences and a sense of exclusion and otherness started appearing for them. Their parental protectionism and the reality of communal threats had made Laltu and his siblings to visualise the world differently.

Laltu had seen several children wait outside the boundary of his house regularly, especially during their play time. They were from the other side of the village. He was foretold by Salman and Hamid that those were the refugee boys. They were never taken in to play by his elder siblings because of their rustic and unruly behaviour, which they did not like. Laltu had seen that some of those boys were his senior schoolmates, who were regularly misbehaving with him and demonizing him calling *kafir* and *malaun*. Sometimes without informing Fakir, Laltu had invited those boys to join the game mainly as patching up effort or generosity. However, once they entered the field, these senior boys would deliberately keep on breaking the rules of the game and start cheating and fighting. Again, he would be addressed by those boys as *kafir* and *malaun* for mistakes made in the game. Once Fakir observed the incidences of mixing up with these outside boys in the game, he instructed the children to stop the game and go inside the house. Though the children had realized that they had broken the disciplinary instructions of their father, they seldom realised the reasons for such instruction.

Significantly, even by that time Laltu did not know the actual meaning of such terms like *kafir* and *malaun*. Once he used these terms to address one of his immediate elder siblings at home, undeterred about its meaning and implication. The result was that of an unexpected magnitude. He was subjected to kneel down as a form of the punishment, even for a reason not known to him. After much scolding, he was strictly forbidden from interacting with those children at the neighbourhood. He could get to know the meaning of these terms, especially for the Hindus there, after several weeks from his elder brother.

Fakir's Increasing Intensity of Social Control, and Realization about Children's Propensity to Break those Control

Fakir did not allow the children to go outside the house alone, and even if permitted, it was under strict supervision. The little Laltu would often peep out of the window to get an opportunity to mix-up with the neighbourhood children as freely as possible. Restrictions, however, were creating their own condition for freedom of these children. As Fakir went away for hours to attend patients, (or neighbouring villages to settle dispute and to local markets for shopping or going to the town for whole day) Laltu and his siblings jumped out of the house to taste of freedom for themselves. Repeatedly, the boundary of his freedom crossed the defined 'boundary of interaction' with outsiders as instructed by his parents and often met with unexpected consequences. As per the household rules, children were neither permitted to eat in anybody's house nor allowed to buy any food items from anywhere. In fact, they were neither allowed to go for any shopping or to marketplace alone, nor were they allowed to use money for any purpose of transaction. Laltu, in fact, had neither used any money so far to purchase anything nor did he know the monetary transactions very clearly.

However, one day while he was playing outside their boundary, he saw a few children purchasing local bread, known as *paon roti* from a local bread seller by paying some coins. This sweet and sour smell of this bread hugely attracted his sense of appetite. Though he was offered a bite by his playmate, he instantly rejected it for the fear of getting punished if someone reported his eating of *paon roti* to his family members. Once he returned home, he expressed his desire to eat *paon roti* to his mother. However, his desire was vehemently opposed by his mother and *pishima*, since these breads were prepared by Muslim workers who applied their dirty legs (*paon*) in making and baking it, and the *bhadralok* (gentlemen) families did not eat such outside stuff. They even cautioned him that eating of *paon roti* would make him sick. However, none of the reprimands worked for him immediately. All these restrictions, however, made his desire for *paon roti* only uncontrollable. He decided to get one somehow and eat it up alone to his total satisfaction. After a few days, he picked up a coin from the table of Fakir silently when nobody was around at home. Next day, he carried that coin with him and sneaked into the other side of the fence secretly and joined the game with other children. While playing, he saw the bread seller. He gave that coin to the bread seller, and the seller, in turn, gave him four pieces of bread instead of one. Laltu kept one piece for himself and distributed the remaining among other playmates.

As he started eating the bread, he found Fakir from the other side of the fence staring at him with a grave face. Fakir called him to come back home. Laltu was in a state of shock as Fakir had caught him committing several mistakes, most importantly, stealing coins and eating of forbidden bread. He, however, followed Fakir silently holding his bread in one hand and holding his slipping pants from his waist by the other, and started weeping out of fear. It appeared to be a long walk for him. As he entered the boundary of their house, Fakir told him to walk faster. After entering the house, Fakir started shouting at him and instructed him to remain seated in the veranda of the house, until he was back. For Laltu, the sky had fallen down on him. His two other elder brothers were already waiting for him inside the house. Weeping was his only language of confession. He changed his *akacha* cloth in the changing room and waited for the punishment to be awarded. There was pin drop silence in the atmosphere and all children started shivering out of fear. Before anyone said anything, *pishima* broke the silence and came to his rescue. She said: 'Our boy has done no mistake. He was lured by bad boys of the neighbourhood. These small boys have no religion till they get the *upanayan sanskar* (sacred thread ceremony) at home'. His mother was silent, but nodded her head in support of her boy. Laltu, however, was getting a guilt feeling that he had taken a coin from the table without informing Fakir. He started weeping profusely and kept on waiting for Fakir's arrival.

Fakir finally returned home from his dispensary quite early that day with a grave face. Generally, there was a presumption that it would be a total silence once he entered home. But on that day the volume of silence was much denser than any other days. Laltu simply started weeping breathlessly and looking at the movement of Fakir, his tears were falling out of his eyes to cheeks, chin, chest, and dripping over his feet. He was clueless as to what would be the possible punishment for him whether heavy slaps, whipping at the back or kneeling down. These were conventional methods of punishment for mistakes committed by his other elder siblings. To his surprise, Fakir sat beside him and gravely asked him to count the mistakes he had committed. Before he started counting, his mother come forward sweepingly and encircled Laltu to her chest and said 'such things would happen, if we remain expounded in this country as a *pardeshi* (foreigner)'. Laltu did not know why his *pishima* and mother started weeping after that. Fakir simply got up and instructed the boy affectionately not to repeat such mistakes again. However, this incident changed the boy and his relationship with his father a lot.

Amazingly, when Fakir went to the town after this incidence, he brought a big piece of *paon roti* wrapped in a glossy paper for the whole family. But his *pishima* never took any outside food. Laltu asked whether these were prepared by the Muslims and legs were used to shape them. Fakir had a very good answer: 'These are machine made breads'. It was a joyous moment for the family and a lesson for the boy. He never tried to purchase bread from outside as long as he was there. Fakir also made it a point to bring bread from the district town as often times as he was visited there.

Interactions through Muslim and Hindu Festivals

Despite having strict social restrictions about social interaction, Fakir allowed his family members to freely interact with the neighbours during the festivals of both the communities. Fakir's wife paid a visit to Jamal's house during the *Eid-ul-Fitr, Milad-un-Nabi* or any other Islamic festivals. On the day of *Muharram*, there was invariably a big festival in front of Fakir's house. The neighbours gathered to see the martial art performances by various local Muslims. Fakir prepared refreshments and gave prize money for the performers. These were the days of enjoyment for the children. However, all children were taken care of by their *pishima* and the *lathel* to ensure that the disciplinary measures were not transgressed.

Hindu festivals were always celebrated in Fakir's house with elaborate rituals. The special *pujas* conducted were *Saraswati*, *Lakshmi*, *Kali*, and *Durga Puja*. Also, the *Pushna* festival was celebrated during the winter months. On all these festive occasions, the whole house was cleaned and moped with thin layer of mud and cow dung. The floor and walls of the house were decorated with *alpana*, which was made with a liquid paste made with white rice powder. Red vermillion was smeared with *alpana* to invite the deities at home on auspicious days. The entire house was purified with sacred Ganga water, oil lamp was lit and placed at the centre of the house, incense smoke was spread all over the house, conch shell was blown repeatedly to invoke various Gods and Goddesses. The *Kali Puja* was a special festival at home that was marked by decorating the house with *diyas* (mud oil lamps). Fakir made a tall bamboo structure with several slabs attached to it and oil lit lamps were put in each of these slabs in vertical and horizontal lines. These lights could be seen from afar. Native Muslim neighbours came in huge numbers to see these lights. It continued till late at night. In all these celebrations, Revati would remain busy in preparing varieties of *laddus* made from coconut, wheat flour, jaggery, and puffed rice, etc. Invariably, a large number of people from their neighbourhood would visit their house during these festivals. The family members of Jamal were the special guests. In fact, doors were kept open for everybody and no invitation was either needed or sent, as formality was rare in those days. If someone could not visit their house during festivals, he was affectionately called by Revati to get his share the next or on subsequent days. Laltu's father was very liberal in those days and allowed the neighbourhood children to stay in his house for longer hours. Little Laltu and his siblings always longed for these days, as they found a longer space for their liberation, interaction and a sense of belonging with their neighbourhood. This festival always gave a sense of closeness and a reassurance of living together with the village community. Laltu had special fun with Hamid, Salman and Amena in those days. However, he had observed that a section of the village boys and their family members, especially from refugee group, didn't come to their house during the festive seasons even, nor were there any concerns about their absence.

Life Cycle Religious Rituals and Knowing the Unknown

Laltu developed an intense friendly relations with Hamid, Salman and Amena in school. The more Laltu got oppressed in the school by these refugee children, the more he became friendly with these three children. Hamid's father was a railway employee, who regularly brought newspaper for Fakir from the town. Hamid always wore white pants and shirts. It was believed that Hamid's clothes were usually made with surplus white railway uniform. Hamid was possessive and proud of the texture and cleanliness of his clothes. Salman's father was a petty businessman and he mostly wore a *lungi*. Amena's father was an agricultural labour. She was mostly wearing loose frock and a *salwar*. Amena was very good at studies, she was very quick in solving mathematical questions and remembered poetry with ease. Her intelligence overshadowed her dress and attire. Laltu wore an oversized loose half pants and shirts. Some of these were discarded by his elder brothers. He had no complaint about his clothes. However, he had the complaint that he was to change his clothes very frequently while going out and coming back to the house. This was not practiced by his other playmates in their respective houses. Notwithstanding the religious, occupational and other social differences, these children became very close friends. Afternoons were the most wonderful moments for them as it was play time. Fakir allowed these children to play in front of his dispensary.

On one afternoon, Hamid and Salman were absent from the game. Amena and Laltu went to Hamid's house to look for them. They peeped through the gate of Hamid's house as they did regularly. They found that many visitors had gathered in Hamid's house and most of them were wearing skull cap and were getting ready to perform *namaz.* Such caps was used by Hamid's brother and father during their prayer time. Amena and Laltu were hesitant to enter the house and they almost took a turn around. However, Hamid's brother came out from house and asked them to come inside. He informed them that there would be a *sunnat* (circumcision) ceremony for Hamid and Salman. These children had no sense and did not know the meaning of this custom. They went inside the house to see that both Hamid and Salman were seated on a decorated bed in a verandah wearing a skull cap, new *lungi* and a new colourful shirt. They were receiving several gifts and were getting good amount of attention from everybody. People were placing their hands on these boy's heads, and both of them were enjoying like a celebrity with lots of gifts like shirts, towels, *lungis*, drinking glasses, plates, etc. (in those days and especially, in this area gift items were not packed and were handed over to the host).

Soon after, Hamid's mother came and told Laltu and Amena, that Hamid and Salman would be taken inside the room, and no other children would be allowed. She also told them that as their entry was barred they should go back home for the day. While they were returning half-heartedly, they could hear something like screaming of Hamid and Salman. But they ignored it and returned home. While returning from Hamid's home, Laltu and Amena discussed that they too should receive gifts, get special treatment. They further asserted that they too should get *sunnat* (circumcision) for themselves and for that, they would talk to their respective parents. They also discussed that though they had not been invited or informed by Salman's and Hamid's parents about their *sunnat* ceremony, they would not repeat the same behaviour. After much discussion, both of them returned to their respective homes.

At home, Laltu expressed his desire in front of his *pishima* for getting a *sunnat* ceremony for him. *Pishima* started laughing at him, but the boy became very baffled. His mother got very annoyed and said in a sarcastic tone that 'this ceremony will be performed for him, if he remains here for some more time. This is the only ceremony that is left out for my children in Pakistan'. The boy got amused by his mother's reactions. . . . He questioned: 'Why not!' *Pishima* told him that, 'Hindus have a different ceremony named *upanayan* and that would be performed for him, when he becomes twelve or above age'. He became frustrated to know why different people have different ceremonies and for that he would have to wait for several years to get such a celebrity status and to get those gifts. His enthusiasm also got a little curtailed as other siblings strongly advised him not to talk about the *sunnat* ceremony any more as his mother was getting upset over such discussions. But his inquisitiveness about Hamid and Salman and their gifts increased.

Amena did not return to play games with him the next day. Salman and Hamid were also not seen around. Laltu was feeling lonely in their absence. None of them was seen in the school either. He peeped into the house of Hamid after either two or three days. He was not interested in games, but to see the gifts received by them. Hamid's mother invited him to come inside the home this time again. He saw Hamid and Salman were lying in a bed and were trying to memorize something uttering them repeatedly '*la ilaha illallah muhammad ur rasool ullah* …'. He went closer to them very silently and inquisitively and asked about their gifts and new dresses. However, they whispered something different to the ear of the boy stating that they had got a ceremonial cut of their foreskins. Laltu was surprised as he never heard of it. Both Hamid and Salman were wearing small *lungis* and were unable to walk properly. There were blood stains on their *lungis* also. However, both of them were very happy. In between their conversations, those boys again engaged in memorizing the same religious verse. They also told him that the *maulavi* (religious cleric) had taught them *namaz* everyday. He became very curious and tried to perform *namaz* with Hamid and Salman. Though Hamid and Salman were unable to move out of the house for a couple of weeks, he kept on coming to their house every day after the school hours. He started playing inside their house and Laltu learnt the Islamic credo *la ilaha illallah muhammad ur rasool ullah* from them very clearly with respect.

Dreaming of *Swadesh* (Own Country) and Mounting Communal Tension

Laltu started feeling a sense of engagement with the neighbourhood with these limited number of friends. At the same time, he felt a contradictory situation in his school. He constantly became the target of communal expression and threat. As he was growing, he became more and more sensitive about the conditions there. His optimistic feeling was getting overshadowed by the treatment he received in the school and in the neighbourhood. Likewise, his family was also becoming a target of such negative communal expressions and threats.

Though his interaction with other students in the school increased, these slurs – *malaun* and *kafir*, remained attached to him. As more boys using these pejorative terms for him increasingly, he started feeling more humiliated, but without getting any sort of a solution. Laltu shared his ordeal with his elder brothers, who were also experiencing similar taunts and humiliations as faced by him. Gradually, these siblings narrated these bad incidences not only among themselves, but also to their parents. Their mother was deeply disturbed by listening to all these humiliations of the young children, that too publicly. She was more perturbed by the fact that such emotional tortures had reached such a certain level. Laltu, however, noticed that his mother listened to their narratives very carefully, and tried to conceal her tears with one edge of her *sari*. She repeatedly, but, firmly pronounced that 'Everything will be alright, when we go to our *nijerdesh* (own country) that is India'. The boy was not familiar with the word *nijerdesh*.

Till date, Laltu had heard of only the term *desh*. He asked his mother, 'what is this *nijerdesh?*' His mother eloquently replied that, 'now we are living in Pakistan. Pakistan is only for the Muslims, but not for Hindus. Pakistan is a *pardesh* (a foreign country) for Hindus. India is our *nijerdesh*, and our *swadesh*.' Being unaware of the differences between the Hindus and the Muslims and the political background of the Partition, Laltu got very confused with the terms: *pardesh* and *swadesh*. He was also not aware of the religious differences between Pakistan and India. His *pishima*, however, objected to the narratives of his mother and said in an emotional tone that, 'these differences will not be there for longer duration and these are going to die soon. This is our *desh*. We are born here and we will die here'. *Pishima* hugged him and started sobbing, her blank eyes looking at the sky. Perhaps, she was remembering her father and her ancestors who had lived in this house.

As the months passed, Laltu kept on asking several questions to his mother and *pishima*. He asked both his mother and *pishima*, 'What is a *pardesh*?' His mother replied that, '*pardesh* is a country where you are surrounded by enemies and live very temporarily'. She considered India as the *swadesh*. However, his *pishima* answered, 'there is no such thing called *pardesh* or *swadesh*. These are unnecessary and artificial creations. There is only one *desh*. The prince would come and unite everybody.' *Pishima* took all the children for a bath at the River Ganga. She said that, 'Look!, this is my *desh*, it is beyond our sight. This is sky, this is the Ganga river, there is gentle breeze, and these are moon, stars, and sun. I was born here. My parents and the prince and princess are born and brought up here. Now, people say that the other side of the river is India, and our side is Pakistan. Can you divide the waters of Ganga, or divide the sun, moon, stars, wind, etc.? If you can divide these, then it is *pardesh* and *swadesh*. Otherwise, we are one.' She continued further. In fact, she became very emotional on the question of division between the *swadesh* and *pardesh* and on the idea of going to India and leaving Pakistan.

Though Laltu got confused, he started bringing in several new elements to his undifferentiated level of understanding of the world. All of a sudden, he started thinking about a wide world with numerous possibilities. On various occasions, when there were discussions at home about their *mamerbari* (maternal uncle's home) in India and had some planning about the visit to India, he never paid much attention to it. During the increasing intensity in the discussion at home about *swadesh* and *pardesh,* he started paying more attention to it. Gradually, the discussions concerning India started getting increased at home. Humiliated and confused Laltu started getting a new ray of hope in his everyday existence. He started talking about India to his siblings. He found they were also enthusiastic about India and a possibility of migration. He started constructing an image of India. His mother called India a *Ramarajya* – a country without hatred, poverty, conflicts and above all, where everyone was happy and treated equally, and nobody interfered with other's religious affairs. He gradually started identifying himself more to be an Indian than to be a Pakistani, or a *malaun* or *kafir* there. This enabled him to construct an illusionary image of an Indian with his own understanding.

He, therefore, started constructing a different meaning about India, and a distinctive identity as an Indian! He started imagining India as his dream land even though he had never visited India. A sweet mystical feeling was attracting him and chripped from within:

Oh My Country

Oh, my Country, oh my land
Oh, blue sky and silver sand
Oh, the rising Sun and glittering floods,
The golden moon and flying birds
Your gentle breeze and majestic green
Dancing flowers of all the season
Now, I dream it all day and night
You are there in my breath and sight!
I am to breath in a fresh air
For all for solace and human care,
I am burdened with all my pain
I look for thy touch again and again.
Would you be as soft as of feather?
Would you be as caring as my mother?
I smell thy odour all through the street
I stand here to touch your feet.
Can now I float on a heavenly stream?
Oh, my country, oh my dream.

Laltu became very enthusiastic about discovering India. But, often his slip of tongue about his newly discovered identity of an Indian invited more hostility from his few playmates in the village and his class mates. The more he became ostracized from the neighbourhood and school playmates, the more he came closer to his 'mother' projecting an ideal and moral image of India.

Internalizing Alienness of the Family

As Laltu was growing up, his thinking and learning horizon were opening up to learn from the live experiences of his surroundings. Earlier, the elders avoided sharing their experiences about incidences of attack and violence on the family with the young children. Laltu, who had only learnt fairy tales from *pishima*, gradually started learning about the horrific incidents of communal attack and violence on their family. He had neither seen nor experienced turmoil faced by his family during the Partition. Now, he started experiencing the fears, anxieties, humiliation and physical threats that a person from religious minority community experiences in a majoritarian theocratic state at that early stage of life. He became a part of this struggle in their everyday experiences of frequent stoning, forceful plucking of fruits from their gardens, illegal grazing of cattle in their courtyards, taunting Hindu women, and verbal threats by some of his Muslim neighbours. These abusers made Laltu's family (including him) feel as if they were in an alien country which were forcing him to leave the country. A psychological wall was, in fact, created between several Muslim neighbours and their family. Laltu frequently asked his mother and *pishima* that 'Why don't we go to our *nijerdesh*?'

Increasing Uncertainties and Shifting of Siblings to India

Various rumours and newspaper reports on communal riots in India, and parts of East Pakistan always created several communal tensions in the neighbourhood, as these were good opportunities for fundamentalists to play their vicious games. Both Fakir and Jamal retained their routine of meeting each other every day. Jamal, not only provided the required security as a part of his commitment to his friend, but also gave advice for higher education of the children. In the village, there was neither a senior secondary school, nor one in the immediate neighbourhood. Jamal had sent his son to England to stay with his younger brother for further studies. On Jamal's advice, Fakir too sent his second eldest son to India to stay with his maternal uncle and to complete his secondary schooling there. Fakir had also shifted his eldest son to a high school, which was located about seven kilometres away from his village to complete the matriculation level. Due to an increase in communal tensions and growing sense of insecurities, Fakir now decided to shift his unmarried teenaged daughter to India to stay with their maternal uncle and complete her further studies.

As Laltu came to know about it, he felt very disturbed. In his imagination, his eldest sister was the most beautiful girl, and she was the princess of *pishima's* story. Her curly long hair, fair complexion, sharp eyes and nose resembled with that of the princess, as described by *pishima.* However, the siblings' separation was unstoppable with the increasing events of communal tension in the neighbourhood. One morning, as he got up from his bed, he noticed a silence in the house and no one was in a hurry to prepare for the sunrise. His *pishima* informed him that by an early morning train his sister, mother, and his youngest brother had gone to their maternal uncle's house in India, to leave his sister there and they would come back very soon. He started weeping profusely and remained uncontrollable for a few days. However, several questions cropped in his mind. 'Why did she have to stay there with a relative, which neither he nor his sibling ever knew?' 'Has she gone because of the similar humiliation that she was facing in school every day for being a Hindu?' He developed mixed feeling about it.

Fakir could easily realise the agony and pain of the boy and became extra careful. In some corner of his heart, Laltu had an expectation that his *didi* would return soon. He kept on waiting for the sound of the train daily, and the passing of the train through the heart of the village and anticipating everyday for a surprising knock in the gate. However, his *didi* never returned to East Pakistan. Revati and Laltu's younger brother returned within a fortnight. Though the return of his family from India was a moment of celebration for him, the departure of his sister made him painful inside. After a spell of emotional turmoil and consolations, Laltu became accustomed to the situation.

Indo-China War and the Hindu Minority Family in East Pakistan

As the days passed, the disciplinary control of Laltu's parents on the children became stricter than ever. It was in the year 1962, when the Indo-China War broke out and became a matter of discussion on the radio, in the newspapers and in public places. A section of Muslim people of the neighbourhood became very jubilant. Many patients of Fakir's dispensary were speaking to him about the outcome of the Indo-China War rather than their ailments. Fakir's friends also started visiting their house regularly to give him all moral support and a feeling of security. Fakir became very alert and started putting several restrictions on the outside movements of the children, especially in outdoor activities.

After sending his eldest son to a far-off village and his second son and daughter to India for further studies, Fakir and his wife started feeling emotionally low. Furthermore, the breaking of Indo-China War added more fuel to the ongoing tension. News of Chinese aggression on India was a matter of celebration of Muslim fundamentalists in the neighbourhood in the day. Anti-Indian slogans were also raised besides humiliating the family. This Hindu family was always an easy target for the attackers, as they were presumed to be the 'supporters of India'. Fakir had strictly instructed the children not to play outside the courtyard of the house, not to talk with the strangers, and to come back from the playground before sunset, and to keep the main gate of the house tightly closed every time and so on and so forth. There was always a sense of tension and threats in their house as some of his neighbours started threatening them regularly in abusive language. Someone would also hide behind the tree or the bushes in the night and shout, 'Quickly go to India, or else you will be butchered here soon. You are *kafirs*, *malauns*, you have no business here, leave Pakistan soon…!' Since the locality was a silent place, such noises were heard inside the house very clearly. The children would rush to their mother and *pishima* for shelter. The *lathel* would try to chase them but in vain. Fakir himself became very annoyed and disgusted and tried to chase and catch them. However, Revati always prevented Fakir from going out of the house, or to chase the miscreants. She instructed everyone neither to retaliate nor to go out of the house. Some miscreants also tried to create a sense of fear with uncertainties and panic in the absence of Fakir from home. Some hooligans were seen breaking the boundaries of their house forcefully, and trying to pluck fruits and vegetable from their garden, and even release cattle inside their boundary to create a quarrel with them. Surprisingly, these anti-social elements tried to question even the citizenship rights of Fakir as a Hindu in an Islamic nation. However, these trespassers tended to disappear, once Fakir appeared on the scene. Often, Jamal complained to the local police about incidents of ambush by goons, but all efforts in vain.

During the night, these tensions rose to such an extent, that even a sound arising out of wind, or movement of wild animals and birds would make children frightened and they would rush to either their mother or *pishima* for refuge. In case, any patients came to Fakir's dispensary in the late evenings or in the midnight, everyone would wake up and sit around a lantern and wait for safe return of Fakir. Some Hindu families in far-off villages had also come in Fakir's house to express their plights. But in these situations, there were least possibilities of extending any help, except from their neighbours and the family friends.

Father's Commitment and Mother's Worry

Though Fakir was internally disturbed, he always projected himself as bold and confident. The sources of his credence were his childhood friends, reliable neighbours and uncountable admirers, whom he extended medical and social help. He was always firm and undeterred about any tension in public life. He would also always console the family members, saying that, 'These problems are nothing. My friends and our good neighbours are there with us to help. Nothing will happen, they are only a limited number, and they speak only out of their own frustrations. Moreover, our *lathels* are also there'. Fakir would also frequently utter, 'I had committed to my father that, I will protect my widowed sister throughout my life. My sister is correct. Why should she leave the *janmabhumi* – where was she born and got married? She desires to take her last breath here. Therefore, I must fulfil it. I have committed to my friend Jamal, and also my patients. How can I forget my promise to all? We will not leave this country'.Fakir, like his sister, was convinced that 'this artificial division of the country would not be a long lasting affair. Netaji Subhas Chandra Bose will come back soon and unite the entire India again'. On the discussion about migration to India, Fakir's sister too had a similar position as that of Fakir. However, Revati had a different view. She was convinced that the whole family would have to be migrated to India if their lives were to be saved; and children were to be educated and lead a dignified life. She frequently repeated the line that, 'Neither am I able to listen to the verbal abuses of miscreants, nor can I see the grim faces of my children anymore'.

Fakir replied, 'I don't want to fight with the people who bark in night.... Let us face them in daylight. These people are cowards, frustrated beings.... They are a few bunches of extremists'. However, Revati was never convinced with Fakir's answer. For her, 'if there are only a few communalists, how and why is the country divided?' Fakir would then counter that, 'Why should we surrender to these fringe elements and forget our commitment to our ancestors, and our neighbours?'

Revati would start weeping frequently remembering the derisive comments and disparaging remarks used by the stone pelters during the night and listening to the tales of everyday humiliation from her little children at school. She would also get into an intense argument with Fakir and Falguni, who, according to her, were unable to realize the everyday threat to life, humiliations and insecurities faced by them. She now stated her desire to go to her brother's place in the northern part of West Bengal in India, where two of her children were already sent for studies on her insistence, and to settle there permanently. Though Fakir never agreed to it, he agreed to her visiting her brother's place in order to meet the children more frequently than before. Gradually, the frequency of Revati's visits to India increased manifold post the end of Indo-China border conflict in 1962.

In the later part of 1964, Fakir again prepared passports and obtained visa for his wife and youngest son for travelling to India. Laltu was informed that it would be a long journey and several enemies would be around on the road. He was always left behind in the custody of his *pishima* to be taken care of in the absence of his mother. This time, however, he was more grown up, had developed discernments about the surroundings. Moreover he had already developed a strong feeling of love for India by considering it as his *swadesh*. In his earlier days, 'India' was a word or a place, now it had a special meaning for him. However, his mother prevailed over him with the promise that she would select a good school for his study and bring a bright red shirt and black pants for him from India. The boy had no option, but to accept the imposition with tearful eyes. His mother again left for India leaving him behind in the custody of his *pishima*.

Mother's Letter, New Confidence, and the Aftermath

Differences and humiliation that Laltu was experiencing in the school were also getting reinforced in him with intense and emotional uncertainites at home. His isolation and humiliation in the school continued as usual. In the absence of his mother, Laltu started finding himself in a lonely environment. As Amena had already got married to an elderly man in another village, he had only Hamid and Salman to play with.

Laltu, in the absence of his mother, had now developed a new understanding of the world around. He was now a grown-up child with his own understanding. He got promoted to third standard in the school. He found, besides Fakir, *pishima* to be more caring, and his ever-quarrelling elder brothers became more affectionate, considerate, and less quarrelsome. Meanwhile, he developed a tacit knowledge and a sense of apathy towards some classmates in the school, because of increasing aggression of pushing him in the class room, isolating him from game and calling him a *kafir* and so forth. In the absence of his mother, he felt that as if he had no escape point from his plights experienced at school.

Meanwhile, Fakir received a letter from his wife stating that, Laltu would be taken back to India next time for an admission in a good school there, and that she would be back soon with the promised gifts of black pants and a red shirt for him. His mother's letter gave a new boost to his personality. His mother's assurance of getting him admission in a school in India gave him further hope for his ambition. He saw in this hope an end to his plight in the school and a new enthusiasm in his life. Next day, he went to the school with a newly acquired confidence and declared in the class that he would be leaving for his 'own country India', soon. He strongly resisted the terms *malaun* and *kafir*. This led to a scuffle in the class with these boys, and, as a result, he received a massive punch on his face and a big cut on his eyebrows. He collapsed on the ground and started bleeding. Those boys ran away as the *maulavi master* came to his rescue. After receiving first aid, he was sent back home with his swollen eyebrows and bleeding face. Looking at the blood strained face of Laltu, Fakir became very upset and furious. His *pishima* started weeping, while two of his elder brothers became shocked by his condition. Elder brothers started removing his clothes soiled with blood stains. Fakir rushed to the school to lodge a complaint, but he got frustrated as the school instructors found more fault with Laltu's behaviour as he was provoking those boys for calling himself an 'Indian' than a 'Pakistani'. Fakir returned without being able to lodge the complaint. As this incidence became a matter of discussion in the neighbourhood villages, Jamal and many of his Muslim neighbours and friends came to console and empathize with Fakir and his family. Fakir decided not to send Laltu to his school until his mother came back from India. After that incident, several of Laltu's Muslim schoolmates also started coming to meet and play with him at his house after the school hours.

Laltu's mother returned from India after a long gap of three and a half months. It was a moment of emotional reunion for the boy. The world had changed a lot for him within these few months. He started weeping profusely hiding his face in the lap of his mother, and his mother too couldn't control her emotions. He started getting a new sense of identity, faith and confidence in himself as he was repeatedly assured that he would be sent to his *nijerdesh* soon for his studies. He became very curious to know more about India, the school there, the people, children, the teachers and so forth. With each touch of his mother, Laltu was trying to find a new sense of elevation in him, as his mother returned from his dream destination. He was extremely eager to touch and feel his gifts from India. He found a new meaning of his existence by wearing an Indian made red shirt and black pants with pride. Though he had never visited India literally, he started running all around his neighbourhood areas proudly wearing his new Indian clothes, showed them to his neighbours and friends. His enthusiastic behaviour was met with a strong rebuke from his elder brothers and cynicism among some of his playmates.

Withdrawal from School and Disruptive Actions

After his mother returned from India, she became much more concerned about the safety and security of the family and she started keeping Laltu under her close watch. Though Laltu's hope of going to *nijerdesh* increased, he was becoming increasingly isolated. He was desperately waiting to go to India and join his sister and brother there to study in a new school. Moreover, he did not want to go to his *nijerdesh* alone, but with his entire family. As he was ostracized, he started getting emotionally attached to his family even more. Though Laltu was happy to see that all members of the family were together, the uncertainty and anxiety was also passed onto him as the days passed by. He developed a feeling that all the family members should leave for his dream country, India as early as possible. His accumulated concern took a surprisingly devastating turn with another incident.

Once he saw a family crossing the village in a bullock cart. His *pishima*, after much probing, told that there was a fire in their house. Everything was burnt, and for that reason they were leaving the village and relocating into a new settlement elsewhere. After a few days, while Laltu's mother was alone at home and busy cooking, she asked him to bring some firewood and to keep it near the hearth. His mother was always trying to keep him engaged. She then immediately left to fetch some water. In the absence of his mother, he developed an evil thought in his mind. On the spur of the moment, he thought that if their house was burnt, everybody would leave for India. He took a piece of burning wood from the hearth and lit fire to the roof of the kitchen. The fire started spreading very fast. He became perplexed after realizing its deadly impacts. He immediately rushed to Fakir and started shouting, 'fire! fire!…'. Every household member rushed fast to extinguish the fire. Though he was pretending his innocence in front of his father but after a few moments he confessed to Fakir about his misdeeds without telling the main reason. Everyone scolded him badly for his mischief. Internally, he was neither convinced of his act, nor was satisfied with the state of his growing isolation. However, his anticipation about his migration to India soon became a reality.

Sudden Attack on Fakir

At the onset of winter, all four children in the house would sit for study in the early morning sunlight. Also, it had always been a pleasant time for the children. Fakir's eldest son had come home after finishing his annual examination. All the family members were in a relaxed mood enjoying the sunshine. After taking his breakfast with the children, Fakir left home to attend a patient in a far-off village on his bicycle. The children at home were excited, as Fakir informed them that he would bring a gramophone in the afternoon. The house was full of laughter as the siblings were tickling each other's tummies to make them laugh. Revati too was having fun with the children and was in the process of preparing some special dish for them.

Suddenly, the joyous mood in the house was disrupted when somebody started banging the main door of the house repeatedly and started screaming loudly, '*naya bhabhijan! naya bhabhijan*! Open the door, open the door…'. As his elder brother hurriedly opened the gate, they found one of their neighbour with a bleeding head and face entered the house and breathlessly started screaming, 'Somebody attacked *doctor babu* and they are trying to kill him; please come!, … come along with us and save him … he may have been killed by now…'.

This created a hysterical situation at home. Fakir's eldest son took a club in his hand and rushed toward the spot. Revati jumped from the kitchen and rushed outside the house leaving behind the burning hearth. She started crying out for help: 'Oh God! Please save him!, save him!…'. Fakir's sister and all his children started screaming and rushed out of the house to the spot, the exact location of the attack. Meanwhile, the news of attack on Fakir spread like a wildfire. Several people, both young and adult from the neighbourhood came with clubs and axes in their hands and rushed towards the railway crossing near the Ganga river-bed, where Fakir was attacked. There was only a single dialogue, *chalo!, chalo!* (Let's go!)…. We will thrash them … come and save *doctor babu*'. Several womenfolk from neighbourhood also immediately came out to hold Revati in their arms, and tried to comfort Falguni, and Fakir's young children. Some neighbours picked up children in their lap and starting consoling them, and moping the tears from their eyes by their hands. And, they repeatedly kept saying that, 'Nothing will happen, we are here; we are still alive, come'.

As they rushed towards the railway crossing, they found a huge crowd had encircled Fakir. He was safe and could be recognized in a white *dhoti-kurta* from a distance by his family members. After the family members found that Fakir was alive and he had got a few scratches in his hand, they breathed a sigh of relief. However, his bicycle, and medical kit had been found damaged. As the crowd saw these, they became enraged and started chasing the perpetrators. The calm and composed Fakir came closer to his family members and his neighbours, and told them to go back home. And, he told slowly that he was perfectly all right and was saved by Rahmat, another Muslim neighbour, who was medically treated by Fakir a long time back. Rahmat was standing silently behind their family with his blood strained clothes and shedding tears. Fakir called Rahmat closer to him and gave him a tight hug. This made everybody emotional at the site. He gave first aid treatment to Rehmat by opening his damaged medical kit and told him to come to the dispensary for further treatment, and started moving towards the house. Meanwhile, the crowd overpowered the attackers. After receiving several thrashes, they were brought in front of Fakir's dispensary with tied hands. The entire neighbourhood joined to pronounce a severe punishment to them and they were handed over to the police. Jamal arrived hurriedly with several people and started hugging his childhood friend with tears in his eyes. He publicly proclaimed for a harsh and deterrent punishment for the attackers and the village court was held thereafter.

The gang-leader of the attackers was a refugee, who had been living in Fakir's neighbourhood and in this area since long. He got immediately roused against Fakir, as the latter objected to their forceful grazing of cattle within his fenced boundary as cattle were damaging the vegetable garden and orchards and posing insecurity for the women and children at home. The denial of free grazing within the boundary was the main issue of aggression by an arrogant Muslim on Hindu, and he therefore decided to teach this family a lesson. The villagers of neighbourhood lauded Rahmat for his brave act and they decided to hand over the attackers to the police.

The villagers questioned, 'how could they raise hand on the *doctor babu,* who is like a God to us and saves lives of the people here?' The attackers pleaded for mercy repeatedly and not to be handed over to the police and accepted their guilt. The attacker's family members also came and joined them too. However, Jamal made these attackers give their undertaking in writing and to make publicly promise, that they would be held responsible, if any attacks/thefts took place on this family in future. The villagers thrashed the attackers very aggressively before they were released. Fakir again intervened between the villagers and the convicts. He let the attackers go only after dressing their injuries with his own hand, put bandages, and applied the required medicine there. The villagers were moved with the sense of forgiveness Fakir had with the assaulters. The crowd gradually promised all security and support to this family in any time of dire need, visitors kept on pouring in even from far off places for the whole day to express support to Fakir and the family. Jamal and his family too remained with them for the whole day.

As an eyewitness to this episode, little Laltu had developed a mixed sense of insecurity and fraternity in the neighbourhood. He discovered the possibilities of further assaults on them by the miscreants at any time, but he also discovered the deep-down bonding that they had developed with the neighbours over the years. Henceforth, the boy received more freedom to meet and play his friends in the neighbourhood.

CHAPTER 4

Laltu's Journey to India with Half Family Struggles against Persecution on other Side of the Borders

Indo-Pak Border Tension in 1965 and a Journey at Midnight

In the middle of March 1965, the increasing Indo-Pak border tensions, rumours and mob violence on the Hindu families in the nearby areas and the district headquarters started reaching Fakir's village also. The local miscreants too became active. Stone pelting on their house at night time became a regular phenomenon again. Jamal and the neighbours tried to identity the stone pelters, but remained unsuccessful. Tensions became so intensified that movements of all members of this family got restricted within their house. Sensing some unwarranted situations around Fakir's house, their Muslim neighbours started patrolling their house along with the *lathels.* However, tensions got heightened further with the information that two members of Hindu families were burnt alive the previous night in a nearby urban area, and that there might be a possible attack on this family too. Miscreants also intensified their aggression and many of them started chanting anti-Hindu slogans in the middle of the night. Revati apprehended an attack on their family. The entire family spent a dark sleepless night in tension and the burden of being a minority. Fakir sent a message to his friend Jamal early in the morning, who arrived quickly and assured Fakir of giving full protection and support.

In view of the heightening tensions, Fakir decided that his wife and their three youngest children would leave for India that midnight itself, and they would be back once normalcy was restored between

India and Pakistan. He decided to stay back in East Pakistan with his sister, his eldest and third eldest son for the time being, and if needed, they would join them temporarily. This was a huge uncertain step taken by Fakir. Nobody was sure how the family would be accommodated by their relative for an uncertain period. Revati and Falguni initially did not agree to accept a hurried decision of Fakir and the family to face an induced separation. Revati was very assertive in stating, 'So far we have survived together, let us also die together, I can't go leaving half of my family members here'. His sister Falguni was also against it and said: 'Don't separate us by sending half of the family members there.... Let us face it here. Our ancestors will save us.' Looking at the increasing tensions, Fakir convinced them, and Revati unwillingly agreed to it. It was decided that this journey would start very secretly, and Jamal would arrange all logistics for the journey. All children in the house were strictly instructed to remain confined to their house and not entertain any outsiders at home, except for the family members of Fakir's friend.

Little Laltu saw Fakir and his *pishima* to be much tensed, while preparing others for a sudden and forced journey. He also saw his mother becoming very tensed and pensive in her mood, but she was firm like a warrior getting ready for an anticipated war. Fakir told all the departing members of the house that they were to leave the house at midnight itself under the disguise of a Muslim family. All the children were instructed not to make any noise throughout the journey. He asked his children to address their mother as *amma* instead of *ma*, *pani* instead of *jal* for water, and to address their elder brothers as *bhai* instead of *dada* to avoid suspicion. The entire day was spent in packing boxes, beds and other necessary items. Fakir made the passport and travel arrangements and cash amount ready for his family. They started disbelieving anybody approaching closer to the boundary of the house. Children started peeping through the window of the house constantly.

Hindu Women Soul inside a *Burqa*

Fakir's friend Jamal came again along with his wife and few other Muslim women from their neighbourhood in the evening. These women gave Revati a black *burqa* (a Muslim woman's attire) to wear. They put lot of *kajal* (kohl) to eyelids and eyebrows to make it darker, and put a big nose-ring on her nose to give her a look like that of a typical Muslim woman. They also requested Revati to remove her *sindoor* (vermilion) from the forehead and red cum-white bangles from her hands as those were the visible symbolic marks of a Hindu woman. As per the Hindu tradition, when a woman becomes a widow, these aforesaid items were removed as part of the ritual. As these items were getting removed from her forehead and hands, Laltu saw his brave mother weeping and she collapsed on the ground saying 'I am neither a Muslim, nor a widow. I am a Hindu, please leave me alone. I will not go to India. I will die with my children and husband here.' It was a very difficult situation for Revati to control herself in the presence of those females present at home. Everybody started weeping after listening to her grief. Fakir, however, made the effective intervention to bring the situation under control. He, after controlling his own emotion, sat beside his wife Revati and slowly convinced her that all these preparations should not go waste. She was supposed to do it for the security of the family for some days, especially for their children. Gradually, but very unwillingly, Revati removed all the Hindu attires and symbols from her body and wore a *burqa*. Now a Hindu women soul started moving inside the *burqa*. Their Muslim women neighbours left Fakir's home after preparations and bid adieu to Revati.

Throughout the day, Laltu remained enclosed inside the house. Though he was looking for an opportunity to meet his playmates for a final time, he was unable to do. He was having mixed feelings of joy of going to the country of his own, but sadness at leaving behind the rest of his family members and his good friends here. Like his other family members, he too was also feeling insecure receiving a list of restrictions for the journey.

The exodus started at midnight. Revati sat on a bullock cart with her other young sons. This bullock cart was escorted by the two bullock carts in the front and two in the rear side with twenty-five *lathels* carrying clubs in their hand. Few *lathels* carrying lanterns were kept at least half-a-kilometre ahead of the bullock carts to counter the possible attackers. The entire team was led by Pontu, the eldest son of Fakir, and a trustworthy Muslim *lathel*. Little Laltu looked behind from the bullock cart only to find that his father was holding hands of his third brother and trying to console his *pishima*. Fakir tried to say a few words, but was unable to say anything. The expedition started for an uncertain destination. The bullock cart carrying Fakir's family avoided the nearest railway station to prevent any possible attack on them. Three hours passed-by, they reached another railway station late in the night. All were instructed to remain seated in the bullock cart silently till the arrival of the train. As the train arrived, the elder brother led them to the railway coach after inspecting the conditions. While his mother, he and other siblings got seated in the train. His eldest brother and a Muslim *lathel* wore a skull cap in their heads to prevent any suspicion.

It was a late-night journey filled with tension. His *burqa*-clad mother was trying to cover all the three children with her unmanageable *burqa* like a hen with her chicks. His elder brother was standing firm on the gate of the coach with a tensed face with readiness to encounter any assaults, so was the *lathel*. In case a new passenger entered their compartment, the tensions further grew. Laltu was so tensed that he was suspecting everybody to be an attacker and was often getting up from sleep. Even a small movement of anybody's arm made him anxious. Though his *pishima* and mother had taught him to chant the *Ramnaam* at house to overcame all fears, he was unable to utter the same with the fear that he would be identified as a Hindu. The sole mode of communication with his mother throughout this journey was through the her firm touch of his head. Nervousness, watery eyes and silence were speaking the language of their uncertainty, separation and frustration. Throughout the journey, the family did not ask for water or food, or expressing the need for the toilet. There was a sense of threat and suspicion. The train arrived at a large railway junction in the morning to interchange for another train to reach India-East Pakistan border. They were to spend their time in a crowded railway platform where everybody was unknown to them, as there was a gap of one-and-a-half hour. The tension was getting mounted, while the ticket-master was asking for the ticket and other relevant details. They gave their false name and address. It was a very difficult experience, but the Muslim *lathel* helped them throughout their journey for everything, from getting train ticket, for entering in train and assembling their baggage, getting a compartment seat, and departure and so forth. After boarding another train around noon, they reached the last station. After getting down from the last train, everyone walked down for another half-a-kilometre to reach the Indian border.

Everyone became very jubilant after reaching the Indian border, since it was a new lease to their life and achievement. They started talking to each other and said 'What a relief!' Revati removed her *burqa*, and applied vermilion on her forehead, and white and red bangle on her hands to remain in her original self. She brought a small pot, full of water rising towards the sun and poured water on the ground. With her folded hands, teary eyes and choked voice, she prayed to the Sun-God saying, 'Oh God! We are safe here. Please guard my children and my husband, whom I have left behind at home'. She shared some food that she had brought with her with everyone. Thus, the relaxing time came to an end, as the remaining part of the journey was yet to take place. It was again time for separation. Revati took her eldest son's hand and put it on the hand of the *lathel* and said to the latter with all emotions and teary eyes, 'I am putting my son into your custody. Protect him, take him home back and protect my husband and others who are alone there. You are a God sent angel for us!'

The *lathel* replied, '*Naya bhabijan,* until I take my last breath, nobody will harm our *doctor babu* and your children. It is the promise of a *musalmaan*. Please go to India without any hesitations.' As the station's bell started to ring, both Pontu and the *lathel* started walking back towards the railway station with tearful eyes to go back to their house. As they disappeared in the crowd by waving their hands, Laltu along with his mother, and his younger and immediate elder brother started walking towards India without knowing that they were heading towards another ordeal and separation. Laltu started getting a mixed feeling out of this separation and developed a new quest:

Parting for New Quest

I was born in the lap of nature,
Grew with siblings and their delicate care,

I was fascinated by stories of prince and princes,
The journey through moon, stars and the milky ways.
Glittering of Sun on morning dew,
Sail board on river and rhyme the new.
Caught little chick and flying feather,
Danced on the rain for fun and showers.

As we were growing in our loving land
We fell prey to the communal hand.
Became isolated because of our faith
Got daily threat of loot, burning and death.
Prepared to leave our land as hatred grew,
Sailing for new shore where known were few.
Leaving behind my father in a haste
We arrived with our mother for a new quest.

Part of our family was left behind,
Several memories of horror still in mind.
My father got surrounded by layers of foe,
Brothers remained there for years to go.
We arrived in a new land facing all odds
Started new life and everyday struggle were fought
My caring mother tried her best
To ensure our life not to go a waste.

Arriving in India: Freedom, Uncertainties and New Plights

These lonely four souls began to head towards the Indian border. Laltu, however, became very excited with each of his step towards India. He forgot all weariness and pain. He was about to enter in his *nijerdesh* and his dream land, India. He was also wearing his Indian-made black pants and red shirt. He rushed leaving behind everybody to reach the border of East Pakistan early, though his mother advised him to walk slowly and remain in a group. There were huge movements of military and para-military forces along the border. He started peeping into the other side of the border, his India, through the iron railings. He was trying to march ahead out of his zeal unknowingly. However, he was surprised that he was stopped at a border check-post by an East Pakistan Rifle guard soldier and asked for his identity proofs. He replied, 'I am a Hindu and I am an Indian'. The security forces smiled at his innocence. His mother followed him to show the passport and other documents. They were allowed to leave East Pakistan. He crossed the no-man's land and entered into the Indian border, well ahead of everyone. He was, however, again stopped by an Indian Border Security Force guard. Before they asked any question, he himself told, 'I am a Hindu and I am an Indian'. Pointing his fingers behind towards his siblings and mother, he said 'My brothers and my mother are also Indians. We are coming to our country.' The Indian Border Security Force guard became so happy with his reply that he hugged the boy, took him onto his shoulder and offered him a few pieces of biscuits to eat. It was a proud moment for him. His love, respect and feeling for India increased manifold. His brothers and mother who were always guiding him with extra care, though liked his enthusiasm, advised him to control his emotions. All of them entered India after completing the necessary formalities at the border check-posts.

Laltu was looking all around. He felt like a liberated bird. He was thinking that all Indian children must be happy like him. He kept on looking all around, the blue sky, flying birds, the green field, silver rivers, grazing animals, glittering ponds, the smiling people and everything. To him, it seemed as if everybody was welcoming him to India. He forgot the separation from his father, other brothers, *pishima*, his playmates and most important, his house in East Pakistan for the time being.

They started on another long journey to reach their destination. They changed two public transports for another four to five hours of journey. Throughout the journey, Laltu never slept. He was enjoying each moment of his journey to India inspite of difficulties and tiresomeness, as it was for others. Thereafter, they rode a bullock cart for another one-and-half hour. They finally reached an unknown remote village in the West Dinajpur district, located in the northern part of West Bengal late in the evening, situated at three kms from the East Pakistan border. The maternal uncle and *didima* (grandmother) received them with a warm welcome, where his second elder brother and second elder sister were already there. He was so cheerful that he had been again reunited with his dear sister and second elder brother, whom he had missed for a long time. They had plenty of questions to ask and so many stories to tell each other about their longing to meet everyone. Laltu had so many plights of their family to share, despite being in a joyful mood. The old village consisted of Laltu's relatives, so he was moving from one house to another without any restrictions from either side.

Encountering the Unexpected

Laltu was extremely happy that he was getting extra attention from his relatives as it was his first visit to India, and that the strict restrictions experienced in East Pakistan were conspicuously absent here. If anybody asked his name, he was excited to introduce himself as, 'I am a Hindu and I am an Indian'. Though his response was a matter of amusement for others, but it was matter of pride for him, because to himself he had arrived in his *nijerdesh*.

Post-arrival to India, Revati sent a letter to Fakir informing her safe arrival in village. She completed her procedures concerning report to the local police station about their arrival from East Pakistan to India, as per the rule. It was around two weeks after their arrival in India, i.e. the second week of April 1965, that they were informed by the local police station that their passport has been confiscated by the local administration and they would not be allowed to go back to East Pakistan immediately as India-Pakistan war had broken out. They were also informed that the life of all Hindus in Pakistan was in danger and, therefore, the border is sealed. Accordingly, they were advised to stay back in India until further notice. Revati was mentally ready to stay in India for a few months temporarily. However, she was not mentally prepared for accepting such uncertainty.

In general, the letters through postal communication, which were the only modes of communication in those days, reached within ten days between West Bengal and East Pakistan. For more than over a month now, there were no letters from Fakir's side. There were no clues from anywhere about the safety of their family members in East Pakistan, since all modes of communication were suspended. In the absence of authentic information, local discussions were predominantly centred on the rumours which were circulated, that the massacre against Hindus in East Pakistan had become widespread.

Revati's Courageous Initiatives

Revati could now realize that she was to stay in India for a long period with such uncertainties and a big responsibility had fallen on her. She was to take care of the safety, food, etc., of five children, who were in India with her. Her second eldest son was to appear for the matriculation from a local school, third son was to be admitted in the seventh class and her daughter in class eight, Laltu in class three, and his youngest brother were enrolled in pre-school. She ensured that education of all her children should not suffer in the absence of their father. Perhaps, she could foresee the complications of human relations. She often remembered her husband's words that, 'Always remain independent and don't be dependent on relatives for too long.' In spite of many uncertainties engulfing her, she gained courage. In consultation with the relatives, she decided to have her own house and a separate living arrangement to stay for an indefinite period. She arranged a new house comprising of two small rooms and a small kitchen with the help of her relatives and adjacent to their house. She had some cultivable land in the village, which she had purchased during her earlier visits to India by selling her ornaments. Besides, she had also brought some cash with her this time. These gave her some confidence to take independent decision and have separate arrangements for their stay. It was in the middle of the academic session and admission was not possible in the senior classes for her third son who accompanied her this time. However, Laltu's admission was finalized in third class at a local school.

Attending New School in India: From Refugeehood to Nationhood

Despite the odd situations, Laltu became very excited about his admission to a local school, and that he would go to the school from next day onwards. For him, his new school would be consisting of new friends and where nobody would push him to the corner and would address him as a *kafir* or *malaun*. Next day morning, he arrived at the school before time with full of enthusiasm, and reached class with a slate and pencil in his hand where he sat on the first row in the class, that was his long cherished desire. As the class teacher entered the room, he stood up with all other students and said *adab*, while other students remained silent. As the teacher asked his introduction, he said in a very loud tone, 'I am a Hindu, and I am an Indian'. The teacher took a back foot. Most fellow students started whispering around and after a few moments, the teacher asked the name of his parents. Before he could say something, some fellow students answered the teacher, 'Sir, he is a refugee boy… a Pakistani refugee'. The little boy could not believe his ears. He started screaming, 'Oh, No! I am an Indian, I am a Hindu'. The teacher smiled and after taking the class, he went away. While fellow students started whispering, he started repeating his proud identity. He tried to convince the classmates, but in vain. Other students declined to accept his utterance any more. They asked him to sing the national anthem of India in order to prove his credentials to be an Indian. He started singing the Pakistani anthem, '*pak sar zamin shad bad…*'. They started laughing at him, as none of them had heard of it. They told him to sing the national song of India. He got confused and failed again in that test, since he recited the Pakistani one: *pakistan ka matlab kya, la ilaha ill-allah*. The result was obvious. The fellow students started laughing at him, as he did neither know *Jana-Gana-Mana*, nor the *Vande Mataram* song. His towering ego got deflated within a few moments. He became highly frustrated and disturbed to be termed as a 'Pakistani refugee', and he returned home with a big burden of humiliation on his shoulders. He started weeping in front his mother, who consoled him and adviced him to memorise the Indian national anthem and not to be disheartened. Following his mother's advice, he remembered the entire Indian national anthem, and partly learned the national song of India overnight to prove his hard earned Indianness among his classmates. His elder siblings started encouraging and helping him in his study and in bringing a new outlook in him.

On the next morning, he sang the national anthem in front of his classmates and he started asking his new classmates the credentials for being an Indian. Their answers were vague as everything else to him was. In his mind, he considered that India was for Hindus and Pakistan was for Muslims, as told to him at his former school. However, in this village school, he found several Muslim students in the class marked by their surnames and were not isolated by others. He was highly moved by the recitation of patriotic poetry by teachers in the classroom for taking him, and other students to an emotional journey of love for brotherhood and sacrifice for the country. Time passed by, he started getting acquainted with the pluralistic surroundings and became engaged with the study in the school, ignoring the tensions, miseries, uncertainties and challenges around.

Increasing Miseries, Missing Festivals, and the Lonely Family

Revati and other members of Fakir's family had arrived in India in the month of April. It was August by now. No communications were received from the other family members living in East Pakistan. Within two-three months of their arrival in India, relatives gradually became non-affectionate and uncooperative. Perhaps, they were realizing that her family member would be a burden on them for long. Once all the money, which Revati brought with her, was exhausted, there were no immediate resources of earning. Those lands, which she purchased, were under the custody of her brothers for more than ten years. However, despite repeated requests, none of them were ready to provide a true account of these lands and of their produce. Her family was left high and dry. At that point, a big help came from a Muslim tenant from the village, who had taken some parts of their land for cultivation under the sharecropping farming system. This sharecropper genuinely came forward to hand over the share that he retained with him. This was the only liquid resource, in the form of paddy, that was made available to them to survive. Revati met all other sharecroppers of the land after collecting the information from various sources. They, however, promised to hand over the share only after the new harvesting season that would commence only in the month of December and January next year. They were to survive on their tiny resources for another four to five months. Revati started curtailing all extra expenditures with no extra food, no new cloth, no luxury and so on.

In the month of September and October 1965, while the whole village wore a festive look for *Durga Puja* celebration, this lonely family – now widely described as a refugee family – became desperate to get information about the other members, whom they had left behind on the other side of the border. Reports of military hostility between India and Pakistan had become a matter of regular discussion in the neighbourhood. In the absence of any newspaper or radio in the village, people visiting the local marketplaces were the only source of getting information about the outside world. Villagers were sharing more rumours than the facts. Some would say that all 'Hindus were butchered and eliminated from Pakistan', 'Hindus are hanged to death in public', 'Hindu women are gang-raped and men are forcefully converted into Islam, they are made to eat beef', and so forth. These were enough to multiply the uncertainty and sadness for this lonely family. Against the backdrops of these uncertainties and tensions and deterioration of economic condition of the family, they decided to celebrate *Durga Puja* without any new clothes, new purchase, sweets and so forth. This was the first time, which was unimaginable for this Bengali family as they were celebrating without much pompousness.

All the children became very unhappy to realize the cloud of uncertainty that was hovering over the family. They were not aware of the whereabouts and well-being of the remaining members of their family. And, they would not be together during the *Durga Puja*. They had always been together during the *Durga Puja* and the several exciting moments during this festival. Little Laltu, however, become very expressive. He was missing his father Fakir very much and started remembering his days celebrating *Durga Puja* with his father, *pishima* and other siblings at his native place.

Laltu Goes Down the Memory Lane: Missing the Celebration of Durga Puja and Baba in East Pakistan

Durga Puja festivities in East Bengal not only marked the arrival of a big Hindu festivity, but also a season marked with beauty and joy everywhere. Arrangement for *Durga Puja* would be in the making with a sense of reunion and joy everywhere. It was always after the rainy season that the colourful cloud was seen across the blue sky with a huge mountain- like formation. With the wind blowing, the cloud would keep on rushing from one corner of the horizon to another. The red Sun would become more soft and shinier now than before. The waves of the river Ganga would glitter profusely with the dazzling rays of the bright sun. Thousands of lotus and lily flower would now start blossoming in the ponds and white *kash* flowers (*saccharum spontaneu*) would blow with the wind all over the field as if the new game was in the making, both in heaven and earth.

Fakir celebrated *Durga Puja* as an occasion to remain rooted to his Hindu heritage. He socialized with the children in its distinctive sense. It was an occasion of family reunion, and neighbourhood interaction. It was an occasion where children were given much liberty in those days. Fakir and his friend Jamal would stand on the high-rising railway tracks and look around the silver water on the mighty River Ganga, the running boats, trees and the greens around in an exciting mood. Throughout this season, they would exclaim, '*puja* is coming!, *puja* is coming!'. Fakir would be very busy in welcoming the Durga's idol. From early September, the potters would come and give new pots, and the whole house would be cleaned and mopped. Bunch of coconuts would be collected from the trees and varieties of new sweets were prepared over the days. Special attractions of *puja* were the new clothes. Fakir would go to the town and would be back in the evening with special shopping for *Durga Puja*. Along with other household items, there would be handful of new clothes. These contained same clothes of same colour for all brothers. Difference would only be for Revati, Falguni and Fakir himself. The local tailor would come and take measurement carefully for all the children. The tailor master would committedly, listen to the instruction of Fakir: 'All the children are growing fast. So, their clothes should be of loose fitting and of extra length'. There was an additional hair cut performed during the *puja* days. It was a special, but a very torturous process.

As per the routine, a dirty *dhoti-kurta* clad authoritative faced barber would arrive to give hair cut to the children. The barber would ask the children to sit in front of him by turns. Even before anyone could sit and bowed his head forward, the barber would take his head within the grip of both his knees for cutting their hair. He was always slow in his action, but was fast in talking to others and threw spit from his mouth all around. Though for the children it was easy to tolerate all these procedures, but the foul body odour of the barber would make them resist him. Some would start sweating and weeping for being grabbed within the grip of the knee of the barber. However, all the children had to bear with this process of hair cutting, as they had no excuse for it in front of their father. Despite this uncomfortable part of the *Durga Puja*, children would wait for the moment of arrival of Durga's idol. Laltu's eldest sister, married in other part of East Pakistan region, would be brought here with her all children to celebrate the *Durga Puja* together.

Laltu was missing all this excitement of *Durga Puja*, as his father, *pishima* and other siblings were not around. He was remembering his first visit to *Durga Puja pandal* wearing new clothes and getting his fresh hair cut last year. There was no *Durga Puja* in the village as there was no other Hindu family who lived here. Fakir took his family members and a few local boys to a *pandal* that was located around 15 kms away from home to show Goddess Durga's idol. A bullock cart was arranged to take them to a railway station from where they were to catch a train to reach a suburb to see *Durga Puja*. For this boy, it was the first experience of travelling in the train with all family members and friends and it was a new and exciting experience for him.

As the abovesaid train would start, their joy would know no bounds. There were no rickshaws or motorcars in his village. For the first time, he was watching them from such a close distance. In his imagination, everything on the train, in the street, in the passing market, and big shop was new for him. He considered himself part of them, as they were for him. He found happiness in each moment with his newly defined 'we-ness' experience. As they reached the *puja pandal*, he would start getting an additional feeling. The whole arena of the *pandal* was full of a unique fresh fragrance of lotus, the priest was dancing with his incense burner (*dhunuchi*) in his hand with rhythmic drums (*dhaks*). Women blowed conch shells. Everything appeared magical to him. He was excited and amazed to watch all the idols of Hindu gods and goddess, their weapons, attires, worshipping paraphernalia inside the *pandal.* He was unable to fix his eyes as everything was attractive and new to him. His *pishima* sat beside him and introduced him the idols of deities – Durga, Lakshmi, Sarasvati, Ganesh and Karttikeya, and the buffalo demon Mahishashura. It was afternoon and he was not ready to come back so soon. His mother dragged him forcefully. Looking at Laltu's blank face, Fakir promised to take him to *durga bisarjan* (immersion of Goddess Durga), that would take place immediately two days later at another place at the banks of river Ganga.

After reaching home, Fakir would start preparation for attending the *durga bisarjan.* This time Fakir's friend Jamal also joined them. Everybody walked along the track for around four to five kilometers to reach the bank of the river, where the immersion of Durga's idol was to take place. A village fair was organized there. The riverbank turned into a crowded place full of activities. Amidst all the activities, Fakir pointedly showed a few boats on the river carrying the idol of Goddess Durga for immersion. Several boats started moving together and gradually started encircling each other keeping the boat with the idol of Goddess Durga at the centre. The colourful blank boats, the descending Sun in the western horizon of the river, the reflection of glittering water waves on the idol of Goddess Durga and dance of people with *dhunuchis* (incense burner) in their hand accompanied with the drum beaters made a deep magical impact in Laltu's mind. He also started chanting along with Fakir, brothers, friends and all the people by saying *Durga ma ki jai!.* Gradually, as the sun was setting down on the horizon, devotees on the boat gently immersed the idol in the river and the devotees standing on the shore started to offer their final respects to the immersed deities with a special prayer to come back again the next year. After the immersion ritual was over, the boy was surprised to see that people started hugging each other. Fakir came first to hug his friend Jamal and thereafter, he hugged all the other children. Laltu for the first time in his life saw the warmth in such festivals. The boys also started hugging each other like Muslims do with each other during the *Eid.* Thereafter, all of them returned home. Although he was thinking about the *Durga*

Puja experience back home, he was becoming more concerned about the safety, security and well-being of his family members back in East Pakistan. Above all, he was missing his father very much.

Missing My Baba

When I go out to play,
Walking alone all the way
I miss my father throughout the day
He was holding my tender hands
Making me walk on rock and sand
Pulling me to walk, not to crawl
Enthuse me to get up if I fall.
He was my father, always strong
To make me happy he walked along.
When I stood alone with my kite to fly
He caught the thread to take it to sky
When my paper boat was rattled in rain
I fall on ground with wound and pain
I repeated it all without fare
He was there to take my care.
To start a game, he would be keen
And he would lose to make me win
He was gloomy to see dirty hand with mess
But he excused all with smile in his face.
I saw the world seating on his shoulder
Even remaining behind all the tall and elders.
As I play game with unknown host
I miss my father the very most.

Fakir Odyssey on the other Side of the Border in East Pakistan

After sending part of his family to India, Fakir became a very disturbed person. He was unable to concentrate on his medical practice. The eldest son Pontu and his fourth son Sadhu were with him. They too became loner. As the villagers came to know about the departure of the remaining family members of Fakir to India, they started looking at the children with a mixed-feeling of apathy and sympathy. Apathy was based on the consideration that this family had developed more allegiance to India than to Pakistan, and sympathy was because of loneliness of the children in the absence of their mother and siblings. Though Falguni was trying her level best to give utmost care to this family, an atmosphere of gloominess, unhappiness and frustration started engulfing the house. Their daily activities became very routinized and mechanical without much feeling of life there. Many hostile refugees started taunting him as a '*hindustani* spy', 'anti-national', *malaun*, *kafir*, and so forth. Though as a mature person he was ignoring these insults hurled at him, it was difficult for his eldest son to tolerate such uncalled for taunting. Fakir and Falguni, however, always advised them to tolerate these nuisances, as they were undergoing very hard time as family.

As the India-Pakistan war broke, the concerns of Fakir eventually got multiplied. Fakir and his sister sometimes wondered, whether they had made a mistake by pushing the remaining family members towards India. Many a times, Fakir was exhaling his deep sigh of silence with drops of tears in his eyes. He was always trying to get reliable information about their safe arrival in India, their security and well-being. Gradually, he started plunging into deep layers of darkness. He wrote them several letters, but received no replies. Invariably, Jamal came almost every afternoon for support and consolation. However, he was unable to provide him a complete sense of assurance and satisfaction. Nights were becoming more torturous for him as he was spending sleepless nights as he remained concerned about physical security, economic condition and general well-being of the other family members in India. Furthermore, there would be regular abuse heard in the nights, 'Hey *malaun*!, Why have you stayed back? We will burn you alive'. These miscreants would often shout in dark and disappears after hurling abuses. The children would encounter the anti-Hindu taunts in the school apart from neighbourhood, 'Go back to India soon, you *kafir*!'. Once, a *lathel* caught a hooligan shouting in an open daylight. He was handed over to the local police station. However, he was released immediately without any punishment. Frustrations were piling up on the family members but they decided to stay back until the situation improved.

Notwithstanding such difficult and hostile situations, Fakir wrote letters to his wife regularly expressing his anxiety. He regularly rushed into the local post office, visited local railway station and even went to the Indo-Pakistan Border with an expectation of getting at least a hint of welfare of his family members from somebody or from some end. Jamal was always with Fakir, but of no avail in getting any information. His uncertainties were getting added by another layer of uncertainties. He would frequently look at the sky, pray to the almighty, seek intercession from his forefathers and console the children to remain contended. Despite the troublesome situation, Fakir maintained his strict disciplinary lifestyle and kept the children engaged in their study seriously.

Meanwhile, Fakir's eldest son Pontu appeared in the matriculation exam. Fakir sent his son to write the exams in the district town staying in the house of his another Hindu friend. Heading towards the town, Pontu again encountered provocative and humiliating taunts regularly like 'bloody Indian stooge', 'anti-national', *kafir*, etc. But the young Pontu tolerated all this as he was a religious minority in a Muslim dominated country, and his father instructed him not to develop any conflicts.

More than five months had passed now. But Fakir's remaining family members received no communications from India. In spite of several difficulties, Pontu had passed the matriculation exam. It was an occasion of big celebration not only in the family, but also in the neighbourhood. In those days, only few students were able to pass the matriculation examination. Several villagers and people from far-off villages also paid visits to Fakir and to give Pontu an appreciation. Being a *doctor babu*'s son, Pontu was already getting an added attention in the neighbourhood. After passing the matriculation examination, he started getting much prominence in the village and around. However, all the members of this remaining family became very unhappy that they were unable to share such important news with all members of the family. The apprehensions about the plight and helplessness of the family members in India made Fakir very eager to reach or at least send some message to them. Pontu also became very restless to reach out to his mother and younger brother somehow. The urge for communication from his immediate family made him restless.

Pontu's Arrest in Sedition Charge and his Plight

As the days for *Durga Puja* started advancing, Fakir was becoming more tense and frustrated. Pontu was also becoming very restless to know about his mother and the other younger siblings. He was especially becoming extremely eager to share the news of his successful passing out of the matriculate exam with his mother and siblings. One day, he took permission of his father to go to the district quarter (that was located around 40 kms away from their house) and to be back by late evening train after meeting some of his teachers. His father agreed, even though it was not usual, considering that a student should meet the teachers after passing the exam.

Pontu left the house at around 4.30 a.m. to take the early morning train. However, Pontu changed the train mid-way to go to Indo-Pakistan border, located in the northern side of Bengal, which was somewhere around 350 kilometres away from his village. His maternal uncle's house was in the northern part of Bengal, where his mother and younger siblings were supposed to be. After getting down from the train in the late afternoon, he started walking towards the border and crossed several villages alone in the hope of getting some information about his mother and siblings. On the way, he met some villagers and started enquiring about India. Some young men became friendly with him and told him that they could take his message to the village in India, where his mother and siblings were staying. They also told him that the Indian village was located only two to three kms away and they could easily bring the message back from them within two hours. They also told him that this was a normal practice there that the East Pakistan Rifle (EPR) and Border Security Force (BSF) of India allowed such exchange, but with some 'payment'. Pontu got tempted and agreed to give the 'payment' to get the required information about his mother and siblings. He instantly wrote a letter to his mother stating that, they are desperate to meet them on the other side of the border and that he has successfully passed the matriculation exam and they are well despite the heightening communal tensions in the neighbourhood and that their movements were strictly observed by the local police. Pontu also quickly purchased some clothes and toys for his younger siblings with whatsoever money that he had with him. Finally, he gave his wrist watch as fee for these exchanges. Those persons took those items from Pontu and advised him to come closer to the border and wait there in a house and they would be back from India within a couple of hours.

However, with all eagerness as he started approaching towards the border, the situation took a devastating turn. All of a sudden, few EPR personnel appeared and caught hold of Pontu by the scruff of his neck and started questioning him. The persons, who promised him help, also disappeared from the scene. Pontu got puzzled and surprised. Though, Pontu spoke the truth by telling his name. As his name and his surname was explicitly Hindu, the EPR personnel held him with more suspicion. As he uttered that he was a Hindu and that he was trying to get information about his family members in India, the EPR became very furious. They instantly started misinterpreting him as a 'bold-faced Hindu Indian spy', who was trying to cross over to India to share a sensitive information. They started beating and kicking him. They also misinterpreted the letter that was written by Pontu to his mother. They shouted at him, naming him as a *malaun*, 'traitor', 'anti-national' and pushed him on the ground, started kicking on his stomach and chest. This young man, who was barely seventeen years of age, started weeping, begging clemency with folded hand. But the security forces were mercilessly beating him. He started screaming in pain, '*Ma, baba, bhagwan* Please help! Please help!' But none came for help. They accused him of being a 'spy with an innocent face' for espionage for Indian government. Pontu became an immediate source for expressing their hatred against India. Thousands of villagers from border areas gathered around. But Pontu's innocence was ignored by everybody in the wake of the enthusiastic aggression of the EPR personnel. Finally, he was handed over to the police in charges of spying for India, anti-national activity and attempt to cross the border illegally. Pontu became shocked as his pleading was of no value to them. He was taken to the district headquarters with blindfolded eyes and handcuffed.

Fakir was worried in the evening and was feeling uneasy for Pontu all through the day. He was waiting for the arrival of Pontu by the late evening train. But Pontu did not return. He kept on waiting for hours. It had never happened for Pontu. Fakir sent the *lathel* to visit the railway station, but he returned after a few hours without any information. Everybody at home became worried. At midnight, Fakir went to his friend Jamal and sent all of his *lathels* and known people to find out Pontu, but in vain. The entire night passed full of anxieties. By early morning train, Fakir reached the district headquarters. He went to Pontu's teachers' house and was surprised to know that Pontu didn't visit them. He again started searching for Pontu here and there with all possible efforts but of no avail. Worried Fakir returned by the late evening train, but without any information about Pontu. Everybody became extremely concerned. While Fakir's sister and younger son were weeping and Fakir was consoling them, this time Fakir also burst in tears in hopelessness and frustration. By this time, the news of Pontu's disappearance spread all over the village. Many villagers came in huge numbers to console them. Jamal and Fakir decided to inform Pontu's missing to the police by next morning. Another worrisome sleepless night passed for the family.

Next morning, Jamal arrived to accompany Fakir to the police station. However, to their surprise, a group of four-five policemen arrived at Fakir's house. Normally, police officers were respectful of Fakir, as many of them got medical treatment from him. But this time, they were very rude to Fakir and instructed him to come to the police station to testify that Fakir and his family were spying for India. Everybody was surprised and shocked as to why they had come and why such an allegation. Fakir got shaken from inside and denied such unexpected allegation. The police informed them that Pontu was arrested for espionage and was trying to cross over to India from the northern part of Indo-Pakistan border. He was already serving in the jail at Dinajpur district and that they had come after getting telegraphic instructions from the police headquarters. One of the policemen exclaimed that, 'Your son is a traitor, a *kafir*. You have nurtured him as an "anti-national", and an "anti-Pakistani" in your house.' Fakir was stunned. He never expected such description of himself or his son. The heavens fell down upon Fakir. He started pleading innocence of Pontu. But these were of no avail. They searched the dispensary of Fakir thoroughly, took his dairy, notebooks, letters received from India and many such items with them. They also ordered Fakir to follow them to police station. In a divided community, there emerged divided opinions about Pontu's behaviour. However, Jamal stood firm with Fakir. The police tried to handcuff Fakir, but Jamal resisted handcuffing Fakir and accompanied him to the police station that was six kms away from the village. Fakir had no option, but to leave behind his sister and young Sadhu alone at home. Fakir's head bowed down to ground because of the shame inflicted on him. He also simultaneously became extremely concerned about Pontu's safety.

As expected, the police personnel became very boorish and hostile towards Fakir and questioned him all through the day about his family members, and his connections with India and other Hindu community members, and reasons for sending the family members to India, sending Pontu to border just before the Indo-Pak War, and so on and so forth. In every question, there was an explicit doubt regarding Fakir's integrity. He was repeatedly pleading his innocence and of Pontu. They kept him in the police station without food, water and even did not offer him a seat till midnight. As the news of arresting Pontu and impounding Fakir in the police station spread across the village, people started visiting police station with lots of curiosity. Ultimately, Fakir was allowed to return home by giving an undertaking that he would not leave East Pakistan, surrender his passport to police station and will not sell or purchase any property there. They also wanted a minimum of two people's guarantee, to which Jamal and another neighbour readily agreed. Frustrated Fakir came out of the police station as a devastated person. Jamal held him tight and consoled him. Few villagers also came close to him, while many tried to avoid him doubting his integrity.

Meanwhile, in the daytime, Jamal sent a communication through telegram with the help of a district administrative officer at Dinajpur. He took the help of his cousin brother, who was a practicing lawyer there in Dinajpur. Incidentally, Jamal's uncle (who arranged Fakir's marriage with Revati from that district), and Jamal's cousin knew Fakir and his family very well. On the following day, Fakir and Jamal planned to rush to Dinajpur on an early morning train. Jamal gave full support in trying to prove Pontu's innocence. Fakir and Jamal reached Dinajpur by next afternoon after changing two trains.

Meanwhile, Jamal's cousin had moved the bail petition in the court for Pontu pleading his innocence, good character and unintended behaviour. The case was slotted for the afternoon. Fakir and Jamal were very eager to see Pontu. Before the court hearing started, Fakir and Pontu had a glimpse of each other for a while. Fragile Pontu was surrounded by a dozen police personnels. Fakir rushed towards him. Both of them broke down. The young Pontu was chained and handcuffed. He was in his soiled clothes, unkempt hair, with black marks on the cheeks, and side of an eye with a swollen face. Stains of blood was already there on his nose and forehead. Fakir rushed to touch him, but police pushed him back. Before the pensive Pontu could weep even in front of his worried father, he was hurriedly taken away by the police. Jamal took Fakir to the court room. The case was placed describing Pontu as an 'Indian spy', 'traitor', 'anti-national', and the sedition charges were levelled against him. The argument of Pontu's lawyer was not even heard and thus, bail was denied. Young Pontu was sent to the Central Jail without giving any opportunity to meet his father. Frustrated Fakir again broke down and fell down on the ground. Jamal and his cousin took care of him and tried to console the inconsolable father. Jamal's cousin promised to send the bail petition again. Both Fakir and Jamal returned home next day without any success.

Fakir started getting frustrated. He stopped attending patients and going outside the village. The refugee population started taunting him as the 'father of a traitor', 'an Indian spy' and many more. Some patients were coming to listen more about his plight and to give bundles of advices than for their treatment. His sister Falguni and son Sadhu also started feeling more and more isolated in the neighbourhood. Everything for Fakir seemed to be a failure. With all uncertainties, along with the sense of separation with his young ones and humiliations, he started feeling that he was in an unknown world. In his own country (*janmabhumi*), whom he loved the most, he was called a traitor, his son was in jail and he was not able to get any information about the remaining members of his family. It was similar to the exile situation with a few friends around.

It is my country whom I loved the most,
Now I have been a traitor,
They have been my host.
We have been parted to save our life,
I don't know the whereabouts of little children
And my dear wife.
We went to meet each other even for a while,
We can't do that, we are in exile
I still work and hold my breath
A long way to go to reach the zenith
Even I am alone in this endless plight
I have still few friends to lit light.

Revati's Plight on the other Side of the Border in India

Tempos containing Durga's idol were in the making in this village. Absence of any communication from Fakir's side made the family live in a state of uncertainty and disdain. Though Revati was trying to maintain a facade of high spirit for the family and to keep the moral of the children high, but internally, she was becoming shattered. She was making it known to the children that the economic stability of the family was only away for a few months. She stated that, 'It would be perfectly all right. Everyone would get new clothes, and food of their choice once the harvesting of the paddy starts. Until such time, you should get satisfied with *dalbhat* (simple rice with pulses). Do hard work and study with all sincerity'.Finally, she would say good news about their parted family was only away from the India-Pakistan border. Once the border reopens, the good news would come, and we would be together again. She would weep silently keeping her face away from the children. In between, she had sold off some of her ornaments to meet the expenditure of the family and children's education. The second elder brother of Laltu was about to appear for the matriculation exam. Though his third elder brother and sister were yet to be admitted in the school, she bought books for their home study. Despite her all uncertainties, she put much emphasis on the value of education for children. Revati tried her best to keep all the children occupied with their study and not to get carried away by the uncertainties in the family. She remained very unhappy by observing the forlorn faces of the children, for whom she was the only protector in India.

This village was situated three kms from the East Pakistan Border. The faint sound of running train in East Pakistan side could also be heard from this village. Many a times, some of the family members would walk toward the border villages with the intention of meeting some people from other side of the border and to get some possible information about East Pakistan. Due to high border alerts, they returned without getting any piece of information. However, just before the beginning of the *Durga Puja*, this family received a huge shock about an unconfirmed information that a young man, resembling their eldest son of their family out in East Pakistan, had been arrested from the border area by the East Pakistan Rifle guards, as he was illegally trying to cross over to India. It was also added that the arrested young men had confessed that he was a Hindu and was carrying new clothes and gifts for his siblings and mother for the *Durga Puja* celebration in this village in West Bengal. It was evening and all were stunned. Even though it was very difficult to confirm the news, the relayed information from words of mouth came closer to their apprehension. The family once again became engulfed in sorrow. It was a long dark night. All relatives came to console them. However, they came without any confirmed piece of information. Rumours started circulating surrounding this event like merciless beating, kicking and torturing of a young man on the border, his screaming and crying for help, etc. Breathlessly, they were waiting for the day break, and someone to come and to say that, that piece of the information was incorrect.

Starting from early dawn, his mother kept on requesting people about the possibility of verifying the information. She started running from pillar to post and met a variety of people including school teachers, postmasters, local revenue collector, village welfare officers, and all senior relatives. But none offered help in view of the tight security and military movements across the border area. Though some village elders also met the Border Security Force official on Revati's request, they came back without any positive outcome. At that moment of heightening tensions and uncertainties, their Muslim sharecropper came forward to take the risk to bring the correct information. He somehow managed to sneak into East Pakistan illegally risking his own life. It was a period of timeless waiting, tension, frustration and multiplication of rumours. The sharecropper came back after a few days only to confirm the information that Pontu was arrested. It was the person with same name and the family name. He also informed that the young man was moving around the borderline to cross the border with some items, and that he was arrested by the East Pakistani border force on charges of espionage. The sharecropper, however, was unable to confirm anything about the whereabouts of Fakir and the other members of their family. He also brought forth additional sensitive news that the East Pakistanis were hostile to the Hindu families and that many such families were wiped out there. This made everyone devastated, their uncertainities increased very fast and they became a loner and subject of sympathy in the village. They also gradually became financially weak, unwelcomed by their close relatives. Eventually, they were mostly left to themselves.

Long Drawn Out Legal Battle to Prove Innocence on other Side of the Border in East Pakistan

Within the darkness in Fakir's life, Jamal and his family, and a few neighbours became the source of light. Pontu was denied bail in one after another hearings. He was also shifted to different prisons. In every lock-up, he was tortured by the prisoners and the prison officers. They tried their level best to force Pontu to write that he was an 'Indian agent' and was spying for India. He was beaten mercilessly to make such confession. Fakir, Jamal and Jamal's cousin regularly visited Pontu at the detention centre. Often, they found Pontu with swollen hands, legs and face. They complained to the judiciary of such physical torture, but the police reported that Pontu was hostile and he tried to attack the jail inmates. As the days passed, it was becoming darker for Fakir. However, after long four-and-half months of struggle and persuasion Pontu was granted bail. It was an occasion of a family reunion with joyful tears. Villagers came in large number to console young Pontu, who had become much darker in complexion, lost weight, and grown beard and looked lost and timid in appearance. For Fakir, Falguni and Sadhu, they found a 'diamond' which was lost in the darkness. Many people also started avoiding Fakir's family as Pontu was branded as an 'alleged spy', 'traitor' and an 'anti-national'. Few friends and classmates of Pontu came to visit him. However, Pontu remained confined to his home mostly.

However, this reunion remained short-lived and Pontu's bail was again revoked. An additional charge of conspiracy against the state was registered against him and he was sent to jail again to undergo all the traumatic experiences. Police started making further enquiries. They visited the house of Fakir repeatedly for interrogation and interrogated several classmates and friends of Pontu to prove the charges levelled against him. The family emerged stigmatized in the locality. To aggravate the matters further, some neighbours started openly taunting this family as 'family of a spy', *kafir*, *malaun*, etc. Often, they felt like running away from this country, but they were unable to do so. Meanwhile, Jamal lost the election and was dislodged from the village council membership. But, Jamal never gave up. He kept on helping Fakir in his effort to prove Pontu's innocence.

Seven months had passed, and more than eight hearings took place and on every occasion bail was denied. While the police became desperate to prove their allegation against Pontu and to punish him severely, Fakir, Jamal and Jamal's cousin became very eager to prove his innocence. Jamal collected signatures of more than 250 neighbours testifying the good character of Pontu. He also highlighted the spotless character of this matriculate, who was denied justice, and whose career and life was put in jeopardy. Finally, Pontu was exonerated from all the charges after a period of eight months. Fakir, Jamal and Jamal's cousin became jubilant by this verdict. Fakir broke down out of happiness after reuniting with Pontu. With all care and emotion he brought Pontu back home. The rejoiced remaining family started feeling a sigh of relief at least on this count. Now Jamal, Jamal's cousin and Fakir started looking for ways and means to develop link with the remaining family, who had left for India and remained incommunicado.

Settling with Obvious in India: Struggle and Hope for the Half Family

For Revati, the possibility of their return to East Pakistan decreased, and getting financial help from any other source further made her bleak and uncertain. Despite several odds, she became more bold and courageous in the face of all these challenges and crisis. With rolling tears in her eyes and pain in heart, she eventually became the sole protector, defender, guardian and friend for all the five members of her family. She remained firm to stay back in India and to protect the life and future of the children here in India. In early 1966, she decided, as the new crop arrived from the sharecroppers, to shift to a newly built tiny house that was located around three kms from her relatives and also near government schools. She repeatedly reminded her children, 'don't get carried away by rumours, your father is alive, see the tip of my red vermilion, it is still red. But my vermilion says he is alive there'. Laltu's indignant, but courageous mother shifted the whole family in that new place with new challenges to counter.

These problems, in turn, made her children remain united, and to be sensitive and obedient to their mother, disciplined and studious. They started following the same routine of study, as they followed back in their East Pakistan days. It was also a remote and silent village. In the evening everyone would remain calm. Revati was neither allowing anybody to go out of the house after sunset, nor allowing anyone to come inside the house. It was a new environment in this new village. However, they started feeling increasing concern and the absence of their father and his guidance, other siblings and *pishima* and her stories. In this new house, Revati took the initiative of telling stories. Her favourite story was taken from *Ramayana*, especially, the abduction of Sita by Ravana. She would narrate the story of Sita's loneliness and would start weeping. As she started to narrate the story of Luv, Kush and Sita's banishment and her exile period, she started crying. Her children also would relate to the plight of their mother with Sita's ordeals and would exhale deep sighs. These brought more pain and a deep-down sense of induced and uncertain separation in them.

Coping up with New Experiences

Life got a fresh start in a new house in new surroundings, even though this newness remained embedded with the accumulated sense of frustration, separation and insecurities. Revati had taken several initiatives following her fresh start in her new house. She took stock of all landed properties, engaged new sharecroppers to cultivate the land and hired few regular farm servants. She started to keep a regular book keeping of the landed produce. As the produce from the land was not enough, she sold her ornament and a piece of land to ensure education for the children. Laltu was admitted to the third standard, his younger brother to the pre-primary, and their immediate elder brother to the high school in the village. The second eldest brother – who passed the matriculation with good results – was admitted into a college in the district town. Their mother also purchased a radio, which was the first radio in the village, especially to listen to the BBC Bangla News, especially on the India-Pakistan situation. Like their father, Revati was sitting regularly in front of the children to supervise their studies. She regularly visited the school to know the progress of the children though that was not a practice in this village. Also, a proposal for marriage came forth for her daughter Kajal. Following a detailed discussion with relatives, she arranged the marriage in a simple manner. Life started moving with a host of new activities and new schedules. However, within all these activities, the absence of Fakir and the remaining family were conspicuously felt by everybody. Over dinner, invariably, they talked about their father, brothers and *pishima*, whose status were unknown to them for more than a year now. Laltu had always seen his mother weeping alone due to such separation and uncertainty but not in front of them.

Laltu was trying to get resettled into a new multicultural village that comprised neighbours from various castes, religious groups and linguistic groups. In this village, little Laltu got acquainted with children of his age group and he started becoming friendly with most of the children. He also himself took the liberty to play various games, run all through the green paddy fields, jump on the pond to pluck lotus, ride on buffalo with other children, playing flute by sitting under the shade of tree with the playmates in the village. Apparently, he could not restrict himself within the boundaries of *bhadralok* and Hindu culture as observed in this new village. The taste of liberation became attractive to him.

Though his character was appreciated by most of his playmates, it was not appreciated by a section of the village elders. They complained to his mother about his overtures. They also said that in the absence of his father, the boy was getting spoiled as there was nobody to control him. One of the influential villagers also offered to regularly monitor this adolescent boy. They were also against his mother's outdoor movement in the village, especially against her going to the school and the market. However, his mother became very assertive and she said very clearly: 'My son has a god and a father, and he does not need a godfather. Don't worry, I will take care of him as his mother. I know myself and my responsibilities'. The village elders disliked the attitude of his mother and her strong sense of independence. They tried to create problems for this family, but she stood firmly against all these odds with calmness, and firm conviction.

Village Teachers, Spirit of Independence Movement and Paradise of Pluralism

As directed by Revati, the village school was the sole place of getting answers to her questions and a direction for lives of the children. It was a little world through which Laltu and his brothers were getting linked to the wider world. The sensitive school teachers of this village were the real bearers of the spirit of independence movement. They were inspiring the whole class of students to dedicate themselves for the cause of the *desh*. For Laltu, *desh* for him was his *swadesh*.

Before taking classes, the teachers made it a point to narrate the sacrifices of the freedom fighters – *shahid* Khudiram Bose, Benoy Bose, Badal Gupta, Dinesh Chandra Gupta, Surya Sen (fondly remembered as '*Master Da*'), Matangini Hazra, Netaji Subhas Chandra Bose, Bhagat Singh, Mahatma Gandhi, Jawaharlal Nehru, Bal Gangadhar Tilak, Lala Lajpat Rai, and many others for championing the cause of freedom for the country. These teachers would speak for hours about the plural essence of the Indian cultural heritage. They highlighted the historical bonds of Hindu-Muslim unity, emphasized social equality, dignity of labour, and the need to seek dedication for society, nationality and humanity. Their inspiring words always echoed in the mind and heart of Laltu: 'None of you are ordinary persons. Every freedom fighter now resides in you. You are them. Every breath you inhale, they touch you. Feel it. Don't commit injustice, do not tolerate injustice'. These teachers professed for an ideal India in tune with the dream of the freedom fighters. They were talking about the *desh* (country) and the people. Their movements and simple lifestyles encouraged the students to imbibe the spirit of patriotism along with the sense of religious pluralism, sensitivity, and respect for all.

Little Laltu was very enthusiastic to ground himself in a pluralistic and secular space with respect for each other, something he was missing in East Pakistan. He was trying to absorb and internalize such spirit from the early part of his childhood in India. However, frustrations and gloominess in the family always bothered this little soul. Many a times, the teacher would personally ask him about his father and would advise him to be brave and to be studious. His father, for him, was an ideal hero in his life. He always had the pain of missing his father in some corner of his heart. This pain was becoming more intense in case of someone enquiring the well-being and information of his father and his brothers. The little boy had firm faith in his mother's utterance that his father was alive and he would join them soon.

A Letter from the Heaven

This family was in the stage of loneliness and disdain in the absence of communication from their father, brothers and *pishima* in East Pakistan for more than two years now. Revati fell ill and lost her health. Many neighbours and relatives promised to do something, to get message about Fakir and other member of that remaining family, but in vain. Even fortune-tellers started getting added attention in the house for a favourable prediction, but without any result. His mother had continued to write to his father with earnest expectation for a reply, but of no use, there were no replies yet. However, despite all odds she was visiting the village post office daily for the same.

In the middle of 1967, they got a surprising visit from the local postmaster himself in their house to deliver a letter. The letter was from London and Revati's name was inscribed on a colourful envelope. There was suspense all around since such a colourful inland letter, that's too from England, seldom came to this remote village. The sender was none other than Zamarul, from London. There was intense curiosity in the village. Some more villagers also arrived. Laltu's second elder brother, who was studying in college in the district headquarter and was available at home that time, anxiously opened the envelope. Surprisingly, there was a covering letter written by Zamarul and there was another small envelope enclosed within the envelope. After controlling all his emotion, Laltu's brother read out the covering letter first that was written in Bengali:

'*Adab naya bhabijan*!, I am Zamarul, the younger brother of one of *doctor babu*'s friends. The *doctor babu*'s letter is there inside the envelope. Every one of them is fine by the grace of the Almighty. They are highly concerned about you all there. Write to me back soon. I will send your letter to my *bhaijan* in East Pakistan, who will pass the same to *doctor babu. Khuda hafiz*'. Then Laltu tried to read out his father's letter that was addressed to his mother:

'My Dear Revati, Love you and the children. I am writing several letters, and I am not sure whether you have received any of these. I am worried how you and my little children … are there.' Laltu partially completed the letter and thereafter, he passed it over to his mother. His mother started sobbing profusely out of joy. Nobody could read out those letters fully at that moment as these were passing on from one hand to another. However, it was enough for them to get the information that their father, brothers and *pishima* were alive in East Pakistsan. It was a joyous and an emotional moment for the family. This letter created an emotionally charged situation for all in the family with the pleasure of finding the missing dearest ones of their lives. Through his hand written letter, they were trying to touch the sentiments of other members of the family, who had coercively remained on other side of the border. It became obvious that

Fakir had sought help of Jamal to send his letter to India through his younger brother Zamarul, who was settled in London. Though the India-Pakistan war had come to an end, the border tensions were yet to be sorted out and the direct postal services were yet to be restored. Passport and permission were yet to be issued for people's visit. Hence, their only option left was to write letter, that is, through London.

Laltu's second eldest brother immediately brought an airmail from the post office. Sitting around a dim lantern, Revati wrote a simple letter after making several drafts on rough papers. Often her tears were beyond her control – why had she not got her husband, children and sister-in-law back in her life. Finally, she wrote the letter stating that they had got their life back getting to know that by the grace of God all of them were alive in East Pakistan. She also wrote among other things that all were well here; all were studying in schools and colleges to fulfil his dream. All of them were alive and miss them so much. She also strongly pleaded that leave everything behind there in East Pakistan come to India without much delay. She was very desperate to know everything on priority about her eldest son Pontu, who had been arrested by the Pakistan's security force.

This letter of their father brought a new sense of hope to them and gave them lot of social recognition among the relatives and neighbours. They got a lifeline of communication through London with active engagement of his father's childhood Muslim friends and their kin. The first letter from London was immediately followed by another letter. The letter brought another relief for the family. In that letter, it was informed that Pontu was falsely charged of espionage and involved in anti-national activities by the East Pakistan state. He was released from the jail, and finally freed and exonerated from all of the legal charges with the help of his friend Jamal and other good neighbours. He was so happy to mention that more than two hundred local people from the surrounding villages had testified about the innocence of Pontu. Over the months, the remaining family members of Fakir, who were living in Indian part of the border came to know through these letters that his friend Jamal and other Muslim neighbours played a big role in securing safety and security of their family in East Pakistan. These letter correspondences with Fakir continued via London for several months, though it was very time taking. Though the intensity of exchange of message increased, there were no visits of the family members from either side of the border in person till late 1967. Though in early 1966, the Tashkent Treaty was signed between India and Pakistan following which the diplomatic relations were established between India and Pakistan; but for the common man the restrictions remained for cross-border movements.

CHAPTER 5

Reunion of Half Family and Legacies for Laltu in India

Waiting for a Reunion

Life began here in India with a new set of enthusiasm. Letters had started coming in directly from East Pakistan by this time, although, most of the envelopes were open and re-sealed. Letters were written in a very short contended language to ensure that their family members were not in danger. However, notwithstanding the language of the letter, they started waiting for the ultimate arrival and reunion with the family members who remained separated on the other side of the Pakistani border.

All were engaged in preparation to meet the remaining members in India. Revati, being a religious person, was regularly offering prayers for their swift arrival in India and instructed all the children to remain as disciplined, academically focused and gentle as was required to meet the expectations of their father. The expectation was growing for the family reunion in Indian part of the border too. Laltu, like all the children at home, was enthusiastic and eager to meet the separated members of their family after such a big gap. While his mother would cook extra foods every day, the boy would wait for the arrival of the local bus from the town and wait till the boarding down of the last passenger from it for their arrival. Their waiting was becoming very intense for everyone, especially on the festive seasons like *Durga Puja*, *Lakshmi Puja*, *Kali Puja*, *Saraswati Puja* and on the occasions like *Nabanno* (Bengali harvest season) *Pushna*, *Nabbarsho* (Bengali New Year). Months and years had passed, but no scope of return.

Pontu's Arrival in the Humble Tenement

Fakir's remaining family in India were living in a very humble shelter. Within the four walls of this humble house, Revati was ensuring discipline, dedication to study and food safely for all the growing children. One evening, while little Laltu along with his siblings were studying in the dim light of the lantern and their mother was preparing food in the kitchen, all of a sudden a young man entered the house and stood in the middle of the courtyard of the house. Nobody could see the face of that person in the dark. All raised their head from their book with a curiosity. He was away from the light of the lantern. His face could not be seen and none could recognise that person with a certainty. It was a silent moment for several seconds. The young man just pronounced *Ma!...* All exclaimed in joy and surprise. *Borda!,... Borda!...* (Pontu was fondly known as *Borda* by his younger siblings). His mother rushed from kitchen and hugged Pontu in her arms and started weeping profusely. Frustrations and pain of a waiting mother emerged out. She became speechless. All encircled their eldest brother and mother in a joyful mood. News of Pontu's arrival had spread all through the village very quickly. People rushed to see him till late night. There were so many things to share and ask each other. His mother was eager to know about his survival, tortures suffered in a Pakistani prison, present condition of his father, *pishima* and Sadhu. It was an emotional affair for few days. Pontu narrated that the help and cooperation of his father's friend Jamal, his family members and other Muslim neighbours made them safe and secure. They had even helped them in getting the passport to come over to India. The happiest news that Pontu gave was that his father had instructed him not to go back to East Pakistan and to take care of the family here in India. Pontu was joyful to meet and be reunited with his mother and other siblings here in India. He was also contented with the educational achievements of all his brothers here. He, however, became very upset with the state of life of their family here. It was a poor life that somehow managed for survival. Agriculture was the only source of income of the family. Economically, the family was totally dependent on the share of the farm produce received from the sharecroppers. He was amazed to see how his younger siblings were adjusting with such simple living without any complaint to anybody.

Since Pontu was a matriculate pass-out, ideally he was supposed to join the college for a degree. However, he started providing private tuitions to the village children to augment the family income. He started doing immense hard work to save the family members from economic hardships. He was trying to compensate through economic and emotional means what was missed over the years. Laltu had seen his elder brother purchasing new clothes and shoes for his younger siblings from his own small earning, but not for himself. Similarly, his mother tirelessly doing all the household chores, like cooking, cleaning, washing, remained engaged in supervising the study of the children and managing the property. However, these were temporary phenomena for them. There was a waiting for bright sunshine at the end of the dark nights.

The Unexpected Arrival of Sadhu and Short Arrival of Fakir

A day arrived after a gap of another two long years. Again, it was in the evening and was time to ignite the lamp. All of a sudden, a little boy with a loose bundle of clothes and a tinned suitcase in his hand knocked the back door of the house. He was not visible properly, but his voice was known, '*Ma!* I have arrived. Open the door!' However, that boy simply started weeping before the gate was opened. All siblings shouted, 'Sadhu has come, Sadhu *da* has come!'. Sadhu was the immediate elder brother of Laltu. He was left behind in 1964 in East Pakistan, when he was only nine-years of age to stay with his father, elder brother and *pishima*. He was thirteen years of age as of now. He was very talkative, simple in nature and never got furious easily. Due to his modest behaviour, he was named as Sadhu. He appeared in the village by availing a local bus, and thereafter, he started looking restlessly to meet his mother and brothers. He did not know the exact location of the house and somehow tried to ask people. He appeared at the backyard of the house. The lantern's light was dim. Nothing could be seen with clarity in this dim light. But the utterance of

Sadhu was enough to electrify the ambience of the house. All the siblings rushed and jumped on him with huge excitement.

Revati gently brought Sadhu inside the house and held him tight close to her chest, as if a small girl had got back her lost dear toy. There was silence inside the house for a while, except for the sobbing of his mother and Sadhu. However, the children gradually started making a big noise to rejoice the arrival of Sadhu. Before Sadhu could say anything, there was an unusual knocking in the main gate. All was about to ignore it and to remain engaged with the arrival of Sadhu. However, the second knocking at the gate and the grave throat clearing sound alerted every one. Sadhu said, 'I have come along with *baba*. He is standing at the gate'. Everyone had a surprised reaction. His mother, who was in an untidy dress, exhausted after whole day's work, suddenly turned back and rushed inside the room. Everyone became alert for the arrival of their father inside the house. As per the social norm, everybody would remain quiet when their father would come inside the house. All children were anxiously looking at the gate. Pontu hurriedly opened the gate. Laltu had in his mind the disciplinarian appearance and gesture of his father. However, his father was a different person this time. As he entered the house and all children touched his feet silently, he took his youngest son and Laltu in his lap and started kissing their foreheads. He had very few words to utter. Fakir had met them after a gap of four years after overcoming several difficulties in their lives. As tears were falling from his eyes on the ground, everybody became dumbstruck. By this time, all the children had developed the ability to learn from their mother, the message that was expressed through tears.

Laltu was surprised that his mother has gone inside the room and had not come out since then. It was a day, for which every one was waiting very passionately. Why is *ma* not coming out? He descended from the arms of his father and rushed inside the room to call his mother. He did not know what had happened. His mother was simply weeping, hiding her face on a pillow. As his elder brother came to his mother, she simply uttered: 'How would I make him comfortable, it is small, broken house. There is no furniture, no proper arrangements for him'.

Fakir came up to the veranda of the room holding all the children by his arm and started looking at his wife like an innocent child. For Laltu, his father's tearful glittering eyes reflected a deep sense of gratefulness to his mother for protecting the family against all odds. His mother, after a little while, just wiped her eyes with her palms. While controlling all emotions, she said, 'Just wait there, I am coming'. His mother closed the door again and came out by wearing a red-bordered white *sari*, red vermilion on her head, bowed down her head at the feet of Fakir and started weeping inconsolably. For all the children it was not only a celebration of reunion of the family, but also a restart with a direction. For Laltu, his father was the real hero of his life, who protected all members of their family in East Pakistan, despite all odds, and was able to unite everybody again. His mother too was a superwoman, who protected him from all problems through her dedication, hard work and leadership. Though their *pishima* was yet to join them, this family reunion brought now a sense of added self-confidence in them. Within all these joys of reunion in this small house, he could realise that his father was becoming very much concerned about the economic well-being of the family.

Fakir came to India only for a fortnight that time as he was given permission only for such limited period. He again went back to East Pakistan, leaving behind the entire family here. Revati was heartbroken. She was not interested in sending him back. She repeatedly said, 'We will rebuild everything here that we had in East Pakistan'. However, Fakir's immediate logic and perception were different. He always reiterated that India and East Pakistan were going to be reunited soon as the people's movement for independence against the domination of West Pakistan had already begun. And that, he and his friends had already been supporters of this movement. He was filled of conviction that these divided nations would be re-united and the whole family would go back to an independent, united India. He also reiterated his commitment to his widowed sister, his friend and his patients. He also expressed the need to protect those properties in East Pakistan for the future of the children in India. As the visa was about to expire and Fakir's overstay would be termed as punishable in East Pakistan, Revati had no option, but to agree to the departure of Fakir to East Pakistan alone leaving behind the whole family here. Fakir, though, started regularly visiting India but the family remained settled in two separate nations.

Bangladesh Liberation Movement and Arousal of New Hope

The political history of Indian subcontinent took a new turn in March 1971. Sheikh Mujibur Rahman became the undisputed leader of Awami League Party of East Pakistan after winning the election with absolute majority. He declared independence for East Pakistan from West Pakistan on 21 March 1971, and announced a mass movement for the independence struggle for the formation of a sovereign Bangladesh. Bangladesh became a dream in the eyes of every Bengali living across the border. People living in this Indian village became very enthusiastic about the liberation of East Pakistan. Various school teachers of all neighbouring schools organized several marches along with school children towards the border in support of the liberation of East Pakistan. Talk concerning undivided India, and a united Bengal movement started spreading across the area. Fakir's entire family saw a new light of hope in this development, as if the dream of *pishima* and the utterances of Fakir were coming to be a reality soon.

As the military oppression increased in East Pakistan, Indian border was opened up for the East Pakistani displaced refugees for taking shelter in India. Millions of Bengali refugees crossed over to Indian side. Because of its location near to the East Pakistani border, Revati's new village witnessed a huge and sudden inflow of the refugee population. Local schools, market places, roadsides, open courtyards and playgrounds became the temporary refugee shelters for these displaced people.

Arrival of Fakir and his Friend Jamal

Hostilities between the Indian and Pakistani governments increased and the postal communication again got terminated. Mujibur Rahman and all other prominent leaders were arrested. News of atrocities against the Bengali-speaking population in East Pakistan by the Pakistani military brought worry for the family once again. However, they were confident that their father would be taken care of by his Muslim friend Jamal and by the neighbours in case of any eventuality. As expected, Fakir arrived after a few weeks in the third week of the April 1971, along with his trusted friend Jamal, undertaking a huge risk. However, their *pishima* did not arrive. She decided to stay back there as per her conviction that India would be united once again. The family was very happy to be reunited. Fakir was very jubilant to see that Bangladesh liberation movement had taken place. He was convinced that a united Bengal and India were in the offing. After a short stay, Fakir's friend left for London. Before leaving, he promised to meet all of them again in the liberated nation of Bangladesh. Subsequently, after a few weeks, he came back to East Pakistan to join the liberation struggle. As the East Pakistani refugee influx increased enormously in that area, Fakir opened a medical dispensary for the treatment of the refugees and joined the relief works for them.

The Bangladesh liberation movement and formation of the anti-Pakistani guerrilla force *Mukti Bahini* invoked a good deal of nationalist spirit in this village. After India won over the Pakistani forces, East Pakistan got separated from West Pakistan and a new independent and sovereign nation was formed on 16 December 1971, known as Bangladesh. Most importantly, it became a secular nation. The Treaty of Friendship was signed between Indira Gandhi and Sheikh Mujibur Rahman for an everlasting peace and goodwill between India and Bangladesh. A new enthusiasm and euphoria started everywhere in West Bengal and Bangladesh. For some years, the Indo-Bangladesh border remained relaxed and people-to-people relationship between these countries became a much-wanted truth. The war-devastated Bangladesh started the journey towards a new path of development.

Visit to Independent Bangladesh: Recounting the Past and Memories

After Bangladesh's independence, Fakir became emotionally charged. He got ready to go back to independent Bangladesh at the earliest to join his lonely sister, trusted friends, needy patients, and dear neighbours. As expected, Fakir received an emotional communication from his friend Jamal, who had requested him to join him immediately with the whole family as whole villager were waiting for their arrival there. There was also an appeal from his sister. Though there was an euphoria and emotional surge to visit Bangladesh immediately, they were hesitant to take a firm decision to go back there and settle permanently. Revati wanted Fakir to stay here in India with them. However, Fakir was very explicit in his feeling: 'How can I forget the land where I was born? I was nurtured in the land, air, water. My father, ancestors were born there. Their souls are there. My ancestors are calling me there. My sister is there. The dichotomy is that how can I leave my wife and my children here? They have suffered a lot in my absence'. Finally, Fakir went back to his *nijerdesh*, the free and secular Bangladesh, in early 1972, where everyone would be considered equal irrespective of his or her religious background. He joined his widowed sister, his old dear friend and the neighbours in his aspiration to be in his own land. As usual, he was getting new inspiration from the soil, air, and water of an independent-cum-secular Bangladesh. He again started his medical practice as committedly as ever.

Fakir's family that remained settled in this part of India started getting repeated communication from their father and request from their close neighbours to go over to Bangladesh. After a few months, Revati, along with Laltu and youngest children, went to their native village in Bangladesh. The border was open too, and passports and visa were not required. They followed the same route that they took in 1964 to come to India in disguise. Laltu was reminded of his experience of leaving the country during the midnight under threat, fears, and anxieties of his mother. Throughout the journey, he was excited to cross over to his erstwhile *nijerdesh*. This time he had another excitement to go back to his native village that he loved as an infant and was compelled to leave behind along with remaining family members because of the resurgence of religious fanaticism. That time he was a small child, now he was more matured as a youth. As expected, Laltu was becoming impatient, which was faster than the speed of the rail and bullock cart in order to reach out to his villagers, friends, his dear *pishima*, and many others.

Around breakfast time, the tiny bullock cart reached the house with dust all around. He jumped from it to meet his waiting father, and then his *pishima* after a gap of one decade. His *pishima* had remained as affectionate to him as ever. She welcomed him in with open arms, as if she was waiting for this moment for around a decade. She was filled with tears to meet Laltu and his mother. This grown-up boy, now started running all around the house – the bedrooms, kitchen, cowshed, *kaltala*, the backward of the house – everywhere. As the news of their arrival in the village spread quickly, the house became a site of a huge fair instantly. Many people from the neighbourhood and around had arrived to meet Laltu and his remaining family. It continued for several days of their stay there.

Though Laltu had grown up now but his fantasy for *pishima's* story was yet to be over. Neither was *pishima* hesitant to tell stories to him. It was as though *pishima* was waiting for many years to narrate the remaining untold stories to little boys. During the childhood days, *pishima* use to feed him with her own hands. He started eating all the foods even without hearing her stories. As Laltu was reminding his *pishima* about the old incidents, she was enthusiastically responding by saying that, 'Oh God! You have not forgotten anything'. He was only observing that as his *pishima* was taking deep sighs out of her joy, tears were coming out her eyes frequently, and was frequently uttering 'God has listened to me! I have everyone now'.

Revati was also busy in meeting several of neighbours, especially, the family members of her husband's childhood friends. On every occasion, there were numerous proposals from the neighbours to come back again in Bangladesh. His *pishima* was insistent that they should not go back to India, but settle down in Bangladesh. Those were the days she was waiting for. She firmly asserted that, 'You have seen that India and Bangladesh have been united again, they again have become friends. The day is not far-off that India would be united again. How could you forget that the souls of our forefathers still blow in the wind and sound there? They sing for all of us, and bless us. So please come back here'.

Several efforts were put on to persuade Revati by Jamal and good neighbours to get settled in Bangladesh permanently along with the rest of family members. However, that has never taken place, as Revati was not convinced of the safety of the children and their educational future back in Bangladesh. After a fortnight, as decided, Revati came back to India with her children, while Fakir and his sister stayed back in Bangladesh, having again become part families across the border. However, because of the waivers in the visa rule, and friendly relations between two countries, the visit to each side of the border became a frequent phenomenon. All the young children visited their family left behind in Bangladesh with a good deal of emotional zeal.

Growth of Fundamentalism in Bangladesh

Against the backdrop of the liberation movement, Jamal was newly elected as the chairman of the village council in his area. He emerged to be a very influential leader and popular too. However, the newly-liberated Bangladesh started experiencing the resurgence of the religious fundamentalist forces within a few years of its existence. Across the country, the fundamentalist groups became active to propagate for an Islamic state instead of becoming a secular one. In many areas, the *razakars* (a secret group of militias that opposed the creation of Bangladesh nation) started actively indulging in revenge killings. They started targeting the participants and supporters of Bangladesh liberation movement. They also threatened Fakir, since he was a Hindu and a staunch supporter of Bangladesh liberation movement and friendly with secular Muslims, who participated in the freedom movement. They specifically instructed him against getting associated with his childhood friend, Jamal, who had emerged as influential political leader there. Similar threats were also given to Jamal for his participation in the Bangladesh independence movement. Often, these threats were communicated either with anonymous letters or midnight knocking on the door and passing slips, therein, by some unknown persons. However, Fakir and Jamal ignored all these threats considering that these to be simply a childish act of frustration by a limited section of anti-liberation reactionaries. They simply lodged police complaints about such incidences. The threats gradually became open and direct for them. Some young members of *razakars* came to Fakir in an open daylight one day and threatened him to leave for India. They also warned him of dire consequences, if he ignored it. However, Fakir was firm in his conviction regarding his commitments. He told them that he would be in Bangladesh, because of his love for his *janmabhumi*, some local people and most important, his commitment to Jamal's friendship, neighbours and his widowed sister. But these sentiments of Fakir had little meaning for the fundamentalists. Gradually, the sectarian and communal politics started gaining ground in Bangladesh, prevailing over the secular value nurtured in the spirit of liberation movement.

Last Days of Fakir's Trusted Childhood Friend

Fakir and Jamal had a daily routine of visiting each other in the evening and joining a small *adda* (chat place). Reading newspapers, discussing national and international affairs with friends and others were the integral part of these evening meetings. The evening meeting spot became a point of target of the *razakars*. Gradually, some young men from outside frequently started appearing there claiming themselves to be members of the *razakar* force, and instructed Jamal and Fakir to stop such discussions as these were 'anti-Islamic'. Everyone present in *adda* firmly rebuked those outsiders and informed the police about this incident. Fakir was alerted by the neighbours to remain watchful but not to be fearful since they were there beside him.

Sporadic incidences of killings by *razakars* also started appearing in the Bengali daily newspapers, making the family members living in the Indian side of the border quite tensed and anxious. In many of his letters, Fakir also narrated to Revati about the emergence of communal threats and tensions in that area. Revati kept on writing to Fakir to come back to India with his sister at the earliest. However, Fakir assured in his letters that he was safe and that everything would improve gradually. His usual sentence was that, 'Don't worry my friend Jamal, all neighbours and patients are there with me. Nothing will happen'. After a certain a period, however, all communication stopped for several weeks from Fakir's side. Revati planned to visit Bangladesh break all uncertainties. However, the things took an opposite turn.

Leaving Friends and the Country Behind Forever

Amidst all these uncertainties, in July 1973, Fakir arrived from Bangladesh on a rainy evening. Everybody was pleasantly surprised. Fakir stood on the main gate of the house without making his usual loud throat clearing sounds and without any indication taking anyone's name. Usually, he brought some potful of Bangladeshi sweets in his hand, when he came to India. This time there was no gifts, sweet packets with Fakir and no smile left on his face. He looked disappointed as if he had encountered a big storm, which surprised most. Fakir was carrying some baggage and a brown marked stethoscope in his hand that was presented to him by Jamal long ago. Somehow, he entered the house, sat in the middle of the courtyard and started weeping hiding his face with both hands. Everybody was puzzled as to what had happened. After a while, he said that his dear childhood friend Jamal and his trusted *lathel*, who were always with him were killed. They were openly assaulted by the *razakars* out of revenge, in front of his eyes, for his direct participation in the Bangladesh liberation struggle and providing refuge to Hindus.

Fakir narrated that it was only two days back in the evening, while Jamal, a few neighbours and he were engaged in a regular discussion, few gun-wielding young men, claiming to be *razakars,* forcefully entered the shop and instructed Jamal to come out of the room at gun point. Once he came out they shouted with a sudden cry of '*allah hu akbar* ... kill this *kafir*!' Fakir – intervened in between, but he was pushed aside forcefully. These *razakars* shouted at Jamal openly calling him a *malaun* and *kafir*. Fakir jumped to hold him with blood flowing from his head and chest. Jamal was trying to say something, but he could not and took his last breath. The attackers intimidated Fakir that, 'Leave India immediately or else you will be killed in a similar manner'. They all disappeared in the dark. Jamal died on the spot and Fakir started shouting for help and tried to grab one of the attackers. The attacker became very aggressive and tried to shoot Fakir. However, his trusted *lathel* came in between to save Fakir. But *lathel* was also shot down and was severely injured.

Sitting on the floor of the courtyard of the house Fakir screamed with anguish: 'I am unable to do anything for them. Those assassins overpowered me.... They are sectarians, fundamentalists, and the terrorists, and the enemy of humanity. Now my friends are no longer alive in Bangladesh, I have no desire to be there anymore. Now, I am back leaving behind everything.... They have not given me the chance to touch my friend, even to mourn for him....' The entire family became shocked and plunged in grief because of the brutal killings of Jamal and their *lathel*, who were the living examples of Hindu-Muslim harmony.

At that time, Fakir decided to leave Bangladesh for India forever with his sister as he had no desire to live in that country as his friend was no more. Despite all such catastrophic experiences, his sister decided to stay back in Bangladesh. She was firm in her conviction to live in Bangladesh until her last breath. Her conviction was that her divided family and her motherland would be united again. Alas! After attending the last rites of his friend and requesting help from the family members of Jamal, neighbours, and tenants to look after his lone widowed sister there, Fakir left for India. He left behind his immovable properties under the custody of the tenants who were taking care of these lands for years. He also wrote to his eldest daughter, who was living in a distant part of Bangladesh to take care of her in his absence.

After settling down in India, Fakir remained a mentally disturbed person. He was dissatisfied with everything in his life and was worried for his sister. Every day, he wrote letters to his friend's family members, neighbours, and others in Bangladesh to know more about his sister's status. His sister was also writing, though infrequently. He regularly read Bengali newspapers especially about the current situation in Bangladesh. He often became tensed, upset and worried about his sister after reading the news of consolidation of the communal forces in Bangladesh. As a common person, he was to pay the price of the Partition at his individual and familial level and was to live the rest of his life with this pain of separation.

Fakir's Resettlement in India with All Pains and Dissatisfaction

Gradually, Fakir started taking interest in family matters and took control of his family. He started his medical practice and continued to socialize and enculture the children in a liberal atmosphere. Soon, he became a friendly figure and gained popularity among all in this rural area. His adherence to a daily routine, good habits, dedication to hard work, sincerity to commitment, and disciplined ways of life became the key characteristics to most of the people in the village. He, however, was very sharp in his comment without a sense of fear and favour to anybody there. Besides, he was apolitical and inclusive in his attitude.

This village was a peaceful, multicultural place, where people engaged in discussing several issues in a group. However, as communalism was growing in the neighbourhood across the border, its ramifications were also felt in West Bengal. Some groups also started organizing people in and around this village in the name of language and religion. Numerous groups repeatedly tried to persuade him to join them in their political venture. Based on his hard-earned and lifelong experience, he resisted the temptation to become a leader for political gain. Some groups projected him as a symbol of 'victim' and 'oppression' by the Muslims in newly-carved Bangladesh. They also made reference to him in a public meeting in that multicultural village. He publicly stopped them from making such depiction of him and alerted people against the spread of communal virus in the neighbourhood. He always replied that he suffered not at the hands of religious people, but religious fundamentalists, and that he vowed to resist communalism as tribute to his deceased friends. Some radical groups even threatened Fakir to deport him back to Bangladesh if he became critical of their group. Fakir, however, remained firm in his conviction for religious tolerance and pluralism.

Falguni's Tragic End

Bangladesh experienced a bloody military coup in 1975, following the barbaric assassination of *Bangabandhu* Sheikh Mujibur Rahman. The new regime eliminated secularism from its constitution in 1977, and accepted Islam as the state religion in 1988. Many who lived on both sides of Indo-Bangladesh border with the expectation of a political miracle for the unity of the two nations started experiencing waves of fundamentalism. However, some were still dreaming of unity. Fakir's sister Falguni regularly wrote to Fakir and his children till the early 1980s. In every letter, Falguni was expressing her hopes of Fakir's family's return to Bangladesh, which was their *pitribhumi*. She desired to see everyone in the same courtyard of the house one day. She was repeatedly writing that she was always waiting for them in the courtyard of their house and sitting and playing with the children below the *neem* tree, where their forefathers once resided. Fakir's children tried to knit several imaginations-cum-fantasies after receiving letters from their *pishima*. However, that has never been fulfilled.

After 1980, letters stopped coming from Falguni for several weeks and then for months as she started suffering from senility. She was unable to see things properly. She, perhaps, became too weak to read and write. In August 1983, children found their father, who was active, now sitting alone in one corner of the house in a remorseful mood. They found that he was only looking at the sky, as if everything had gone out of his hand. When Revati passed in front of him, he started weeping like a child. He was holding several things to his chest by hiding something from them. After much interrogation, he presented a letter to Revati, written by one of his neighbours from Bangladesh. The letter was posted around ten days ago. It narrated that Falguni was no more and she died of old-age ailments. During her last days, some Muslim neighbours had taken care of her and the last rites were performed by some Hindu people, who were living in a distant village. He simply uttered: 'I have not been able to do anything for my widowed sister. I was not present with her when she died. When my father died, she was only seven-years-old. I vowed to my father that I would take care of her throughout her life, but failed to do. What a shame! Communalism has separated both of us and has given her a death like a destitute. I have not been able to conduct her funeral. So unfortunate! Had the country not been divided, I would have upheld my commitment'. Every member of the family started comforting Fakir, but he was not able to control his emotions. He remained confined in a single room of the house for several days in grief. Revati also started accusing herself saying that, perhaps, she should have been more persuasive in bringing her back to India. Children too became saddened after listening to the unfortunate demise of their *pishima*. Fakir remarked that, 'It is the cost of the Partition that we are paying for the upcoming generations. She was mad in her conviction and affection towards her *pitribhimi*, her *desh*'.

The Last Days of Fakir

Fakir's Frustration and Sad Demise

After the death of his sister Falguni, Fakir remained very disturbed. Despite the full attention of the family, he preferred to be a loner. He started speaking optimum with everybody and often got agitated very easily. But he always waited for someone. He would read the whole newspaper twice. Happenings in Bangladesh were his special interests. He was fond of listening to news from BBC, All India Radio, and Dhaka Radio Station and others. If someone spoke about the happenings in Bangladesh, he took special interest not only on the issue, but also the person concerned. People from his native village wrote letters to him by remembering the days of his selfless service, eloquence, social sensibility and fearlessness. Many remembered him as a valuable village elder present among them through his critical eloquence.

The eloquent critic:

As generations over the years
They tend to miss some of their near and dear
Some are remembered not as kith and kin.
Even not being part of our thick and thin
The whole village remembers this village elder
Who was neither headman nor a stupid, either.
He was critic of everyone without causing any harm
But he was loved by all for his eloquent charm.
He was eager to discuss all new subject
He would look everyone with a sense of respect.
He would deeply engage with a weekly newspaper
Once he asked young villagers with a sense of despair:

'I saw men are going to moon,
Will we have relations with the universe soon?'
He said 'I am perplexed,
It appears to be very complex.
As an ignorant, in asking this question I feel shy
Men are going to moon? Tell me why?'

The young villagers looked at his face,
He was calm, composed and full of grace.
They faltered, but gather small courage.
They are educated but may not be up to his age!
Some said: 'About the moon, we have little knowledge, or a few
Men are going there in search of new'.
He was not satisfied, again raised his eye,
'That's okay, but there are going there tell me why?'

Some started organising their thought
Became hesitant whether it would satisfy him or not.
Some said:
'Over the centuries we have made scientific progress,
We should conquer universe, leaving narrow obsess.
Men are going there to discover life and its new source
They will go to Mars, Venus, Jupiter in due course.
They will bring for humanity hope of new ocean
We will connect with the whole universe with new relation'.

After fixing his eye on the hanging specs
With deep sigh he looked at their face
He said in his loud clear voice,
'For helping humanity, don't they have other choice?
For discovering human relation
You cross millions miles destination?
Don't you look your poor neighbour, fellow and friends?
Who are sick, homeless and starve very often,
They look for help on the earth and heaven.
Many are unable to lit their hearth

Many have remained untouchables by birth
They need every day dignity and human touch
They too possess life, love and aspiration very much.
Don't fly too high forgetting the nest
Have love first for your neighbour in your chest'.
On the beaming sun the elder stood alone
All heard his feeling that was their own.
The Villagers still remember their village elder
Who was not head but a big message sender!

Many letters from Bangladesh were flooded with request for a visit. Someone would write to go there to take possession or to sell properties. But he had least interest in the property matters as he was highly moved by the bereavements of Jamal and Falguni. As a loner, he was always engaged in reconstructing the memory of his past.

Remembering the Treasures of Childhood

When I looked back at my childhood,
It appears to be a tale of lost and found
I wanted to be Robin Hood for my friends,
Who conquered my life very often.
I was among these innocent cowboys
With dreamy eyes and heart full of joys
Sitting under tree with green and glories
Made priceless tools and mouthful of stories
We were carefree to hop and roam around,
Ran after the butterflies and falling flowers on ground.
We gathered together our priceless treasures
The glass ball, kite, paper boats with heartful of pleasure.
We were chased by dogs and honey bee
For stealing poppies and poking honeycomb on tree
We jumped into fishpond to pluck lotus and lily.
Got punished by elders for mistakes and being silly.
We repeated these mistakes playing hide and seek
And waited for friends for our heart to speak

I left my village and my friends long ago
Carrying all sweet memories as my shadow.
Till I get calls from my village,
It's always a heavenly privilege,
With chocked voice from opposite end,
In tumbling tune utters my forgotten friend,
'It's for decades, where have you been,
All ask about you, you are not seen?
O dear, Oh stupid Awesome!
Tell me please when will you come?'
It was full of nostalgic noise,
I reciprocate with cracking voice
I promise to return there for a rest
I look back; my childhood has not gone a waste.

Fakir sometimes becomes humorous, but also full of laments. But, he rejoiced with the family members narrating his stories, although he developed mixed feelings while narrating these old memories.

Aspiring for Reunion with Left behind Motherland

It is evening, I like to sit alone
Chewing memories of the days bygone.
As I occupy on a rocking chair,
Remembering my childhood and the village fair,
Soft hands of my mother on my head,
Father pointer on the rainbow shade
Getting lost on the game of hide and seek,
Rushing towards greens from down to peak.
I keep on floating on boat of sweet pain
Holding my breath again and again.
My wife lit the evening lamp.
She still sings with rhythmic clap
Friends still come without knocking the gate,
We assemble, raise toast to celebrate.
We still hug old friends with tears in eye,

Miss each other after bidding goodbye
Children have grown up for a new world to view,
I try to redefine my world that I knew.
To please me at home now and then,
They still repeat again and again,
'Papa you are strong, you are the best'.
With a proud full chest
I thank God for being blessed.
I pick up my pen and old note book
To pretend my avoidance from their look.
All I get is the courage for a peaceful rest
I struggled to make my life not a waste!
I miss my motherland on the other side of border
She becomes dearer to me as grow older and older,
The rising sun, golden river, gentle breeze
Rhythm her lullaby with the swarm of bees
I am still awake to hear the voice of friend
I will breath for them till my life comes to an end.

Years passed by, Fakir's children had grown up. All of them got settled, married and had their own children. Some stayed at home, while others were away in district headquarters, state capital and in the national capital. Fakir was always in touch with the children via postal letters. In his letters, he often wrote few sentences about Bangladesh by expressing his anguish against the religious fundamentalism and intolerance. In his daily routine, he performed the *surya namaskar* pose with the same hymn, *janani janmabhumishcha svargadapi gariyasi* after his morning walk and taking his bath. He always said that his *janmabhumi* was undivided Bengal. In one of his letters to Laltu, he expressed his desire to pay his last tribute to his birthplace at least once in his lifetime standing on the banks of River Ganga, where the Sun would rise in the east, and the sunlight would shine on his head, and wind would blow all fragrance of the mother earth.

Fakir was fond of writing letters. In one of his letters, he wrote to Laltu stating the same desire of his mother. In that letter, he also enquired about the required formalities for reviving his old passport and process of getting visa to go to Bangladesh. But, that had not happened. Before any of these were processed, Falguni died and his dream of visiting the native village and meeting his sister remained unfulfilled.

Fakir was feeling a sense of emptiness from within despite having his wife, two children and grandchildren always around. On one afternoon, he was refering to a letter that he had received from neighbours in Bangladesh to his wife Revati. He was very excited and started remembering his *janmabhumi*. He became very emotional. He was repeatedly pleading to take him to his village in Bangladesh for a visit. After reading the letters, he suffered a massive heart attack and instantly took his last breath with a deep sigh. It was shocking news for everybody. Moreover, he had not been able to visit to his native village for a final time.

Last Days of Revati and her Painful Nostalgia

Revati always tried to live in the future even at the cost of present. For her, the understanding of the future was totally circumscribed. Her world was the future of her children and the welfare of her husband. She had very little to think or preserve for herself. After Fakir's death, she became very lonely. She frequently remembered her old memories of companionship, lifelong struggles and separation and reunion with close acquaintances. However, she found very few listeners of her tales, except her regular domestic helps. By this time, she had got a hard earned realization that the future and direction of lives of her children were not under her command but somewhere else. They were grown up now and had their own families. They were busy with themselves, their careers, aspirations, autonomy and leaving little space for her in those domains. All of her children, except the youngest one moved out of the house because of professional commitments. She preferred to stay in the village with her youngest son only. She had always been an independent-minded person with a deep sense of self-respect and dignity. Though at times, she paid visits to the houses of her children, but her heart always remained in the village, which was her own house. However, she found herself in her own house to be a neglected person and her desires had become matters of non-priority and sheer attention seeking overtures among the daughters-in-law. Her sons had become very busy with their own careers and their grandchildren also started living in a different world.

As long as her husband was alive, Revati life always revolved around him throughout the day, to arrange all the things as per his specific requirements. In the expanding joint family like hers, where individualism was visibly growing, she was cautious that her husband should not be ignored in a situation of extensive engagements of other members of the family with their own affairs. In the evenings, when most of her children were engaged in their own affairs, she kept herself busy with her lonely husband talking about their past in East Pakistan, their struggle for reunion and survival sitting in one corner of the house. At times, both laughed like children and even burst to tears remembering their past events. Often Fakir had proposed to Revati to go for a long vacation to his Bangladeshi village with him and to convince his sister Falguni to come back to India at least in the last days of her life. He was of the hope that Falguni would have also agreed to the proposal with all enthusiasm with a feeling that the elderly generation would be together again. Revati also conveyed their proposal to other children too. Sadly, there were few serious takers of their proposal and to implement it.

Revati was fond of making telephonic calls from the village. With great enthusiasm, she discussed her plan with Laltu in order to visit Bangladesh. She said: 'Laltu!, You come home urgently and arrange passport and visa for your father and me. Both of us, your father and myself will cross over to Bangladesh by the Hilly Border (the nearest border between India and Bangladesh). From there, we will start our journey by a train, followed by a ferry to cross the River Ganga, then we will take the bullock cart to reach our home. We will visit all around the places. We will pay a visit to Jamal's house and family of neighbours and other friends. I am sure that our neighbours will be very happy by the surprise visit and to meet their *naya bhabijan*...'. In the morning, I will see the River Ganga, take bath there and bring along a potful of holy Ganga water for the house. We will see below all the trees we have left behind.... In the evening I will blow conch shell standing in front of the *tulsivedi*.... Thereafter, I will cook food in the evening and wait for the train to pass the village and then we will take our dinner.... We will come back to India with your *pishima*. This time we will not listen to any objections. Hence, we should be together at this stage of life'.

As Revati started feeling very lonely, forlorn and insecure after the death of her husband, she was making frequent requests to Laltu to pay her a visit. During one of his visits, Revati narrated a dream to Laltu that she had dreamt the previous night:

In the dream, I am wearing a spotless red bordered white *sari*, with a red vermilion spot on my forehead and red bangles in my hand. Your father caught my hand and took me on a boat to cross the river Ganga to go to our house in Bangladesh. *Pishima* was standing on the other side of the river to welcome us with a broad smiling face. Your father was so happy that we were ultimately going back to our village. As we were seating on a boat, a gentle breeze was touching us from all side. The splendid view – the boat was sailing on flowing water surrounded by a colourful cloud, flying birds, the mist and a huge rainbow formation.... But, before we could get down the boat my dream got interrupted....

After that, she started insisting that she should be taken to Bangladesh so that she could go there to see her village and meet all those places and people there – her rooms, kitchens, garden, courtyard, *tulsivedi*, the dispensary ... the Ganga River, the sail boat, the neighbours and so on and so forth.

Unfortunately, her desire remained unfulfilled. After a few days, she fell down in the house and broke her limb and got her head banged. She recovered physically. She started consistently nagging her children to take her to Bangladesh to fulfil her cherished desire. Many started giving her false assurance and making false promise to take her to Bangladesh to purchase a momentary peace. Perhaps, she was in a position to realize the shallowness in those promises and started becoming insistent in her demand to everyone, to visitors, relatives and, of course, the children, but of no avail. Most people around her and the caregiver started describing her as 'crazy'. Sadly, Laltu's heroine mother, Revati died of mental instability after a couple of months. Laltu rushed to the village only to perform her last rites.

It was a deep winter month. Revati ashes were to be immersed in the river. Laltu reached the bank of River Ganga with those mortal remains in an urn, as per the Hindu tradition. He crossed the Farakka Barrage to touch that water of Ganga that goes to Bangladesh and touched his parental village. As he offered those ashes to River Ganga from the Indian side, he remembered chanting of early morning hymns by his father back in the East Pakistan by offering a handful of water to the River Ganga saying, *janani janmabhumischa svargadapi gariyasi.* Distressed Laltu got a deep down feeling that his patriotic parents became persecuted following displacement from their *janmabhumi* and forced to live on the other side of the border by the forces of communalism and sectarian nationalism. Throughout their lives, they struggled to get united with their *janmabhumi*, but could not. Now, they would get united with their *janmabhumi* again in spirit as River Ganga would touch their village with these body remains, though not in life. *Tathastu.*

Grown-up Laltu with Generational Reflexivity

Fakir and Revati's life had strongly influenced the growing up process of their children and inculcated several cultural legacies. Laltu, has experienced the cost and pleasure of living with these legacies. The hard-earned experience of plight as a religious minority in a religious fundamentalist country has made Laltu realize the plights of the religion minorities, who are made the victims of forced isolation, displacement, alienness, suspicion, and apathy. He has also learned through the experience of his family how communalism and religious fundamentalism are the products of vested interests, which engulf the feelings of common person and how a commoner becomes a victim of sectarian political interests. The courage and hard work of his mother to combat all challenges, deep sense of social commitment of his father, a strict disciplinarian at home, combined with the overall pluralist and liberal ambiance of this small village in India and the spirit of independence movement and liberalism imbibed from the school teachers helped Laltu to uphold his identity as a patriot in a plural social order. His patriotism is founded on his love for his *nijerdesh*, which he imagined and was inculcated in him, since his childhood days in East Pakistan, as a refugee child and as a naturalised Indian, thereafter. His articulation of patriotism always remains his commitment for an inter-community bond like millions of Indians, which was evident between his father and Jamal.

In his growing up process, Laltu has remained a *gainya* (rural folk) as his little village has remained a source for his plural foundation. He is possessive and arrogant of his identity, founded on the commitments to simplicity and inclusivity. In case of any questioning and threat to his commitment for simplicity and inclusivity, he firmly stands against all odds to uphold these commitments by singing Rabindranath Tagore's composition *Ekla Chalo Re* (let us move alone). He retained a similar attitude throughout his education and professional journey. Like millions of ordinary Indians, his commitment for hard work has made him a self-made man, though he has also encountered the undercurrents of political, ethnic, religious and regional politics in his daily life. His experiences make it explicit to him and to many others that the traditional plural fabric of Indian society that is founded on the language, religion, region and ethnicity are also manipulated by the sectarian and communal forces as tool to serve their interests. They construct a boundary of 'we' and 'they' in the name of exclusivity, name and shame people in the name of faith.

Laltu deeply realizes that India, despite becoming a knowledge hub for superpower, phenomenally modernized, global and a transitional society, its formal institutional arrangements, and their functioning have remained primordially conditioned to a huge extent. These reflect both in the informal setup and in the formal organizations. Both, sectarian and communal forces – those are active within the formal organization – encourage the formation of primordial solidarity to fulfil their interests. By emerging as a dominant group, these forces influence the organizational culture and norms, break the established rules and procedures to satisfy their vested interest. They even use physical violence and threat to demonize the 'others', and are always hungry for power and authority. They try to control the organization and unleash a reign of terror to get complacent support of middle-class sections, who follow a similar trail to avoid the possibility of victimization and political incorrectness. Significantly, in the shifting political atmospheres, these communal forces are quick to change their political affiliations to be the part of the ruling order. They first pressurize the authority for individual positions through manipulation, even at the cost of violation of rules and procedures. However, when denied, they use all kinds of possible political and sectarian means to change the authority to have control over the organization. To gain legitimacy for their act, they form a community of cultural 'we-ness' on the basis of language, region, religion and caste-based communal hatred. They close the space of analysing critical enquiry and start to identify the critics as their 'opponents'. They are eager to show their political potentials, and start targeting the others by shaming them in order to create an environment of unforeseen fears, and threat.

Laltu, as per his social conviction, kept his straightforwardness and joined a group to dissent against the communal shaming of people and against trial of few people on account of rumours. This apolitical group of people collectively asserted for patriotism and social inclusion without any prejudices for class, caste, religion and region, and stood for institutional interests and against the so-called 'trial' by rumour. The powerful, egoistic-cum-domineering group started threatening the members of this small group of people, who stood against their narratives. They started targeting Laltu and made him a *persona non grata* within the organization to give the message of their strength in the organization. While Laltu remained uncompromising in his attitude, they used all means including public and physical threats to demonize him and tried to choke his voice. Undeterred by the consequence, this man developed a confrontational attitude against the domineering characters.

While the domineering forces shifted their political affiliations quickly from left to right to develop alignment with political parties in power, he remained fixed to his commitment to the individual autonomy and patriotism as cherished values. While the domineering group tried to mobilize the organization by securing consent through coercion and tried to demolish the disagreement and dissent by the tyranny of their constructed majority, he contested through democratic means and kept on voicing his dissent as a citizen and as patriot by risking his life. They tried to isolate him, while others came to his refuge as fellow citizens. They put him in extreme humiliation, isolation and shame with the allegation of being a 'traitor'. They influenced the organization to initiate one enquiry after another against him with false charges, but they were frustrated finding no substance in their charges levelled against him. They even conspired to deny him the space of professional mobility, influenced the organization by denying his position in gross violation of the rules and procedures, he accepted the denial by giving a dissent. They suggested him to be dynamic by changing his conviction, he suggested them to be inclusive, plural and accommodative to be Indians by conviction. These fringe groups tried to provoke others to malign, marginalize and shame him, through whims, politicking and manipulation, but others came forward to reveal their design as fellow companions.

A grown-up Laltu remembers the plights of his parents. He keeps on asking questions. However, his questioning is not only projected as a 'pariah', but also seen as 'anti-establishment' position and a 'pseudo-intellectual' in nature. They celebrate their capacity of manipulation. He, however, does not mourn for his ostracization. He keeps his head high as for him he has not failed, he has been failed by the institution, and by failing him the institution has failed itself. Despite being denied, isolated and humiliated, based on the experience of his father, he insists them to be inclusive by conviction. They felt that he was paying a cost for his dissent, but he feels an enjoyment as he upholds the conviction of his parents.

My mother's courage and love for self-esteem
Inspired me to move and cherish her dream,
I was prepared for a journey to see new dawn
Carrying with me all the native longings that I adorned.

My parents blessed me with all tearful eye
Villagers stood there to bid me goodbye
They inspired me to discover the world more and more
Life started moving to a new seashore.
Many midnight candles burn into flame
Unfolding the life to another stage of game.
I encounter in life new game and threat
I prefer love, than go for hate
They gave punishment to me and near and dear
They pushed me in a world of unforeseen fear.
Firmly, I started walking alone
In the company of flower and stone.
I uphold my parents having no fear at all
Even risking my life, and obvious downfall.
Even I look back the life left behind
Sufferings of my parents occupy my mind.
Fulfilling their dream always in my chest
I have not let my life to go to a waste.
As I get a glimpse of new sun shine
I celebrate the blessing of my parents the divine

As a religious minority, Laltu has already experienced the victimhood of his parents back in East Pakistan. He has witnessed the friendship and commitment of his father's friend Jamal, during the days of their crisis. He has been a part of those sufferings, communal tension, but with an inter-faith assurance. He has observed the increase in communalism in India, in the neighbourhood and in the functioning of the organisation. Now, a grown-up Laltu, based on his own experience, has put his life on test as an average Indian does. For him, his parents were heroes of his life. Their ideals were the source of motivation for his life. However, he questions himself as to whether his parent's life has gone waste? Will he be punished for questioning again for being a common man? But he celebrates his manhood upholding the example of his parents' life.

I am an innocent byestander on the street
I smile by habit, and stand for others to greet.

I make the way to run other's chariot
I love my country, my fellowmen, I am a patriot.
I feel for all with sensitivity and passion
I am a common man, I am a part of my nation.

I have seen my father's agony and mothers tears
Keeping them awake with night full of fears.
They have been victims of threat, hatred and riot,
Got persecuted in their own land by communal zealot.
They taught me brotherhood, and hate for none
Remain simple and a proud common man.
I loved my dignity and freedom
Always hated coercion and serfdom.
Now faith has factored in friendship and foe,
To make a choice for here or elsewhere go.

I am a common man, a patriot of the bay
Unimagined of our division of 'we' and the 'they'.
They hate me and design me as an 'other'
Since I do not call them 'my godfather'.
They took my name, put me on shame
Tried to be victorious in cruel game.
They were always longing to dominate
I have the weapon of truth only to celebrate.
They tried to punish me and my friend,
Wanted to bring our life to an end.
Keeping our head high without fear
We common men stood for love to share

I am a common man, a simple idiot.
I stand for justice as a natural patriot
I live with the legacy of my parent and their zest,
My father's friend's sacrifice and his inclusive quest
My inner self always rises in hope
Standing alone for all situations to cope.
I stood alone on a descending shore,

Many darkness to cross, and storms many more.
Now we stand together for those quest
To make sure, my parents sacrifice was not a waste.
Though life moves with new colour and taste
I uphold their spirit, they are the best.

CHAPTER 6

Conclusion

Human beings are an innovative creatures and have created varieties of social groups to remain linked to the society at several levels. Social groups which are founded on the familial, kinship, caste, racial, religious, linguistic, ethnic, regional, nationality, and citizenship, etc., relations have been integral parts of such innovations. There have been institutional arrangements for the sustenance and functionality of these groups. Conventionally, by associating with the functioning of these groups people get linked to the wider society, at times cross-cutting the boundaries of each of these groups. These associations give, in many ways, the joy of doing things together, enjoyment in the collective success and also sadness in collective failures. These were not only actions and roles and status for those who have remained involved in the association with these groups, but also a process of deriving emotion, reflexivity and meaning out of such associations. Association with many of these groups have remained historically and traditionally rooted, and have provided the deep-down foundation for subjective attachment and for making sacrifices for these groups. It is the capacity of these groups for deriving meaning, emotional attachment and invoking sacrifice that these groups have acquired significance in human societies.

One's association to one's country through the emotional relation of patriotism has always remained a special and an integral part of such a process. Very often patriotism subsumes the boundaries of family, kinship, neighbourhood, linguistic and religious and other ethnic groups in its expression. It has always remained an integral part of people's existential and spiritual attachment to the land, nature, people, history and culture of the motherland with an inherent spirit of accommodation and inclusivity and apoliticality of social concerns. In a multicultural society, patriotism as a subjective articulation has naturally remained inclusive in its orientation to integrate communities of all religion, colour, language, caste, class, occupation and creed living in that territory with its shared cultural ethos, heritage and practices. It provides a feeling of emotional attachment, cultural meaning, collective belonging and an identity for one's association to the people and to the land historically pre-existed. Patriotism is, thus, *sui generis* that has evolved on its own and has remained one such moral innovation. Over the centuries, it has acquired enormous strength to unite and keep the people grounded with their own geography, culture and compatriots.

Human being converted a part of the patriotism into nationalism and have linked it with the modern state formation through the process of political construction. Historically, nationalism has emerged to be a powerful force to politically mobilize people against the dominant forces of colonialism and external aggressions, inner-oppressions and the counter political forces operating both within and outside the country. It has also been a part of the emancipatory force of the modernization project. However, as nationalism is not an autonomous construct and it undergoes a long process of construction and transformation, it gets intersected with the forces of ethnocentrism and communalism.

In a multicultural society, at time and places, ethnicity and ethnic identities are brought into the forefront to underline the issues of cultural neglect, social insecurity, marginalization, economic exploitation, and political domination, etc., of one ethnic group(s) by the others. The politically conscious ethnic assertions many times take the form of ethnocentrism to express the exclusivity of identity of the asserting ethnic group carving out a boundary for in-group vis-a vis out group(s) leading to the formation of a nationality within wider nationality formation in the country. The mobilised ethnic groups by acquiring politicality of social concern articulate subjective feeling of admiration, well-being, accommodation, egalitarianism and fellow feeling in the group, while hostility and segregation for out-groups. Ultimately, by asserting their association with specific territory, they may develop aspiration for nationhood leading to a nation-state formation. Communalism, that overtly and covertly expresses exclusive love for own religious, linguistic or racial community, is rooted in ethnocentrism in many ways. It emphasises exclusivity for the other community, underlines distrust and hatred for them and develops binaries, uses threat or victimhood from others as its vehicle for its propagation, tries to recast the glorious past and propagate fundamentalism to strengthen its social base, takes the form of political ideology to capture the state power, and influences the course of formation and expression of nationalism in a country. In the South Asian context, in general and in Indian subcontinent in particular, the dominant basis of communalism, has historically been religion since the middle of nineteenth century and it has influenced enormously the process of shaping up of nationalism therein.

In view of its intersectionalities with diverse ethnic, communal, civic, cultural and political forces over the centuries nationalism has emerged to be multifaceted. In this changing trajectory, nationalism has got transformed from civic to political, liberal to communal, secular to religious, inclusive to exclusive, etc., facets. The ethnic exclusivist or communal nationalism are circumscribed by the consolidation of communities within communities with political aspirations. It has converted social and natural differences into politically and culturally defined 'we' and 'them' communities; and the communities of common 'friends' and common 'enemies, inflicted cultural and economic uprooting and forced migration of millions of people across the border as refugees. Importantly, the colossal attainment of such victimhood of vast section of people is linked to the evolving politicality of construction of the ideology of ethnocentrism, nationalism and communalism and their changing formation across the globe. Notwithstanding the resurgence of ethnocentrisms, communalism and also the exclusivist communal nationalism, patriotism still occupies a distinctive social space in the individual and collective minds of millions of people.

India has borne witness not only to the consolidation of the forces of nationalism through the anti-colonial struggle, but also the changing course of nationalism over the centuries. With the resurgence of communalism and ethnocentrisms, India experienced the proliferation of multiple nationalities as political realities, propagation of two nation theory and ultimately the attainment of Independence in 1947 through the division of the country with a secular India on one side, and a theocratic Pakistan with two parts – West and East Pakistan, on the other. Though India was politically partitioned in 1947, the efforts of partitioning the country were made historically deep seated through varieties of administrative, political and social means. Broadly speaking, these efforts had taken shape within the broad processes of colonialism and their divide and rule policy on the one hand, and articulation of Indian nationalism, anticolonial movement and resurgence of communalism in the country on the other.

The strength of Indian society, which was founded on its plural religious, ethnic, linguistic, cultural and geographic fabric, was often used by the colonial forces as points of weakness of India for its unity and the growth of nationalism. To counter the tide of nationalism as aroused through the Indian Mutiny of 1857, in 1860, the British explicitly noted its adherence to the divide and rule policy for India. From the very inception, the Census of India was used as much as a mechanism to collect information on India society, as much as a tool to show the religious and racial etc. divisions in Indian society to suffice their divisive administrative purpose. As the spirit of nationalism started getting consolidated since late 19th and early 20th century, the colonial administration engaged itself with the communal forces to keep people divided in communal terms and by promoting communalism, especially religious communalism. They panned Partition of Bengal on Communal line in 1905. In 1909, the Morley Minto Reforms Act was enacted to give separate electorate for the Muslims. Subsequently, the kept on encouraging the formation of communal associations to counter the growth of pan India nationalism. In 1932, the British announced the Communal Award giving reservation for the religious minorities, cultural and caste groups. As their coercive and divisive policies failed to stop spread of pan-Indian nationalism, they made efforts to balkanise India by creating not only two nations, but also more than two nations by giving the provinces and Princely States the option of remaining independent of either India, or Pakistan.

The communal forces have also tried to get an opportunity to expand their support base within their community following the path of populism. They have articulated the threat and danger to their specific religious, ethnic and cultural practices and identities from the other primordial communities. The communitarian political mobilisation of religious minority and majority to thwart the perceived threat have taken the form of ethnocentrism and ethno-nationalism. The communalism, thus, emerged out of the divide and rule policy of the British, furthered the social and political divides in Indian society paving the way for the articulation of India nationalism through varieties of shades like that of Muslim nationalism, Hindu nationalism and secular nationalism.

Congress was formed in 1885 for the consolidation of national unity, in 1887, Sir Syed Ahmed Khan declared Hindus and Muslims are two different nations. In 1906, All India Muslim League was formed with encouragement from the British. In 1907, Arya Pratinidhi Sabha, in 1909 Punjab Hindu Sabha and Provincial Hindu Sabhas in 1913, All India Hindu Sabha, in 1915 Sarvadeshak Hindu Sabha were formed. Savarkar asserted for arousal of Hindu consciousness across India from 1906 onwards. Though the Congress was formed on secular basis, many Congress leaders stared giving Congress a Hindu colour. In 1916, Congress conceded the demand of Muslim League for separate electorate for the Muslims in the Muslim minority provinces. In 1920, Gandhi supported the Khilafat movement, Hedgewar opposed it. RSS was formed in 1925 for the protection of Hindu *Dharma*. On 1929, Congress demanded full independence and an action plan was worked out. However, the Muslim League developed its own action plan demanding effective representation of the minorities in the Central Legislature. In 1930, Congress launched the Civil Disobedience movement, the Muslim League and Hindu Mahasabha remained firm in promoting their own objectives. In the 1937 provincial elections, Communal divides got institutionalised as election was held on the basis of communal representation. Starting from 1937, while Congress was for the withdrawal of colonial forces from India, Muslim League remained silent on such demand, while Congress was raising issues for the whole people of India, Muslim League was raising the issues of the Muslims and questioning the credentials of Congress for speaking for whole of India. As Congress formed government in most of the provinces after the 1937 election, Muslim League stated raising the issues of atrocities against the Muslim minorities in the Congress ruled provinces, and promoting Hindu Raj and urged the British government to initiate enquiry against the Congress governments. In 1939, as the British entered the Second World War the Congress asked for the war aim and the future of democracy in India, the Muslim League offered its support. In response of the British government's reluctance for clarification, all Congress provincial governments resigned, the Muslim League celebrated it as day of deliverance. The British used all the opportunity to patronise Muslim League against the Congress to smooth sale its divide and rule policy to prolong colonialism in India. In 1940, Muslim League demanded separate Pakistan, Congress discarded such demand. Liaquat Ali declared Pakistan or death. As communal tension increased, British sent mission for the transfer of power in 1946. India experienced the holocaust of communal riots in 1946; the Great Calcutta Killing and Noakhali massacre shook the moral of the nation. In the Partition Plan, the Muslim League demanded whole of Punjab and Bengal in Pakistan as Muslims were in majority in these provinces. However, the Congress was for only the parts of the provinces with Muslims majority should go to Pakistan. Jinnah also argued for similar partition to have Muslim enclave in every province of India, and a corridor connecting East and West Pakistan.

Meanwhile, the 1947 proposal of Suhrawardy, the Muslim League leader and Prime Minister of Bengal Province and a section of the Bengal Pradesh Congress Committee for independent undivided Sovereign Bengal was vehemently opposed by the Congress high command and Hindu Mahasabha as 'a trap to incorporate Hindu dominated Bengal into Pakistan' and 'a poly to force the Hindus to live under Muslim domination'. Against the backdrop of vitiating political environment and heightening communal tension aroused out of the Direct Action Plan of Muslim League, Calcutta Killing and Noakhali riots, the Hindu Mahasabha fierce campaign for Partition of Bengal and the inability of Congress to launch counter mass campaign for united India, the Partition Plan was announced in June 1947 causing unprecedented riots, looting, migration and death of people across the border of the newly created nations. The impact of partition was felt and is felt by the common man through their everyday plights, uncertainties, miseries, loss of life and livelihood and deep sense of separation from their own motherlands.

The newly emerged independent country paid a heavy cost for the resurgence of communalism and exclusivist communal nationalism by witnessing mass exodus across the border with unprecedented human tragedy. In the same country, where people were born and lived for generations with patriotic feelings became the insecure religious minority, and some became secured majority in the name of religion. The migrants on the other side of the border acquired the status of 'refugees'. The imagination of communal threat and identity became a reality for vast sections of people. Looting, genocide, rape, murder, open torture and humiliation of religious minorities became rampant across the border. Many became confused and felt threatened as to how to protect the life and security of the innocent family members. Though at the wider level of the politics Partition was planned, for the common man migration was not planned. It was left to themselves to decide the fate to their destiny by themselves. How can a family get uprooted from the land where they have remained attached socially, culturally, economically and spiritually for generations?

Despite such confusion and heightening tension and insecurities, like many Hindu families, a lonely Hindu family headed by a person called Fakir of Bheramara Thana of Kushtia District of newly created East Pakistan stayed back as religious/ethnic minority in their 'own country' because of their historical and lifelong emotional attachment to their motherland and the habitat where they were born. Closeness with their neighbours and friends, and the hope of normalization and reversal of the situation and fear of loss of property and livelihood security made them stay on even after being known as minority. However, in the wake of resurgence of communal nationalism, the family members of Fakir encountered a variety of communal violence in the form of organized attack on the house and property, physical attack, stone pelting on the house, forceful encroachment, regular derogatory comments as *malaun*, *kafir* and so on.

Meanwhile, a new generation is born. They experienced early sunny days and started getting rooted with their '*desh*' – the motherland, its nature, surroundings, people, its air, water and earth. For them, an fledgling practicing patriotism at the gross root knew no boundary of religious majoritarianism. However, the victimhood of communalism, its related violence and humiliation were also passed on to them. As they grew up, they started experiencing cultural isolation, every day humiliation and physical threat. They encountered humiliating addressing of them in the school and neighbourhood as *kafir* and *malaun*. They also witnessed physical attacks on the family members, attempt to burn them to death. However, despite all these threats and isolation, they also simultaneously experienced unconditional spring of love and support in all moments of crisis from the friendly neighbours. At times, some friends and neighbours even risked their own lives to provide security to this lonely Hindu religious minority family there. As the border tensions increased between India and Pakistan, this family started experiencing more communal threats. Their life became precarious during the Indo-China war of 1962, Indo-Pakistan war of 1947, 1965 and thereafter. More the border tensions increased, more this family got isolated and became the victims of communal threats despite regular support and cooperation from friendly patriotic neighbours.

Though Fakir's wife Revati was vehemently interested in migrating to India, Fakir and his widowed sister Falguni were not, because of their cultural and spiritual attachments to that land and the people there. Fakir and Jamal were childhood friends. They had promised to each other during the pre-Partition days that whatever the outcome of the political Partition of the country might be, they would not leave that village at all. Furthermore, Fakir also publicly promised Jamal to stay in that village as he had saved that family from an attempt to burn to death in the wake of Partition of the country and attack on Fakir's family by the refugees. To Fakir and his widowed sister Falguni, the division of the country, rising communal tensions were very temporary phenomenon, they believed that the country would be united again. Revati had always perceived the communal threat and violence against her family to be a sustained one. She was broken-hearted to see the victimhood of her innocent children with the aggressions of the communal forces there. For her, India was the *nijerdesh/swadesh*; so was it for her children. She repeatedly uttered and insisted her understanding of the threats to the family members. The emotionally insecure, physically threatened children started getting an unexpected light of hope in the utterances of their mother that their motherland was India that was located on the other side the border. They stared developing love and fascination for India, the dreamland that remained unseen and unrealised by them. They got new confidence in their existence, but invited more hostility from the neighbourhood children and in the school.

With the turn of the events, as this family became extremely vulnerable because of communal threats Fakir, with the help of his childhood Muslim friend Jamal, shifted half of his family headed by his wife Revati to India, undertaking an odious journey in the darkness of the midnight against the backdrop of 1965 Indo-Pakistan war. It was an unplanned migration, executed in haste only to save the innocent lives of some of the family members. They arrived in India with all enthusiasm. However, the outbreak of Indo-Pakistan war in 1965 closed the border and common men strictly restricted from visiting other side of the border. This stopped all channels of communication for these half families living on both side of the border. These threw open heaps of social, emotional and economic plights on the family. The migrant families living on the Indian side of the border emerged refugees or half-refugees, economically insecure, poverty ridden and emotionally shattered. On the other hand, those who remained on the other side of the border started experiencing unprecedented torture by the state and administration, communalists and religious fundamentalists. The eldest son of the family, Pontu, who had just passed his matriculation exam became desperate to share the joyful news with his parted family members in India. Out of desperation without informing his father he attempted to cross over to India illegally. He got arrested by the East Pakistani Rifles, beaten mercilessly, shifted from one jail to another for allegedly espionaging. The half family also become stigmatized as 'traitors' and 'anti-Pakistanis'. The case continued for years before he was exonerated from all charges. This half family, however, overcame all the blames and violence with the help of their Muslim friend Jamal and his family and several neighbours. On the other side of the border, with the courage of Revati, children encountered all uncertainties, poverty and isolation years after years. Along with mounting plights, this half families became desperate to communicate and to know about each other's whereabouts, livelihoods, safely and security. Finally, a line of communication was ultimately developed between these half families by Fakir via London with the help of his Muslim childhood friend Jamal, and they could experience the emotional reunion of after several years. Though the Bangladeshi war of independence brought a long lasting union of these families, and their association with neighbours and the left behind land, it however became very short-lived in the wake of the assassination of Sheikh Mujibur Rahman and resurgence of religious fundamentalism there. Jamal was killed in open daylight in front of Fakir by the religious fundamentalists for participating in the Bangladesh Liberation movement and helping a Hindu family. This incident shook Fakir the most and he therefore, left his beloved country forever apparently leaving behind all emotions and attachment.

But on the contrary, Fakir's sister Falguni never shifted anywhere with the belief that her ancestors would visit her house to bless her and the hope that India would be re-united. However, Falguni died on the other side of the border alone without having any chance to meet her beloved parted family. Fakir became a loner in India without his friend, became a depressed and restless person and died on this side of the border, always longing to be united with his lost motherland, and his childhood friends. Revati also died on this side of the border with her last desire to visit her own house, where she went as a newly-wed bride and to meet all those neighbours for whom she was their '*naya bhabijan*'.

For Fakir, Revati, Falguni, Jamal, Rehmat (the traditional body guard) and many others, patriotism and nationalism was not founded on any political motives or personal understanding. It was founded on ingrained love for the country and compatriots and brotherhood. The lifelong friendship between Fakir and Jamal is such an example, which stood against all odds without having any vested interest. It is also the dedication for others' life which is exemplified in the case of the *lathel*, who stood for Fakir's family in East Pakistan. It was a feeling of bondage which is personified in the Muslim sharecropper, who helped Revati during her hardship days in India. They understood that to be a patriot, you need not be a chest thumping powerful person, in order to be a nationalist or you need not be the first person in the line or a public stage occupier, but a commoner. One must have the capacity to love and to accommodate others and empathy for others. The exclusivist form of nationalism and communism has not only developed hatred and intolerance among the communities, it has also divided the nations. Fakir, Revati, Jamal, Rehmat and others have become victims of the exclusivist nationalism and communalism in the Indian subcontinent. Notwithstanding this victimhood sense, they have lived with the legacy of compassion and brotherhood with a deep sense of patriotism and unconditional love for their motherland.

The political history of Partition of India is well documented across the borders with archival facts and interpretations and perspectives. People's history seldom get a place in the political history even though they are parts of the history. People's history are founded on humanitarian concerns and the everyday lived in experiences of the people. However, they are not autonomous of the broad and phenomenal events taking place in the wider political frame of reference of the society. In fact, the course of the political events of the larger society and the state often influence the course of life history of common men. It is not to say that people always remain a product of history, they also create history. There are also autonomous efforts by the people at the grass root to withstand the influences of the wider society, and create space for their own social history whatsoever short-lived and episodic these may be.

Though historical events stands as social facts for the common man, they also create their own history through lived in experiences. The influences of broad historical processes are not only situationally contextualised, they are also made to sustain and to get a space of legitimacy among common man through varieties of ideological and conceptual formulations like those of communalism, ethnocentrism and nationalism. Many historical processes are staged for legitimacy founded on communitarian populism and communitarian mobilisation. As the communitarian political mobilisation is founded on the politics of religious majority and minority, the humanitarian concerns and the everyday lived inexperience of common man seldom get full scope of expression in those history. However, notwithstanding these limitations a common man creates space for its own history which are practiced, experienced and mutually shared through patriotic ideals. These are founded on the events of their own personal life situations and in memories gathered.

For the victims of partition, these memories are located within the live-in experiences of separation, uncertainties, threats, tortures, physical violence and prolong struggle for their survival. These memories are link to the processes of fragmentation of the identity of nationality on the one hand, and consolidation of the identity of the ethnicity, language and religion, expressed through communalism on the other. These are also the memories of binary of 'we' and 'they' articulated through the identities religious majority and minority. These are also memories of struggle against communalism, and victimhood of communal consolidation of society. These are also the memories of growing up in a mixed community, living together in shared neighbourhood and friendship, help and support during crisis situation as naturally practiced through the spirit of patriotism. The life history of Fakir is reflective of not of isolated individual identity, but reflective of collective identity founded on patriotism. This is a part of legacy those are left behind by Fakir and carried forward by many as part of people's history.

In a multi-cultural and multi-ethnic society like India, the identities of patriotism, ethnocentrism, exclusivist communal nationalism and civic nationalism continually get consolidated at one end and fragmented at the other largely through political and other situational mediations. Patriotism preexisted in India and continues as an apolitical, non-specific and moral constructs. National identity on the other hand, as a historical product, achieved through political engagements initiated by the political elites, intellectuals and gradually spread among the middle-class workers, peasants, farmers, and the common masses alike supposedly subsumed all the pre-existing identities within its ambit and became a powerful force against anti-colonial struggle. Importantly, the growth of nationalism was also accompanied by ethnocentrism, communalism and exclusivist communal nationalism and acquired political significance by constructing community within community, 'us' and 'them', 'insiders' and 'outsiders' in terms of cultural, geographical and ethnic boundaries (SinghaRoy, 2018). People become a part of these identities because of their cultural and ethnic locations, but assert them selectively. Even though most of these identities are founded on inherited cultural essentials, they tend to undergo frequent reconstructions and reconfigurations in association with other identities, making identity as matter of heart at one point and matter of mind at another. Indeed, people make choices for getting associated to any or more of these identities (Sen, 1999) either in terms of cost -benefit calculation, or emotion, subjectivity, humanism, cognition of the self and the historical experiences of coexistence. Many of them also make choices based on lived in experiences and shared memories.

In the wake of the partition of the country and the communal holocaust thereafter, as the exclusivist communal nationalism triumphed to create the political urgency for its communal collective assertion, to propagate binary, hate, exclusion and otherness in the name of religion, to unlatch emotional upsurge for brutal violence, physical attack and murder, looting and burning of property of the religious minorities, and to compel them for exodus from their own motherland, the silent, but firm eternal spirit and soul of the patriotism also emerged from among some compatriots upholding the life-force of humanism, morality, conscience and historical legacies of coexistence. They came forward to protect the endangered religious minorities from all brutal aggression and attacks, to provide them safely and security and to restore their faith on the inherited patriotic bondage of living together even encountering threats to their own lives.

Such patriotic efforts of conscience and humanism, being essentially apolitical, have created deeprooted lived in experiences and memories of assurance against communalism inflected uncertainty, injury against healing, peace against violence, love against hate, care against neglect, dignity against humiliation, and inclusion against exclusion and aggression against friendship for the victims of partition. These lived-in experiences and the engrained memories still provide them zest for life in this naturalized land and longing for those friends on the other side of the border and nostalgia for the left behind idealized motherland. These experiences and memories have been parts of people's entrenched legacies. They uphold and replicate them, pay cost for them and celebrate their success in upholding the valued nostalgia of patriotism, its soul and spirit as tribute to those compatriots who created those good memories and feelings and experiences. When life has experienced the unrepairable injury of violence, up-rootedness, separation and humiliation inflicted by exclusivist communal nationalism, and when other identities also appear to be shaky, the inherited lived in experiences and memories those have emerged out of the self-sacrificing efforts of the compatriots bring for them the possible hope of reflexivity in collective living.

Bibliography

Aggarwal, M., 2014, 'Communal Politics and Genesis of Pakistan', History Discussion.net (https://www.historydiscussion.net/history-of-india/communal-politics-and-genesis-of-pakistan/654.) Accessed on 11 March 2020.

Ahmad, Jamil-ud-din (ed.), 1960, *Speeches and Writings of Jinnah*, Shaikh Muhammad Asharaf, Lahore.

Ahmed, I., 2011, *The Punjab Bloodied, Partitioned and Cleansed: Unravelling the 1947 Tragedy Through Secret British Reports and First Person Accounts,* Rupa & Co., New Delhi.

———, 1996, *State, Nation and Ethnicity in South Contemporary Asia*, Pinter, New York.

———, 2020, *Jinnah: His Successes, Failures and Role in History,* Penguin Viking, New Delhi.

Aikant, S.C., 2006, 'Rethinking the Nation', *Indian Literature*, 235, Sept.-Oct.: 169-78.

Ali, M., 1907, *Green Book No. 1*, Delhi Telegraph Press, Lucknow.

Ali, R., T.K. Saint and D. Sengupta (eds.), 2017, *Looking Back: The 1947 Partition of India, 70 Years on*, Orient Blackswan, Hyderabad.

Bandyopadhyay, S., 2014, *From Plassey to Partition and After,* Orient Blackswan, New Delhi.

Banerjee, S., 2002, 'Civil and Cultural Nationalism in India', in P. Brass, and A. Vanaik (eds.), *Competing Nationalism in South Asia: Essays for Asghar Ali Engineer*, Orient Longman, New Delhi.

Barth, Frederick (ed.), 1969, *Ethnic Groups and Boundaries*, Allen and Unwin, London.

Bass, P. and A. Vanaik (eds.), 2002, *Competing Nationalisms in South Asia: Essays for Asghar Ali Engineer*, Orient Longman, New Delhi.

Basu, J. and A. Roland, 2011, *Reconstructing the Bengal Partition: The Psyche Under a Different Violence*, Bhatkal & Sen, Kolkata.

Beteille, Andre, 1999, 'Citizen, State and Civil Society', *Economic and Political Weekly*, pp. 2588-91.

Bhardwaj, P., A. Khwaja and A. Mian, 2008, 'The Big March: Migratory Flows after the Partition', Harvard Kennedy School, *Faculty Research Working Paper Series*, J.F. Kennedy School of Government, University of Harvard. https://research.hks.harvard.edu

Bhatia, M., 2021, *The Partition/India-Pakistan*, Bluerose Publishers, Noida.

Bose, N.K., 1953, *My Days with Gandhi*, Nishana, Calcutta.

Butalia, U., 1998, *The Other Side of Silence, Voices From the Partition of India*, Duke University Press, Durham.

Chakrabarty, B., 2004, *Partition of Bengal and Assam 1932-1947: Contour of Freedom*, Routledge Curzon, London.

———, 2012, *The 1947 United Bengal Movement: A Thesis Without Synthesis* in K. Roy (eds.), *Partition of India: Why 1947?*, Oxford University Press, New Delhi.

———, 2016, *The Partition of Bengal and Assam, 1932-1947: Contour of Freedom*, Routledge, London.

Chakravartty, G., 1987, *Gandhi: A Challenge to Communalism: A Study of Gandhi and the Hindu Muslim Problem 1919-1929*, Eastern Book Centre, New Delhi.

Chandra, B., 1993, *Essays on Contemporary India*, Har Anand Publications, New Delhi.

Chaterjee, J., 2019, *Partition Legacies*, Permanent Black and Ashoka University, Ranikhet.

Chatterjee, P., 1994, *The Nation and its Fragments: Colonial and Postcolonial Histories*, Oxford University Press, Delhi.

Chatterji, J. 2007, *The Spoils of Partition: Bengal and India, 1947-1967*, Cambridge University Press, Cambridge.

Curran, J.A. (Jr.), 1951, *Militant Hinduism in Indian Politics: A Study of RSS*, Institute of Pacific Relations, New York, 20 February 2021.

Devos, George and L. Romanucci Rose (eds.), 1975, *Cultural Continuities and Change*, C.A. Mayfield, Palo Alto.

Encyclopedia Britannica, 1985, Ethnic Group, University of Chicago Press, Chicago, vol. 4.

Francis, E.K., 1976, *Interethnic Relations: An Essay in Sociological Theory*, Elsevier, New York.

Giesen, B. and K. Eder, 2001, 'European Citizenship: An Avenue for the Social Integration of Europe', in K. Eder and B. Giesen (eds.), *European Citizenship between National Legacies and Post National Projects*, Oxford University Press, Oxford.

Godbole, M., 2006, *The Holocaust of Indian Partition: An Inquest*; Rupa & Co., New Delhi.

Gopal, S. (ed.), 1975, 'Presidential Address to the Lucknow Congress 12 April 1936', *Selected Works of Jawaharlal Nehru*, New Delhi (https://en.wikipedia.org/wiki/1945_Indian_general_election). Accessed on 16 June 2020.

Gosewinkel, D., 2010, 'Citizenship', in H.K. Anheier and S. Toepler (eds.), *International Encyclopedia of Civil Society*, vol. I, Supringer, Berlin.

Gould, W., 2005, *Hindu Nationalism and the Language of Politics in Late Colonial India*, Cambridge University Press, New Delhi.

Hobsbawm, E.J., 1990, *Nation and Nationalism Since 1780*, Cambridge University Press, Cambridge.

Jaffrelot, C., (ed.), 2002, *Pakistan: Nationalism without a Nation*, Zed Book, New York.

Jalal, A., 2014, *Struggle for Pakistan: A Muslim Home Land and Global Politics*, The Belknap Press of Harvard University Press, Cambridge.

Jenkin, Richard, 2007, 'Ethnicity', in G. Ritzer (ed.), *Blackwell Encyclopedia of Sociology*, Vol. 111, Blackwell, Oxford.

Kaviraj, S., 1995, 'Religion, Politics and Modernity', in Upendra Baxi and Bhikhu Parekh (eds.), *Crisis and Change in Contemporary India*, New Delhi: Sage Publications, 1995.

Khalique, K.A., 2002, 'Genesis of Partition', in S. Settar and I.B. Gupta (eds.), *Pangs of Partition: The Parting Ways*, ICSSR and Manohar, New Delhi.

Kripalani, J.B., 1976, *Gandhi: His Life and Thought*, Publications Division, Government of India, New Delhi.

Mahajan, S., 2000, 'Congress and the Partition of the Provinces', in A. Singh (ed.), *The Partition in Retrospect*, Anamika Publishers and Distributors, New Delhi.

Malhotra, A., 2018, *Remnants of a Separation: A History of the Partition through Material Memory*, HarperCollins, New York.

Mill, J.S., 1861/1958, 'Consideartion of Representative Government, Liberal Arts: New Work', op. cit., D. Rustow, *International Encyclopedia of Social Sciences*, Vol. II, New York: Macmillan and Free Press.

Mujahid, S.A., 1981, 'Quaid-I-Azam Jinnah and World Muslim Unity: An Interpretation', *Pakistan Horizon*, 16-28.

Mukherjee, B., 2021, *Bengal and its Partition,* Rupa & Co: New Delhi, Manohar reprint.

Nairn, T., 1977, *The Break-up of Britain*, New Left Books, London.

Nanda, B.R., 2002, 'Tragedy and Triumph: The Last Days of Mahatma Gandhi', in S. Settar and I.B. Gupta (eds.), *Pangs of Partition: The Parting of Ways*, ICSSR and Manohar, New Delhi.

Nandi, A., 2006, 'Nationalism, Genuine and Spurious: Mourning Two Early Post-Nationalist Strains', *Economic and Political Weekly*, vol. 41, no. 32: 3500-4.

Nehru to Krishna Menon, 23 Feb. 1947, JNWS, Second Series, vol 2: 44. op. cit., Mahajan 2000:224.

Neogoy A.K., 1987, *Partition of Bengal*, A Mukherjee and Company: Kolkata.

NMML, SP Mukherjee papers subject file no. 139; Mukherjee to Mountbatten, 2nd May 1947 op. cit., Chakrabarty 2012: 176.

Noorani, A.G., 2000, 'United Bengal Plan: Pipe Dream or Missed Opportunity', in A. Singh (ed.), *The Partition in Retrospect*, Anamika Publishers and Distributors, David Page, New Delhi.

Nora, P., 1996, *Realms of Memory: Rethinking the French Past*, Vol. 1: *Conflicts and Divisions*, Columbia University Press, New York.

Olzak, S., 2007, 'Ethnic, Racial and Nationalist Movements', in G. Ritzer, (ed.), *Blackwell Encyclopedia of Sociology*, Vol. 111, Blackwell, Oxford.

Oommen, T.K., 'Demystifying the Nation and Nationalism', *India International Quarterly*, Vol. 29, no. 4, pp. 259-74.

Pandey, G., 2001, *Remembering Partition: Violence, Nationalism and History in India*, Cambridge University Press: New Delhi.

_____, 2012, *Nationalism Versus Communalism* in K. Roy (ed.), *Partition of India: Why 1947?* Oxford University Press, New Delhi.

Parekh, Bhikhu, 1989, *Colonialism, Tradition and Reform: An Analysis of Gandhi's Political Discourse*, Sage Publications, New Delhi, pp. 34-70.

Raju, A.R., 1993, 'A Raghurama Raju', *Economic and Political Weekly*, 3-10 July 1993.

Ramu, P.S., 1995, *Gandhi-Subhash and Quit India*, S.S. Publishers, New Delhi.

Renan, Ernest, 'What is a Nation', text of a conference delivered at the Sorbonne on 11 March 1882, in Ernest Renan, *Qu' est-ce qu' une nation?*, Presses-Pocket, Paris, 1992 (tr. Ethan Rundell).

Roy, K., 2012, *Partition of India: Why 1947?*, Oxford University Press, New Delhi.

Runciman, W.G. (ed.), 1978, *Weber, Selections in Translation*, Cambridge University Press, Cambridge.

Sarkar, S. 2014, *Modern India 1885-1947*, Pearson, New Delhi.

Savarkar, V.D., *Hindutva: Who is a Hindu?* (1923; rpt. New Delhi: Bharatiya Sahitya Sadan, 1989), pp. 4-12, 42-6, 90-2, 113-15.

Sen, A., 1999, *Reasons Behind Identity*, Oxford University Press, New Delhi.

Sengupta, D., 2016, *Partition of Bengal: Fragile Border and New Identities*, Cambridge University Press: New Delhi.

Settar, S. and I.B. Gupta (eds.), 2002 *Pangs of Partition: The Parting Ways*, ICSSR and Manohar, New Delhi.

Singh, A.I., 2006, *The Partition of India* , National Book Trust, New Delhi

Singh, A.I., P. Moon, G.D. Khosla and M. Hasan, 2004, *The Partition Omnibus,* Oxford University Press: New Delhi.

Singh, I., 1987, *The Origins of Partition of India 1936-47*, Oxford University Press, New Delhi.

SinghaRoy, D.K., 2018, *Identity, Society and Transformative Social Categories: Dynamics of Construction, Configuration and Contestation*, Sage Publications, New Delhi.

Smith, A., 1995, *Nations and Nationalism in Global Era*, Polity Press, Cambridge.

Smith, A.D., 1991, *National Identity*, Penguin, Harmondsworth.

Smith, Anthony D., 1971, *Theories of Nationalism* (1st edn.), Duck-worth, London.

Soysal, Y., 1994, *Limits of Citizenship, Migrants and Post-National Membership in Europe*, Chicago Press, Chicago II.

Spencer, P. and H. Wollman, 1998, 'Good and Bad Nationalisms: A Critique of Dualism', *Journal of Political Ideologies,* vol. 3, no. 3: 255-74.

Stone, J. and B. Piya, 2007, 'Ethnic Group', in G. Ritzer (ed.), *Blackwell Encyclopedia of Sociology*, vol. 111, Blackwell, Oxford.

Sunderland, J.T., 1928, 'Hindu-Mohammedan Riots', *Modern Review*, vol. 43, January: 2.

Tagore, R., 1958, *Nationalism*, New York: Macmillan.

White-Spunner, B., 2018, *Partition: The Story of Indian Independence and the Creation of Pakistan in 1947*, Simon & Schuster, London.

Yusufi, K.A.K., 1996, 'Speeches, Statements and Messages of Quaidaeazam', vol. 2, Bazm-e Iqbal, Lahore.

Zaidi, A.N., 1970, 'All Indian Muslim League Resolution no. IV, 1906', vol. I, 393, Karachi.

Zaidi, Z.H., 1970, 'Aspects of the Development of Muslim League Policy', in C.H. Philips and M.D. Wain Wright (eds.), *The Partition of India: Policies and Perspectives 1935-1947*, George Allen and Unwin Ltd., London.

Index